ReFocus: The Films of Roberta Findlay

ReFocus: The American Directors Series

Series Editors: Robert Singer, Frances Smith, and Gary D. Rhodes

Editorial board: Kelly Basilio, Donna Campbell, Claire Perkins, Christopher Sharrett, and Yannis Tzioumakis

ReFocus is a series of contemporary methodological and theoretical approaches to the interdisciplinary analyses and interpretations of neglected American directors, from the once-famous to the ignored, in direct relationship to American culture—its myths, values, and historical precepts.

Titles in the series include:

edinburghuniversitypress.com/series/refoc

ReFocus
The Films of Roberta Findlay

Edited by Peter Alilunas and Whitney Strub

EDINBURGH
University Press

Edinburgh University Press is one of the leading university presses in the UK. We publish academic books and journals in our selected subject areas across the humanities and social sciences, combining cutting-edge scholarship with high editorial and production values to produce academic works of lasting importance. For more information visit our website: edinburghuniversitypress.com

Edinburgh University Press Ltd
The Tun—Holyrood Road
12 (2f) Jackson's Entry
Edinburgh EH8 8PJ

Typeset in 11/13 Ehrhardt MT by
IDSUK (DataConnection) Ltd, and
printed and bound in Great Britain

A CIP record for this book is available from the British Library

ISBN 978 1 4744 9746 6 (hardback)
ISBN 978 1 4744 9748 0 (webready PDF)
ISBN 978 1 4744 9749 7 (epub)

Contents

Figures

Notes on Contributors

Peter Alilunas is Associate Professor of Cinema Studies at the University of Oregon. He is the author of *Smutty Little Movies: The Creation and Regulation of Adult Video* (2016), and co-editor of *Screening Adult Cinema* with Desirae Embree and Finley Freibert (forthcoming), and *The Intellect Handbook of Adult Film and Media* with Patrick Keilty and Darshana Mini (forthcoming). His work on adult film history can be found in various journals and collections.

Kevin John Bozelka is Assistant Professor of Communication Arts & Sciences at Bronx Community College. He has written music criticism for *The Village Voice*, *The Chicago Reader*, *The Dallas Morning News*, and MTV.com. His research interests include genre, popular music, avant-garde cinema, pornography, and queer theory.

Finley Freibert is an Assistant Professor at Southern Illinois University-Carbondale and, with Alicia Kozma, is co-editor of *ReFocus: The Films of Doris Wishman* (Edinburgh University Press, 2021). With work published in peer-reviewed journals such as *Film Criticism, The Journal of Anime and Manga Studies, Porn Studies, Synoptique,* and *Spectator,* Finley researches and teaches at the intersection of media industry studies, critical legal studies, and LGBTQ+ history.

Derek Gaskill is a New York City-based activist, filmmaker, and urban planner. His work focuses on the relationship between the body, gender, sexuality, and the built environment. Recently he has written about the impact of policies and politics on the curation, creation and preservation of Queer spaces. He holds two Bachelor of Arts from Purchase College in Gender Studies and Cinema Studies and a Master of Science in Urban Policy from Hunter College.

Alexandra Heller-Nicholas has published nine books on cult, horror and exploitation cinema with an emphasis on gender politics, including *Rape-Revenge Films: A Critical Study* (2011) and its tenth-anniversary second edition released in 2021, books on Dario Argento's *Suspiria* (2015), Abel Ferrara's *Ms. 45* (2017) and Robert Harmon's *The Hitcher* (2018), and the Bram Stoker Award finalists *Masks in Horror Cinema: Eyes Without Faces* (2019) and *1000 Women in Horror, 1895–2018* (2021), the latter of which was named one of Esquire Magazine's 125 best books about Hollywood in 2022. She is a member of the Alliance of Women Film Journalists, a top critic at Rotten Tomatoes, and a four-time winner of writing awards from the Australian Film Critics Association. She holds a PhD in Screen Studies from the University of Melbourne and is an Adjunct Professor in Film and Television at Deakin University.

Neil Jackson is a Senior Lecturer in Film at the University of Lincoln, UK, and is the co-editor and a chief contributor to *Snuff: Real Death and Screen Media* (2015). He recently contributed chapters to *Grindhouse: Cultural Exchange on 42nd Street and Beyond* (2016), *The Routledge Companion to Media, Sex and Sexuality* (2018), *The Jaws Book: New Perspectives on the Classic Summer Blockbuster* (2020), *New Blood: Critical Approaches to Contemporary Horror* (2020), and *Shockers: The 70s Cinema of Trash Terror and Exploitation* (2021). He has also recently contributed articles to *Porn Studies* journal and *Screening Sex* online academic journal. He is currently preparing a monograph entitled *Combat Shocks: Exploitation Cinema and the Vietnam War* (Bloomsbury, forthcoming).

Kier-La Janisse is a film writer, programmer, producer and founder of the Miskatonic Institute of Horror Studies. She is the author of *House of Psychotic Women: An Autobiographical Topography of Female Neurosis in Horror and Exploitation Films* (2012) and *A Violent Professional: The Films of Luciano Rossi* (2007), and has been an editor on numerous books including *Warped & Faded: Weird Wednesday and the Birth of the American Genre Film Archive* (2021) and *Satanic Panic: Pop-Cultural Paranoia in the 1980s* (2015). She was a producer on David Gregory's *Tales of the Uncanny* (2020) and wrote, directed and produced the award-winning documentary *Woodlands Dark and Days Bewitched: A History of Folk Horror* (2021) for Severin Films.

Jennifer Moorman is Assistant Professor of Communication and Media Studies at Fordham University. Her research focuses on gender, sexuality, race, class, and disability in popular media texts and industries. She is currently completing a book manuscript entitled *The Softer Side of Hardcore? Women Filmmakers in Pornographic Production Cultures*. Her work appears in *Camera Obscura*, *Signs*, *Synoptique*, and several edited volumes.

Giuseppe Previtali is Postdoctoral Research Fellow in Film Studies and Visual Culture at the University of Bergamo, where he teaches Film Studies. He holds a PhD in Intercultural Studies in Humanities. His main research interests are connected with the extreme forms of contemporary visual culture and with the issue of visual literacy. He published extensively on these topics and attended several international conferences. He is the author of the books *Pikadon: Memories of Hiroshima in Japanese Visual Culture* (2017), *The Last Taboo: Filming Death between Spectacularization and Political Usage* (2020), and *Visual Literacy* (2021).

Whitney Strub is Associate Professor in History at Rutgers University-Newark. His books include *Perversion for Profit: The Politics of Pornography and the Rise of the New Right* (2011), *Obscenity Rules: Roth v. United States and the Long Struggle over Sexual Expression* (2013), and the collection *Porno Chic and the Sex Wars: American Sexual Representation in the 1970s* (2016), edited with Carolyn Bronstein. His work has appeared in such scholarly journals as *Radical History Review, American Quarterly*, and *Journal of the History of Sexuality*, as well as popular venues including *Vice, Washington Post*, and *Temple of Schlock*.

Johnny Walker is Associate Professor in the Department of Arts at Northumbria University. His books include, as author, *Rewind, Replay: Britain and the Video Boom, 1978–92* (2022), *Contemporary British Horror Cinema: Industry, Genre and Society* (2015), as editor, *Hammer and Beyond: The British Horror Film* (2021), and as co-editor, *Grindhouse: Cultural Exchange on 42nd Street, and Beyond* (2016). His scholarship can be found in numerous journals and anthologies.

Acknowledgments

Roberta Findlay does not make for easy subject matter—a status we are certain she would appreciate—but her films and career provided an ideal opportunity for a fruitful and rewarding alliance. Our thanks to everyone at Edinburgh University Press, and particularly the series editors, Gary D. Rhodes, Robert Singer, and Frances Smith, for supporting our vision. Friends Alicia Kozma and Finley Freibert inspired this project with their own *ReFocus* volume on the similarly neglected filmmaker Doris Wishman, which provided the perfect lantern to light our way.

The process of creating this book was a pleasant and pleasurable one, marked by collaborations with the good folk who make this kind of work such a joy to do. We have deep gratitude for the tremendous roster of contributors whose work fills these pages—not just colleagues, but compatriots in a community of like-minded sleaze surveyors. Anyone who takes Roberta Findlay's work seriously needs to read both scholarly work in porn studies and also message boards and *Fangoria*. To that end, we thank our many friends and colleagues in the Society for Cinema and Media Studies Adult Film History Scholarly Interest Group who have built such an inviting and supportive community, and also the posters at places such as the old DVDManiacs (later AVManiacs) board who collectively built one of the best sources of Findlay knowledge out there. No work on Findlay could be complete without the committed research of Casey Scott, as well as the endless riches April Hall and Ashley West have imbued within *The Rialto Report*. When we hit a brick wall regarding the facts of Findlay's biography, Andy McCarthy at the New York Public Library solved our methodological quandary, while Steve Puchalski at *Shock Cinema* and John Sirabella at Media Blasters provided otherwise elusive copies of Findlay's films. Our completist urges would otherwise never have been sated.

We also thank Karen Sperling for her willingness to speak about her own over-looked career, as well as her generosity with the images that appear in this book. Joe Rubin didn't just write the Foreword, or create and operate the mighty Vinegar Syndrome, with its vital film preservation mission, he also continues to be a valued and trusted friend and colleague. Robin Bougie deserves a special note of appreciation, as a key contributor to Findlay knowledge in his brilliant *Cinema Sewer* and elsewhere. We owe him a lot; he knows why.

We also thank Roberta Findlay. She cuts a daunting figure in the mythologies and urban legends of the fan world, and we were a bit intimidated to reach out to her. But once we connected, she was nothing but pure delight, even in her withering sarcasm toward the worth of this book. Our affection for her doesn't mean these chapters aren't critical—they certainly are, though not nearly as severe as her own judgment of her work. We hope she finds the analyses here meritorious, but barring that, that she meets them with a good quip.

Finally, the people in our lives, who provided crucial support beyond the visible page. This entire book was conceived, written, and published during the worst global pandemic in a century, and everyone who in any way contributed to ameliorating its ravages has our profound gratitude. Indeed, working on *Roberta Findlay* at times offered a welcome respite from the fears and anxieties of our times. It's rare that scholarly labor is also *fun*, but as friends and mutual admirers, we both really enjoyed this and hit the exact right groove for rewarding and productive collaboration, so we thank one another for that. Peter thanks his students and colleagues at the University of Oregon, who unflaggingly support projects such as this one without hesitation. Whit thanks his students and colleagues at Rutgers University-Newark and comrades at North New Jersey Democratic Socialists of America (a better world is possible!). We also thank our cats: for Peter, the late, great, and incomparable Holmes, who died during this book's production but will live forever in the cat hall of fame; for Whit, the distinctly unambitious Polly, Persimmon (RIP), and Dusty, despite their sloth-ful and filthy ways. Last, but never least, we are grateful for the endless good humor and encouragement of our respective partners, Erin Hanna and Mary Rizzo, themselves distinguished scholars (and best possible sounding boards), who at times seemed to secretly suspect this project was nothing more than an alibi for us to hang out with people we like and admire and watch trashy mov-ies. They may know us better than we know ourselves.

Foreword

Joe Rubin
Founder, Vinegar Syndrome

The first time I met Roberta Findlay in person was to go down to lower Manhattan and inventory a storage unit she'd rented to house the various negatives which, for years, had languished behind a wall at a recording equipment museum in Brooklyn. She'd brought along one of her male studio technicians to do the heavy lifting part of the job, noting (with her always slightly cynical humor) that such a task was only suitable for a man. Our "helper" for the day was completely floored by the revelation that his boss had once enjoyed a prolific career directing and shooting "porno movies" (among other things) and, on the taxi ride back to Sear Sound, kept inquiring about details on the subject, eventually asking how exactly she went about directing sex scenes. Without missing a beat, Roberta loudly shot back: "I told them to screw, and they screwed!" The resulting gasp on the taxi driver's face was truly priceless.

Summarizing the life and career of someone like Roberta Findlay is a bundle of contradictions: artistically, politically, and at times even morally. For a filmmaker who has worked on projects in nearly every imaginable genre, and having held nearly every key creative position in the medium of cinema itself (sometimes close to half a dozen on a single project), Findlay has often tried—quite deliberately—to remove herself from her work.

Be it through the use of pseudonyms; focusing on genres and subject matter that, by her own admission, she found boring at best, distasteful at worst, it can seem difficult to find the artist reflected in the art. That, coupled with her deliberate avoidance of prospective interviewers and well-known distaste for the very concept of academic interest in the areas of film in which she toiled has, unfortunately, left her incredible career of directing over thirty theatrical features and nearly double that number in cinematography credits, out of much of the recent collective "rediscovery" of key genre-based filmmakers (a wrong that my company Vinegar Syndrome has been actively trying to right through our ongoing preservation and release efforts for both her hardcore and horror films).

However, Findlay is and was never anything less than an astute and primarily self-taught master craftsman who delighted in using the cinematic form for equal parts creative release and commercial gain, frequently devising ingenious and economical methods of making movies under the most inhospitable conditions.

The ten chapters in this collection offer an initial opportunity for scholars and cinephiles alike to begin finally exploring one of New York exploitation cinema's most challenging and key figureheads. From examinations of some of her most iconic directorial efforts, to studies of the subtly and consistently present themes across her vast body of work, to deconstructions of the more notorious and controversial titles in her filmography, *ReFocus: The Films of Roberta Findlay* fills a crucial gap in the history and culture of independent movie making while shedding light on a woman who has proudly not cared about any of it.

Introduction: Sleazy Honesty

Whitney Strub and Peter Alilunas

> People expect me to be something that I'm not.
>
> Roberta Findlay, 2005[1]

Roberta Findlay's *Angel on Fire* (1975) inspired what might be the first published close scholarly reading of a hardcore porn film. Its author harbored some doubts about her existence. Her name "is possibly a pseudonym," warned Dennis Giles in a 1976 *Velvet Light Trap* article, as he clung to a psychoanalytic reading suspicious that the film "may well present only the appearance of a female subjectivity." His doubts were not inane—plenty of male pornographers adopted female pseudonyms as marketing hooks, as Laura Helen Marks notes of Shaun Costello crediting himself as "Amanda Barton" to bestow a perceived "woman's touch" in marketing strategies—but they also bore traces of his own sublimated desire, that of maintaining the coherence of a phallic Freudianism where "the unconscious fantasy of *Angel on Fire* is a masculine megalomania in which the sadist gives birth to his victim."[2] Or maybe it was the film's success that prevented Giles from accepting that a woman could have made it; in New York, in its opening weekend, *Angel* was the top grosser, beating out *Lenny* (1974, dir. Bob Fosse) and *Amarcord* (1973, dir. Federico Fellini).[3]

Pioneering feminist film critic Molly Haskell saw it quite differently, and in a rare moment of attention to pornography in her *Village Voice* column, she noted that having "two women greet their lovers with the unwelcome news that they are pregnant" was not only a "definite downer to Don Juan fantasies of quickie, no-fault sex" but also a potential indicator of female consciousness.[4] What might have evolved into a robust interpretive debate—particularly given the ways in which many of Findlay's films combined those explorations of female consciousness with unabashed "definite downer" narratives—instead dissolved into indifference, as scholars and critics alike outside the world of adult film magazines largely passed over Findlay for the next several decades.

Yet here was a filmmaker who helped build the hardcore porn industry, and who shaped softcore sexploitation cinema before that, an enormously talented craftsman who worked in front of the camera as a performer and behind it in multiple crew positions, and who regularly received onscreen credit for writing, producing, directing, and photographing a single film. That she did all of this as a woman in a male-dominated industry (not so much pornography as film itself) has often made gender and feminism inescapable lenses for assessing her work in ways not paralleled by reception of such contemporaries as Gerard Damiano or Joseph Sarno, sometimes in ways that obscure her sheer virtuosity as a culture worker. Even though Findlay has long actively resisted any sort of gendered analysis of her work, both Haskell and Giles—and many of the authors in this collection—were right to center gender, because Findlay's work forces such an interrogation on its own terms.

Those terms are fiercely anti-feminist, even as her work simultaneously offers a scathing critique of hetero-patriarchal relations. "I'd rather be dead than be a woman," says the smug male chauvinist protagonist of *Angel on Fire*— he is, in fact, dead at the time, and facing reincarnation as exactly that—but far from using the line to score points against him, the film emphatically *supports* his position. It wouldn't be the last time a Findlay film made such a move. To be a woman, in Findlay's world, is to suffer; indeed, "I can't take it any longer, the pain of being a woman is too severe," this one concludes, too weak to hack it in feminine form. And while hardcore pornography is often understood as a utopian genre, for Findlay sex is frequently dismal—and decidedly unerotic. "Okay Lou, be quick and be quiet," says a wife to a husband in *From Holly with Love* (1978), before he rolls on top of her for precisely sixty seconds of abjectly lackluster marital coitus. Similar scenes recur throughout Findlay's films; after all, she titled one *Anyone But My Husband* (1975), while the frustrated wife of *A Woman's Torment* (1977) begins the film by delivering a postcoital assessment to her negligent spouse: "you just masturbated inside me" (for the film's second sex scene, performer Crystal Sync offers an equally rousing "alright, let's get it over with").

"Abjectly lackluster" might also describe Findlay's level of interest in shooting the hardcore scenes. "I was always disgusted by the sex scenes so I'd say 'Okay, everybody screw.' That would be it," she told Jill Nelson in 2010.[5] Her disinterest manifests in a sort of creative negligence, much of her work hitting its required generic marks of explicitness with little investment in genuine erotic heat. For a generally careful craftsman, Findlay could be quite sloppy in shooting sex, from the poorly simulated scenes in *Altar of Lust* whose humping and thrusting are occasionally belied by mistimed pans revealing Harry Reems clearly not engaged in actual penetration, to the visible tube used to fake a money shot in the otherwise austerely composed *A Woman's Torment*. In her comedic register, *Love, in Strange Places* includes not one but two scenes sexually involving a banana, sex played for yukks and slapdash pratfalls rather than carnal desire, and the opening scene of *Anyone But My Husband* best embodies Findlay's sneer at both her genre and her audience, as the sex is intercut with the distinctly less enticing preparation of a chicken for dinner. Such contradictions and complications litter Findlay's erotic worlds, making for a rich body of work that has yet to receive sustained scholarly attention. The chapters in this volume rectify that oversight, bestowing upon Findlay's films the careful analysis they merit as the work of a groundbreaking exploitation filmmaker. In this introduction, we set the chapters up by arguing for her importance as a culture worker—in spite of her own long-expressed disagreement with that very claim.

FINDLAY'S FILMS

The daughter of Hungarian Jewish immigrants, Roberta Hershkowitz was born, according to most accounts, in 1948. In actuality, her 1962 marriage license dates her birth to December 30, 1943—but is available only by request from the city clerk of New York, the facts of her life thus anticipating the unstable footing her cryptic filmography will also impose on the researcher.[6] Raised in the Bronx with her two older siblings and talented on the piano from a very young age, she attended Music and Art High School after skipping fourth and eighth grade, and then enrolled simultaneously in the City College of New York and the Manhattan School of Music, planning for a successful future as a concert pianist. Instead, she met Michael Findlay, ten years older and a cinephile who organized screenings in the CCNY library and in Greenwich Village coffeehouses. He recruited her to record piano scores to accompany the films, which she improvised from the various pieces of music that she had studied. That irritated her professors, who thought she was tarnishing the music department's reputation, but it endeared her to Michael, whom she married after turning eighteen (as she recounted in our 2021 interview with her, included at the end of this collection, "his mother said, well, you'd better get married. I'd rather you marry a Jew than live in sin").[7]

Roberta entered filmmaking rather passively, when Mike and their friends John and Lem Amero, brothers from Massachusetts eager to get into the exploitation game, collaborated on what became their collective debut, *Body of a Female* (1964). By her own account, "I was just tagging along," though her career-long tendency was to downplay (and occasionally deny) her own contributions.[8] Taking the screen name Anna Riva, she played the lead role; while shooting striptease and skinny-dipping scenes with her husband and male

friends proved awkward, the Ameros' joint coming out as gay helped ame-
liorate Mike's masculine possessiveness, and John Amero recalled Roberta as
"a good sport and quite fearless."[9]

She subsequently appeared in a string of films from Mike and the Ameros,
separately and apart. For *Satan's Bed* (1965), Mike acquired *Judas City*, a
meandering film with Japanese artist Yoko Ono playing the newly arrived fian-
cée of a sleazy drug-runner, shot new scenes of dope-fiend criminals malinger-
ing, and released it under a new title. The footage never connected, but with
heavy doses of rape and sadism on both sides (to become a staple of Mike's
and Roberta's collaborative and individual work), it fit cohesively into the
"roughie" genre then popular in grindhouse theaters. Roberta appeared briefly
as a woman stripped, beaten, and tied spread-eagle on a pool table by the drug
gang. Meanwhile, while *Body of a Female* remains lost, footage from its shoot
cropped up in the Ameros' pseudo-documentary *Lusting Hours* (1968), where
Roberta also appeared in new scenes as a prostitute fighting another woman in a
brothel and a stripper with a crown on a candlelit stage, performing for sweaty
and leering men (see Figure I.1). Neither enthused nor particularly reluctant
in her onscreen embodiment, she offered the "fleshy documentary facticity"
that film scholar Elena Gorfinkel argues constitutes "the body's failed labor"
in sexploitation cinema, where *acting* often collapses into an unwitting exposure of the sheer *work* of performing, in the bored gyrations of the women

Figure I.1 Roberta Findlay in *Lusting Hours* (1968). From Something Weird Video DVD.

onscreen.[10] That work extended beyond performing, as Roberta also did the lighting for *Satan's Bed*—the first of many times she would take on the part of filmmaking that she would later say she most enjoyed, its technical side.[11]

By the time of *Take Me Naked* (1966), the Findlays had already carved out a place on the cutting edge of sexploitation's march toward ever-greater explicitness. Driven primarily by Mike's lurid fixations—on lesbianism, perversion, murder, and despair—and offering Roberta's high-contrast arthouse lighting, the film presented a gutter poetics capturing the rain-soaked street scenes of New York's grimy Bowery. "The loneliness of the self-isolation still empties him," Mike narrates gloomily over his own hangdog face in the film's opening moments, "and he feels an occasional desire for another human being to share a part of his perverted life." Alongside vivid, overwrought beatnik ravings were gauzy lesbian scenes featuring Roberta and emerging grindhouse stars June Roberts and Darlene Bennett, set to narrated lyrics from French poet Pierre Louÿs's fabricated ancient Greek translation of *Songs of Bilitis* (1894), which had also inspired the more high-minded Daughters of Bilitis, the first US lesbian-rights group, established in 1955. After opening the film by disrobing, writhing autoerotically, and showering, Roberta's character is ultimately murdered by a scuzzy male voyeur. She also increased her role behind the camera, sharing writing, producing, and directing credit with Mike (as "Julian Marsh"), as well as cobbling together a stolen soundtrack consisting of everything from Czech composer Bohuslav Martinů's *Double Concerto for Two String Orchestras, Piano, and Timpani* (written in 1938 to capture the feeling of Europe imploding) to music from the B-movie *The Blob* (1958).

As Anna Riva, Roberta became a minor grindhouse sex symbol, her face appearing on the ad mat for *Take Me Naked* as it circulated the nation— though in more modest titular form for some markets, appearing as *That's Me* at Detroit's Gem Art in late 1966 and the Minnesota-nice *Please, Take Me* when it hit Minneapolis in early 1967 (see Figure I.2).[12] While Roberta would continue to appear in small roles—a shrill wife stabbed to death by aggrieved husband Mike in his *A Thousand Pleasures* (1968), a bitter woman taunting her boyfriend's "teenage tramp" daughter with a "Came to screw your daddy, huh?" before being strangled with a belt in *Janie* (1970)—her full migration toward the other side of the camera lens was already well underway, replete with a variety of additional aliases and slippery duties.

Indeed, as Alexandra Heller-Nicholas notes, a certain "authorial haze" hovers around Findlay's precise roles and credits. Exploitation production moved quickly, and the Findlay/Amero nexus was broadly collaborative.[13] Findlay herself has roundly disavowed her contributions. "I had nothing to do with those pictures," she told Ashley West of *The Rialto Report* regarding Mike's signature trilogy *The Touch of Her Flesh* (1967), *The Curse of Her Flesh*, and *The Kiss of Her Flesh* (both 1968), films with which she has not only long

Figure 1.2 Roberta Findlay as part of the original advertising for *Take Me Naked* (1966).
From Whitney Strub's personal collection, courtesy Something Weird Video.

been associated, but also variously credited on for photography, co-writer, and co-producer. Devoted fans on the Something Weird Video Facebook group, however, caught a fleeting frame of *Kiss* with the crew reflected in a window, Roberta seemingly included.[14] Credible accounts sometimes diverge; Jack Bravman, who co-authored the incestuous proto-slasher *Janie* (1970), recalled it as "one of the first films that Roberta directed herself," while production assistant John Amero remembered her as cinematographer and Michael as director.[15]

Findlay's own self-declared directorial debut poses immediate challenges to scholars of her work. *Erotikon* (1967) is not even listed on the Internet Movie Database as of this writing. In a 1978 interview, Findlay explained that she and Michael traveled to Belgium for him to make a film, but because she knew French and he didn't, she took over, both writing and directing. "In Belgium they didn't screw in movies at that time," so she composed "a real script" instead. Beginning with a man's attempted suicide, thwarted when his gun misfires into his stomach, the film (which shares a title with Mauritz Stiller's boundary-pushing 1920 Swedish sex comedy) follows "a series of aural impressions" that lead the protagonist through various memories—particularly his sustained gay panic—until his eventual death. Findlay also cut and edited the film in Holland, before US customs officials seized it upon entry.[16]

The case received extensive attention from *Variety* in 1968, as its judge publicly prepared by studying such cutting-edge films of the sexual revolution as Michelangelo Antonioni's *Blow-Up* (1966) and Mac Ahlberg's *I, a Woman* (1965). At trial, the director of customs compliance argued that fifty-five of the film's ninety minutes were obscene, but after seven hours of deliberation a hung jury could not reach consensus. The government moved for a new trial, but once a libertarian-leaning judge was assigned, it dropped the case, perhaps preferring to focus on the upcoming trial of Grove Press's erotic import *I am Curious (Yellow)* (1967, dir. Vilgot Sjöman). Despite winning the case, distributor Stanley Borden apparently chose not to circulate *Erotikon*, and today it remains a lost film. Findlay was never mentioned by name in the press coverage and it has rarely been referenced since (for that matter, her only other known published comment on the matter also shows the tendencies of her narratives to shift over time: in a 2017 *Flavorwire* interview, she attributed the script to Michael).[17]

Further complicating any exact breakdown is the disappearance of several films Roberta allegedly shot for Michael (*Crack-Up*, 1969; *The Closer to the Bone, the Sweeter the Meat*, 1971; *Vice Versa*, 1971), and the elusiveness of some of her own early directorial work, such as 1973's *Teenage Milkmaid*, nearly impossible to see outside the Kinsey Institute's rare surviving print. *Take My Head* (1970) perfectly crystallizes the imprecision of the Findlay filmography: credited to Roberta as director in the American Film Institute Catalog, it was flatly rejected by her when we asked about it in our 2021 interview. Michael Findlay's unmistakable voice narrates, with his typically overheated prose rhapsodizing about the "tender slit of love itself" and "the endless ecstasy of oral satisfaction," and a lesbian scene is shot with the same Vaseline-smeared lens that marked Roberta's photography in *Mnasidika* (1969) and arguably *Take Me Naked*. A series of cutaways to sexual sketches echo customs officials' descriptions of "ancient drawings . . . which reportedly depict sexual intercourse in graphic detail" in *Erotikon*, and the presence of performer Ariana Blue also links it to several of Roberta's immediately subsequent films. Is *Take My Head* a Roberta Findlay film? Probably—but it's nearly an impossible point to debate, as it also reflects the poorly preserved nature of Findlay's work. Though Alpha Blue Archives released an incomplete version on a softcore VHS double-feature in 1997 alongside *Janie*, the tape is held in no libraries, was not available on tube or torrent sites until its streaming debut on HotMovies.com in early 2022, and cannot be found for purchase on online sites such as eBay (which purged its adult content as this book coalesced, making such research even harder). We were only able to obtain a copy through the generosity of *Shock Cinema* publisher Steven Puchalski, who reviewed the VHS release in 1998.[18]

What is clear is that she came out from behind her pseudonyms in the early 1970s with a string of films explicitly credited to Roberta Findlay as writer, producer, director, and photographer. *Altar of Lust* (1971), *Rosebud* (1972), and the aforementioned *Angel on Fire* (1974) charted a course from the waning days of softcore sexploitation toward the full graphic sex of hardcore, with explicit oral sex in the first two but no penetrative sex in their tales of intrafamilial psychosexual angst, and full of rape, incest, and death-bound desire. Once in auteurist motion, Findlay maintained a rigorous filmmaking pace, becoming one of the defining producers of New York City pornography in the 1970s.

Even as she was steadily directing her own films, Findlay continued working for other filmmakers, a practice that continued throughout her career. Most of the early gigs were within familiar orbits, alongside Michael. That included stints as cinematographer on ultra-low budget horror films and exploitation films, such as *Shriek of the Mutilated* (1974), produced by Ed Adlum and directed by Michael, and later an oddball ostensible documentary about ordinary people enacting their sexual fantasies on camera, *Acting Out* (1978, dir. Carl Gurevich and Ralph Rosenblum). She frequently collaborated with the Amero brothers, Lem and John, and Jack Bravman, with the latter churning out a series of so-called "one day wonders" that showed Findlay at her most careless, such as an opening driving scene for *The Honeymooners* (1976) with a shakily held camera that didn't merit a second take. Given the chance, though, Findlay delivered far sharper images. On Chuck Vincent's *Visions* (1977), surreal sets shrouded in darkness allowed her to play with sources of light, as did a candlelit lesbian scene in the otherwise unexceptional Bravman production *Honey Throat* (1980). And when conditions truly afforded it, as on Henri Pachard's *Babylon Pink* (1979) or the Ameros' *Blonde Ambition* (1981), Findlay shot in a gleaming classical style that belied the films' still humble budgets, also editing the former film's lovely opening-credit city-symphony.

The year 1973 perfectly captures the freewheeling Findlay filmography. That year she directed her own *Teenage Milkmaid* and shot three other films: *All in the Sex Family*, shoddy, bottom-of-the-barrel filler for Bravman; *Checkmate*, a failed action-comedy would-be crossover for the Ameros; and a true outlier in her career, the independent feminist film *The Waiting Room*, which deserves sustained attention.

The Waiting Room had nothing to do with sexploitation, pornography, or horror; ironically, given Findlay's well-established feelings about women in the industry, it also marks an important feminist moment in film history. Director Karen Sperling set out in 1973 to create a film that would capture an experiential perspective on women's lives, and in particular the expectations (and consequences) surrounding marriage. Key to that process, Sperling believed, would be to shoot the film with an all-woman crew: "I felt that since the film is about women, why not make it entirely in a women's environment and from their point of view?"[19] It was a follow-up to Sperling's debut film, *Make a Face* (1971) which had garnered some minor acclaim and steady publicity, including a runner-up prize for Best First Feature at the Atlanta Film Festival, putting her on a

Figure 1.3   Roberta Findlay, to the right of camera, on the set of *The Waiting Room* (1973). Photo courtesy of Karen Sperling.

trajectory with other groundbreaking women filmmakers such as Barbara Loden, whose film *Wanda* was playing on the festival circuit at the same time and with whom she occasionally appeared on panels and in interviews.[20] Filmed on sets built on Ward's Island and presenting loosely connected, mostly abstract scenes, *The Waiting Room* follows a woman (played by Sperling) at her job in a hospital, in her home, and at a wedding and funeral. Audacious and creative, the film features several inventive sequences photographed by Findlay, and feels very much at home in the experimental and boundary-pushing era of the early 1970s. Molly Haskell, after a set visit, described the all-woman crew as exhibiting a "tremendous feeling of confidence and mutual respect."[21] Ultimately, however, the film was nearly completely unseen, playing only a single time in Los Angeles before quietly slipping, along with Sperling, who never made another film, into forgotten history.[22]

Like Roger Corman and Jess Franco, Findlay was an economical filmmaker who made efficient use of casts and locations, often shooting in clusters—after the early 1970s familial sex dramas, she met Walter Sear, who would become her partner of several decades through his death in 2010, and together they produced a series of anarchic hospital-based comedies (*Love, in Strange Places* [1976], *Sweet, Sweet Freedom* [1976], *The New York City Woman* [1977], etc.), which recycled so much footage that they barely stand alone as discrete textual units; an orgy scene with a band playing recurs endlessly across these films. Authorship blurs in the collaborations of Findlay and Sear (as Derek Gaskill notes in his chapter here), but Findlay is quite clearly the animating cinematic force and has acknowledged as much, even when attributing directorship to Sear on occasion, as she did for the madcap *Dear Pam* (1976) when we mentioned it to her. The humor can be puerile in these films—*Love, in Strange Places* is not the only one of them to use bananas for groan-inducing penis jokes—but Findlay's very crassness could also afford genuine laughs, as when *"Sweet Punkin" I Love You . . .* (1976) opens with the well-endowed John C. Holmes and Tony "the Hook" Perez arguing over who's better hung as artist Jennifer Jordan sculpts a phallus. Holmes boasts in a badly exaggerated Russian accent, until Perez intervenes, "you pinko prick, that cock ain't got no dignity, it's downright trash." The Broadway-style quips of porno-chic auteur Radley Metzger this is not, but as a low-rent comedy of manners of the sort where a wedding cake is introduced and the audience knows immediately that it will receive an ejaculatory icing, it hits both its comedic and sexual marks with panache.

In Findlay's next cycle of moody, mournful hardcore films, her New York rooftop garden and a rented Fire Island beach house became visual staples, with the same rooms eerily serving as a familiar touchstone as background in different plots. *A Woman's Torment* (1977), *From Holly with Love* (1978), *Mystique* (1979), and *The Tiffany Minx* (1981) shift from zaniness to bleak existential angst, and offer some of her most pointed depictions of patriarchal constraints on women. *Mystique*, written by Roger Watkins (who also directed his own downbeat hardcore, such as the fatalistic *Her Name was Lisa* [1979]), begins with an onscreen poem by Paul Valéry before two lonely women discuss composer Gustav Mahler ("songs about dead children") in a forlorn seaside cottage, one of them battling a serious cancer diagnosis; having set up this high-culture framework, the film then shifts toward brutality with a home-invasion rape scenario and ultimately resolves into elegiac lament.

These films sit uneasily beside the wild comedies. *Tiffany Minx* ends on a rare triumphant note of conspiratorial lesbian usurpation of the male privilege that so chokes the women of Findlay's universe, and other seemingly feminist interventions sometimes punctuate her work, as when Nora, the protagonist of *Anyone But My Husband*, finally interrupts a blathering and condescending psychiatrist with "I don't know what the fuck you're talking about! . . . what garbage!" (a diatribe made all the more delightful coming from star C. J. Laing, who took her *nom de porn* from anti-psychiatry radical R. D. Laing). She then lets her lazy, philandering husband know that "washing and cleaning" all day drain her of desire, and the film ends with him staring into the mirror, classical melodrama that is shattered by a cartoon image of a man masturbating on a toilet as the end credit arrives. But how to reconcile this feminist Findlay with the rape played for laughs in *Love, in Strange Places* or the adult man having sex with his sleeping teenage daughter in *Dear Pam* (retroactively secured as consensual when she conveys to the audience that she had been awake, a typical recuperative gesture of 1970s hetero-hardcore)?

Findlay left any such queries unresolved at the time, hidden behind her pseudonyms. The contemporaneous porn press engaged in a sort of double-consciousness; her authorship was clearly widely known, but coverage generally avoided direct attribution, with occasional exceptions as when *Hustler*'s critic praised her "skillful editing" on *New York City Woman* despite her name never appearing in its credits (Anna Riva took the onscreen credit).[23] *Adam Film World* gave *Mystique* a five-page promotional spread upon its release without ever referring to a filmmaker, but when it interviewed Findlay a year later, they discussed the film as if Robert W. Norman's actual identity was simply a matter of common knowledge.[24] Authorship could also be amorphous in the films she shot for producer Jack Bravman and director John Christopher in the late 1970s: the same threesome on the bed of a pickup from *Candi Girl* (1979) and a pastoral coupling of Serena and John Holmes from *Summertime Blue* (1979) both recur in Findlay's own *Honeysuckle Rose* (1979), blurring the question of who directed them—a question that neither Findlay nor anyone else has ever shown great concern over, to be sure, but one that again highlights the fuzzy boundaries of her filmography.

As a filmmaker, Findlay elicited a certain loyalty from a recurring cast that became something of a troupe, with such performers as Crystal Sync, Eric Edwards, and Jeffrey Hurst staples of hardcore Findlay, while the viscerally well-endowed Tony "the Hook" Perez delivered all six of his credited performances in Findlay films. Still, she never hid her contempt for the form, in a 1981 interview describing "most porn films" as "boring, dull, stupid, childish and inane," and adding, in a sideswipe, "there's little real talent in the business, and the screenplays are insipid." She argued that "knowing the characters makes a movie erotic . . . Understanding, empathy, compassion, sympathy for the characters are necessary."[25] For her final hardcore cycle in the early 1980s, she implemented this argument, again shifting registers from the dour late-1970s films to a glossier, more romantic framing. If *A Woman's Torment* and its ilk fit nicely alongside a broader Jimmy Carter-era hardcore malaise (seen too in Gerard Damiano's and Anthony Spinelli's work of the time), Findlay's hardcore home stretch of *The Playgirl* (1982), *Liquid A$$ets* (1982), *Mascara* (1983), and *Glitter* (1983) offered classical Hollywood inflections for one last gasp of the porno-chic theatrical era.

These films perhaps most paralleled the contemporaneous work of onetime Orson Welles cinematographer-turned-hardcore director Gary Graver, who like Findlay shot his own films, and the bright polish of his *Indecent Exposure* (1982), *Centerspread Girls* (1983), and others resonated with her newly adopted style. For the opening scene of *Glitter*, in which Kelly Nichols dominates Jerry Butler before making him lick his come off her fingers, Findlay seemed for possibly the first time genuinely invested in infusing a sex scene with actual eros. In predictable Findlay fashion she then burned those aesthetic and industrial bridges with *Shauna: Every Man's Fantasy* (1985), which exploited the recent suicide of Colleen Applegate, who performed in hardcore as Shauna Grant, for a leering pseudo-documentary. Using outtakes from *Glitter* alongside a framing narrative of Joyce James (then the real-life editor of *Cinema Blue* magazine), ostensibly trying to understand Applegate's death, the film also featured new hardcore sequences playing over performers' narrated recollections and memories. Findlay has long offered no defense for the cruel and cynical film, instead providing her own blunt, shrugging assessment. "This shows you my moral ethical code," she later told Jill Nelson. "I pretended it was real and that it was something of homage to her, but it wasn't. I just put it together figuring we could make some money from it."[26]

By the early 1980s, home video and cable television had dramatically changed the landscape for adult film production and distribution, creating an oversupply of material. As early as 1983, Findlay saw the bottom falling out of the market for adult films. "We may just get out of the adult field entirely," she told a reporter. "It may just make more sense to move exclusively into R-rated product."[27] That's exactly what she did, pivoting away from adult films to a string of low-budget films. First up was *Tenement* (aka *Game of Survival*, 1985), which offered a different kind of X-rated spectacle, that of trashy action cinema too violent for an R rating. It partook of then-prevalent urban-decay sensationalism, with families in a South Bronx apartment complex held hostage by freakish miscreants. A police officer in the opening scene summarized Findlay's misanthropic worldview, declaring, "somebody oughta drop a bomb on this place."

Conventional horror films followed, with *The Oracle* (1985), *Lurkers* (1987), and *Prime Evil* (1988). As Johnny Walker points out in this collection, these were designed to emulate the popularity of the horror films then in circulation, both in theaters and even more profitability on home video. They also contribute to a deeper understanding of Findlay's overall body of work. For example, *The Oracle*, a story about a spirit terrorizing a young woman (Caroline Capers Powers) from beyond the grave in the hopes of solving his murder, features as its central villain a character described in the film's marketing as a "a psychotic transvestite lesbian."[28] This is Farkas (Pam La Testa), an assassin hired by the spirit's widow, who prowls 42nd Street to murder women sex workers in gruesome fashion. The stereotype-laden Farkas surely brings to mind an encounter between Findlay and two women at the premiere of *Angel Number 9* in 1974, which she later described to journalist Timothy Green Beckley:

These two women—and I use the term loosely—came in—real bulldykes—and started to rant and rave. They had seen a press release which quoted me as saying I would never under any circumstances hire a woman on my crew. This monster of a gal sticks her finger in my nose and shouts, "How the hell do you come off saying something like that? How're the rest of us going to get ahead?" I shrugged my shoulders and tried to walk away. At this point I thought the dyke was going to push my face in. Luckily the film started. They stormed out after 30 seconds.[29]

Such context adds much to understand the vitriol embedded in the character of Farkas, as well as a more complete portrait of the long-simmering layers of misogyny and homophobia that circulate within Findlay's work. Other works of this era carried less thematic depth; she cobbled together *Blood Sisters* (1987) on the advice of her accountant to beat out the fiscal year for advantageous tax returns, and the disinterest shows.

Tax advice was similarly the impetus for the final film Findlay has directed to date, *Banned* (1989), which shifted into the comedic-horror register of contemporaneous Troma films such as *The Toxic Avenger* (1985, dir. Lloyd Kaufman and Michael Herz) and *Class of Nuke 'Em High* (1986, dir. Richard W. Haines and Michael Herz), with the murderous spirit of a punk rocker

Figure I.4 Sear Sound in New York City, September 2021. Photo by Whitney Strub.

escaping through a toilet into the body of a gentler musician. It never found a distributor, and as that niche began to wither, Findlay left film behind to return to her original passion, music, managing New York's Sear Studio for several decades. With that, the filmmaking book closed for the woman who had been part of the transformative period between sexploitation and hardcore, directing more than twenty-five films and being part of the crew on at least thirty more. As she told us in 2021, some of the musicians who record at Sear Sound know about her past, and posters from her horror films are still on the studio's walls, even if she is no longer behind the camera.

Roberta Findlay is an outlaw filmmaker in the most literal sense: her work was frequently deemed obscene and she was repeatedly arrested in the course of producing sexual imagery. Her very first film, *Body of a Female*, led to an Illinois case in which the state supreme court affirmed the film's obscenity. Shortly thereafter a judge in San Bernardino, California, shut down a local theater for showing the "extremely pornographic" *Take Me Naked* and another film. *Anyone But My Husband*, with its bondage and fisting scenes, came under repeated legal attack as part of a New Orleans "hardcore pic crackdown" in 1975 and charges were directed at an Indiana drive-in two years later. Canadian Mounties even erased video copies in 1984, and as late as 1989 Iowa video store owners narrowly averted criminal charges when the state supreme court determined that obscenity law covered only sales, not rentals. Meanwhile, Findlay was arrested in 1974 after shooting Jack Bravman's *All in the Sex Family* (1973) and faced felony obscenity charges when outraged Suffolk County, New York, officials recognized local scenery in the film's locations. She and most of the cast and crew of *Honey Throat* (shot in 1978, released in 1980) spent two nights in jail after police in Point Pleasant, New Jersey, peeped through curtains as she shot a sex scene in a hair salon.[30]

Findlay beat the charges. Yet instead of taking pride in staring down the state itself at far greater personal risk than most "transgressive"-labeled filmmakers, for most of her career, she has openly scorned her films, her fans, and the very idea of scholarly interest in her work. "I don't find any academic merit in any of this stuff," she told us in our 2021 interview, though she reluctantly admitted there might be some First Amendment importance. Yet her historical significance in shaping exploitation and hardcore cinema is simply undeniable— and in one of the many ironies of her career, this anti-feminist pornographer helped spark the feminist anti-pornography movement with her work on the controversial *Snuff* (1976), which played a key role in mobilizing activism against cinematic depictions of sexualized violence. Had only Women Against Pornography members paid closer attention to Findlay's bitter, acerbic hardcore films—or to her life and work experiences—they might have imbued their analyses with more nuance. With this volume, we hope film scholars will do the same; the chapters here grapple with the complications and contradictions of her work in ways that firmly establish her as a major filmmaker of lowbrow cinema and resist easy conclusions about her rich, problematic, sleazy, grim, and also hilarious films.

THE FINDLAY ARCHIVE

The knowledge base for work on Findlay had to come, of necessity, almost entirely from outside academia. ArchiveGrid, the largest online compendium of archival finding aids, contains precisely zero hits for her as of this writing, reflecting the larger collective failure to properly preserve hardcore history and often the history of sexuality more broadly. This is a topic that has engaged both of us in our respective work, and which pertains rather viscerally to Findlay.[31] Here is a filmmaker not only without an available archive but even whose first (*Body of a Female*, 1964) and last (*Banned*, 1989) films remain currently unavailable, whose filmography may never be fully documented because of her profusion of aliases and the rapid conditions of production for so many sexploitation and hardcore films.[32] Until recent restorations by such cult-oriented labels as Vinegar Syndrome and Media Blasters, her films have been treated poorly by distributors; beyond the lost films, many existing ones have had footage excised from VHS and DVD releases, from fisting scenes in *Anyone But My Husband* to a narratively important rape scene in *From Holly with Love*. With the Reagan-era turn toward child protection, her moral-guardian-baiting *Underage* (1977) became *Raw Footage* on video—a titular shift that may have led to some confusion when she denied appearing as a custodian in the film's final sequence.[33]

While that formal challenge offers much on which to meditate about the incompleteness and unknowability of even recent film history, so too is this institutional invisibility combated by the work of fan culture. From 1970s adult magazines to *Fangoria* in the 1980s, and on to an assortment of cult and porn message boards, Facebook groups, and blogs, fan communities have long served as the de facto public historians of scholarly disregarded topics, and Roberta Findlay is a case study in this form of knowledge production. From Bill Landis's *Sleazoid Express* in the 1980s to Robin Bougie's *Cinema Sewer* (est. 1997), and later from Casey Scott's reviews on the website *DVD Drive-In* to the *DVDManiacs* and *Rock! Shock! Pop!* message boards and Facebook cult fan clubs, it is outside the Ivory Tower that Findlay's history has best been preserved. More recently, Jill C. Nelson's monumental book *Golden Goddesses*, centered on long-form interviews with women from adult film history, and Ashley West and April Hall's *Rialto Report* website, which began as an oral history project and expanded into an expansive digital library of once-elusive magazines, out-of-print books, and previously unpublished manuscripts, have further developed a Findlay archive.

With endless diligence, fans have scanned posters and pressbooks, dug through newspaper advertisements, and carefully tracked developments in digitization, so that when the City College of New York's student newspaper found its way online, Michelle Alexander was there to quickly locate young Roberta Hershkowitz's 1961 appearance and share "Coed Records Mood Music for Silent Film Program" on her blog, *Chelle's Inferno*. As a sophomore music-education major, Roberta kept "several themes in mind," with "fear" and "panic" being her favorites, though she also noted that "love, of course, is in all movies."[34] That particular trait would rarely appear in her own. Findlay's own relationship to her fans and their interest in her films has often been ambivalent at best. "People who like those old movies seem to have deep psychological problems," she noted in one career retrospective.[35]

Scholars have been slower to recognize Findlay's contributions. She made the most fleeting of cameo appearances in Linda Williams's foundational *Hard Core: Power, Pleasure, and the "Frenzy of the Visible"* (1989); *Snuff* drew attention from early exploitation historians Eithne Johnson and Eric Schaefer; and the conspicuous presence of Yoko Ono in *Satan's Bed* led Joan Hawkins to consider the tantalizing avant-garde/grindhouse intersection in *Cutting Edge: Art-Horror and the Horrific Avant-garde* (2000).[36] Later, such influential exploitation scholars as Elena Gorfinkel and David Church would include Findlay in their analyses, but it was not until Alexandra Heller-Nicholas's 2016 *Senses of Cinema* article "What's Inside a Girl?: Porn, Horror and the Films of Roberta Findlay" that she received sustained attention.[37]

By way of contrast, Findlay's approximate peer Doris Wishman, the other most prominent female exploitation/porn director, first drew a scholarly article devoted to her work in 1997, and indeed this volume follows in the footsteps of Alicia Kozma's and Finley Freibert's 2021 *ReFocus* volume on Wishman.[38] Wishman and Findlay share much as rare female filmmakers in male-dominated spaces with often similarly reactionary views, but stylistically they diverge rather dramatically, with Wishman's wild, vertiginous camera and jolting, fetishistic editing lending itself to experimental and auteurist analyses, whereas Findlay's more classical craftsmanship ultimately solicits more industrially oriented readings. Kozma and Freibert compellingly reject centering the question of whether Wishman was a feminist as "unanswerable, and ultimately unhelpful," though in Findlay's case the question is both more easily resolved and also somewhat unavoidable given her own extensive commentary on the matter.[39]

We hope this book will put Roberta Findlay on the map not just of porn studies and exploitation film scholars but also film historians more broadly. Maya Montañez Smukler's vibrant and necessary recent book *Liberating Hollywood: Women Directors and the Feminist Reform of 1970s American Cinema*, for instance, specifically noted that Findlay was not within its purview—but it can be productive to think of her work alongside her precise contemporaries Joan Micklin Silver and Joan Tewkesbury.[40]

OVERVIEW OF CHAPTERS

The chapters amassed here offer both interpretive overviews and focused case studies of much of Findlay's career, from 1960s roughies through 1980s horror. As suggested above, sexual and gender politics occupy a central—though not monopolizing—analytical position, and the authors approach related questions from very different angles (indeed, the Giles and Haskell *Angel Number 9* responses that we began with reappear throughout—a matter not so much of redundancy as motif, used to varying analytical ends). Instead of reducing Findlay's often misogynistic and at times antigay personal comments to a matter of personal pathology, Finley Freibert argues for reading such utterances as strategic marketing communications that helped maintain what today's parlance would call a brand. Indeed, Freibert notes her fascinating participation on the crew of the exclusively women-made independent film *The Waiting Room* (1973)—and her disparaging words about female crew members. Using different theoretical tools, Jennifer Moorman locates in Findlay's films an "ambivalent feminism," one that does not necessarily resolve into fixed ideological clarity, yet whose consistent depictions of male supremacy enforced through violence offer complicated and problematic texts far more nuanced than their maker's more puerile public commentary.

Kevin Bozelka, meanwhile, tracks queer and avant-garde genealogies through Findlay's grindhouse years, from the relatively familiar *Take Me Naked* to the utterly obscure *Mnasidika* (1969), possibly the world's first and only arthouse beaver film.[41] Bozelka reads these works as so evacuated of legible interiority that their radical externality shatters the Lacanian Symbolic Order itself—an unstainable fever pitch of perversity that could perhaps only collapse in later works into camp.

While *Snuff* (1976) has proven to be well-trodden territory for scholars, particularly given its centrality as a cultural flashpoint for the anti-pornography feminist movement of the 1970s, its origins as a different film, directed by Michael Findlay with cinematography by Roberta in 1971 and titled *Slaughter*, has usually been relegated to passing mentions or footnotes. Here, Giuseppe Previtali gives the kind of overdue, detailed analysis of *Slaughter* that puts the film—and the concept of "snuff films" more generally—into the historical contexts of its production moment, including the role Charles Manson and his "family" had in creating the cultural meanings of violence.

Derek Gaskill's chapter examines the commodification of women, including Findlay, during the "porno-chic" era of the 1970s, as well as weaving in a history of Findlay's relationship with Walter Sear, and the unique films on which they collaborated, including *Love, in Strange Places*, *Sweet, Sweet Freedom*, and *Dear Pam* (all 1976). That Gaskill is Sear's grandson adds a unique, personal touch to the chapter, and to this collection.

Roberta Findlay made a fleeting appearance in Kier-La Janisse's searing *House of Psychotic Women*, a self-described "autobiographical topography of female neurosis in horror and exploitation films," and here Janisse returns to Findlay's least ethical effort, the notorious *Shauna: Every Man's Fantasy*.[42] What can one say about a fake documentary that exploited the suicide of performer Colleen Applegate? Rather than condemning (or, worse, defending) the film, Janisse burrows into its various resonances within Findlay's career and avant-garde practice to in some ways read the film as a documentary not about the tragedy at its center but rather Findlay's own working methods.

While Findlay's sexploitation and hardcore films have typically garnered the most interest, her turn toward non-adult cinema at the end of her career presents equally rich and vivid historical terrain. Neil Jackson argues that *Game of Survival* (aka *Tenement*, 1985) represents a curious outlier in Findlay's filmography—not a sexploitation or adult film, and not a horror film, the two periods typically associated with her work. Jackson argues that the violent exploitation film, set in the Bronx, where Findlay herself grew up, offers a portrait of, as he puts it, "defiant outsiders" made by one. Johnny Walker, along similar lines, explores the four horror films that came at the end of Findlay's career: *The Oracle* (1985), *Blood Sisters* (1987), *Lurkers* (1988), and *Prime Evil* (1988). Positioning them within the larger context of home video and horror films in the late 1980s as the theatrical market was rapidly changing, Walker illustrates how these films were more than just the final entries in Findlay's filmography, they were part and parcel of an economic landscape specific to that particular time period.

As noted above, it was Alexandra Heller-Nicholas's 2016 *Senses of Cinema* essay that inaugurated contemporary scholarship into Findlay's films—making her presence in this collection most welcome. In this original contribution, Heller-Nicholas examines *Banned* (1989), Findlay's final, unreleased film, tracing that film's turbulent production history and its historical role in ending Findlay's work as a filmmaker, as well as her subsequent (and ongoing) career as the manager of the Sear Sound recording studio. In doing so, Heller-Nicholas fills in long-neglected gaps and offers the first detailed analysis of one of Findlay's most bizarre and sought-after films.

This collection concludes with our interview with Findlay, done in September 2021 at Sear Sound in New York. Covering a wide range of topics, she spoke to us with her typical, familiar candor, offering thoughtful (and at times humorous) responses to our questions, which we developed in the hopes of avoiding the familiar ground of the interviews she has done over the last four decades, though we did return to areas that might offer insights into her complicated perspectives. While she may not agree that her films deserve an analysis of the type we've tried to present here, she proved willing to engage us on any terrain on which we approached, and gamely accepted that we do find merit and historical value in her work. Findlay expanded our knowledge of her oeuvre, casually mentioning that, contrary to the familiar narrative,

Shauna did not end her hardcore career, which in fact extended to directing two further films in 1985, *Wet Dreams* and *Climax!*, both credited onscreen to Henri Pachard (just as her *Fantasex* had been to Cecil Howard in 1976) and not previously attributed to her. Clearly shot in close proximity—they share cast members and even a beige couch with a winding geometrical pattern—the two films resonate with some of Findlay's recursive themes, both opening with masculine heterosexual failure. *Wet Dreams*, whose thin narrative of people in a bar/restaurant fantasizing about sex (a sort of bargain-basement rendition of Radley Metzger's porno-chic classic *Barbara Broadcast* [1977]) is so desultory that it's effectively a loop-carrier, opens with performer Eric Edwards initially unable to achieve an erection; the slightly more ambitious *Climax!* makes vivid use of Atlantic City B-roll footage to spice up its own set-bound sex scenes and offers more narrative development, but also begins with performer Cody Nicole delivering a postcoital assessment to her male partner: "I don't mean to upset you or anything, but that wasn't that good," a line that would have been right at home in Findlay's mid-to-late 1970s films. While these are decidedly minor works, we are pleased to expand the Findlay universe ever so slightly by claiming them for her.

In a gesture that startled us, she also casually handed over a leather volume containing hundreds of pages of distributional records from approximately 1978 to 1985, and suggested more were to be found scattered around the filing cabinets and closets of Sear Sound, thus leaving hope for an accessible Findlay archive to come—something that would not only collect and preserve invaluable materials for scholars working on hardcore film history, but also on independent filmmaking, home video distribution, and all kinds of New York histories. We hope the publication of this book might help inspire a proper archival acquisition by a publicly accessible repository.

CONCLUSION: DIFFERENT LEVELS OF JUNK

Among its other goals, this collection acknowledges Findlay's work, her literal labor in front of, behind, and holding the camera, labor that for decades went almost entirely unacknowledged or seen primarily in relation to the various men surrounding her at different points in her career. For all the contradictions that define the narratives in her unquestionably divisive filmography—not to mention the web of aliases, lost films, dismissals, and denials—there can be no doubt that she *worked* as a filmmaker. That also happens to be one of the few things she acknowledges, too. Her performers recognized her pleasure in craftsmanship even despite her disdain for porn; as an unnamed cast member of *Angel Number 9* told an interviewer in 1975, "At one point she told me, 'Take your, uh, masculinity and do so-and-so.' I think she gets her real kicks out of the film itself and making it all come together technically."[43] While she has never expressed more than tepid and bemused derision for her films, one of her most plaintive confessions of professional disappointment pertains to her failure to get into the cameraman's union, IATSE Local 644. Findlay created a non-sex reel, found two sponsors, and was provisionally accepted, before one of her legal busts derailed the process. "They asked me to withdraw," she recounted to historian Jill Nelson; "I did, and I was ashamed."[44]

While physically unimposing, Findlay nevertheless developed a reputation for simply hoisting the heavy cameras onto her shoulder and becoming what she called a "human tripod," moving around the set and saving production costs and time.[45] That detail could help explain the misogyny embedded in Findlay's production discourses, such as her long-standing "absolute rule" not to hire women for technical positions on her crews, which might be understood via the intense self-reliance that she clearly felt had to define her own complicated career. "I've worked pretty hard and I don't rely on anybody else—women or men—to do anything for me, so I don't see why I should help anybody else," she defiantly argued in a 1975 interview. "It's a very unpopular position, I know, but it's unfortunately true."[46] That perception hasn't changed in the years since, as our 2021 interview with her attests.

It was also true that Findlay's work took a physical toll. The camera on her shoulder—the machine at the heart of the "human tripod" so instrumental in creating her hardworking, gender-defying persona—also hurt her body. The camera's motor, sitting on her breast, created a cyst that needed to be removed. "I'd break every camera cable because they were not meant for females," she later described.[47] Surely a more ideal metaphor would be difficult to concoct for the women of Findlay's era who wanted to become filmmakers: even the *equipment* was seemingly against them. That wound also neatly symbolizes the simultaneous, paradoxical tension in her career, exemplified by her desire to ignore, avoid, and deny any possibility that being a woman meant anything at all (and certainly, in her mind, it did not hold her back), alongside her unmistakable narrative choices that were often unquestionably rooted in that very thing. How else are we to understand that the same Findlay who made *A Woman's Torment* in 1977—the raw portrait of a woman broken by an uncompromising, misogynistic world that she later called "the story of my life"—also said, only two years earlier, "I'm not a feminist. I don't feel responsible for any other women in the world"?[48] Her career and work has long been defined by such contradictory layers, as well as her active and ongoing refusal of any nudge trying to get her to take sides.

Heller-Nicholas, in a turn of phrase that gives us the title for this introduction, intended to honor her work, argues that Findlay's films are "marked by a unique blend of sleazy honesty: they are what they are, and never seek to apologise for it," and that has also been the case with her own attitudes toward them, the toll they have taken on her, and what they all mean in a broader context.[49] Perhaps the work that best embodies her ethos is the little-known *Beach House* (1978), one of what she calls her "free films," compilations constructed from outtakes, reused material, and other surplus footage. Findlay (hidden behind her Robert W. Norman pseudonym) uses four women talking, often about male sexual inadequacy, as the stage for a series of banal sexual encounters that they describe to one another. The women nearly renounce unsatisfying heterosexuality ("poor girl, she should've tried a woman," one reflects, while another later muses, "perhaps the best joys of sex could be had from another woman"), before a sudden closing reassertion of hetero-phallic sexual supremacy, as a narrator concludes, "but no, as we touched each other my mind kept seeing that immense tool . . . if only Harry were here in bed with us now, what real pleasure we could have. This was just a substitute for a rigid prick in my poor burning cunt." What begins as a feminist consciousness-raising session tending toward lesbianism devolves into a paean for the very normative system whose fundamental failure has been on ample display all along—and this self-defeating diegetic level sits bound within Findlay's cynical rip-off of her performers' recycled labor at the structural level. Sleazy honesty, indeed.

In Findlay's telling, there is not much worth remembering about her career or her films, complicating any discussions of legacy. "I accomplished nothing," she said in 2015 in response to one such attempt to define her work, preferring instead to think of it all as the consequences of the childhood time wasted playing the piano, a view she has held for decades; as far back as 1978, for example, she said that "the only reason I make these pictures is because I'm not talented enough to be a concert pianist."[50] Her references tend toward the classical, in fact. In our interview with her, she describes narrative film structure in terms of opera (one of her abiding interests), references John Ford, Billy Wilder, and William Wyler's films as influences, and confirms that Herman Melville's *Pierre; or, the Ambiguities* (1952) would be her dream film project. A certain level of embarrassment permeates any discussion that veers back toward her own films, the only exception emerging for cinematography, which she has always tended toward highlighting in her own work.[51] Nevertheless, Findlay has consistently fended off attempts to label her as a pioneer, trailblazer, or groundbreaker, particularly as career retrospectives (including this collection) have begun to appear. "I don't know what it is that I discovered, learned or did that was new or something that had never been done before," she said in one retrospective, while in another she argued that "a pioneer is someone with a conscious effort trying to make a breakthrough and I was not."[52]

Perhaps, in the end, we might consider Findlay, her films, and her career in terms that decenter conventional espousals of ideological leadership, particularly when overlaid with essentialist feminist politics, neither of which have ever remotely interested her. Doing so allows for an acknowledgment of the difficult conditions in which she worked, the technical mastery she exhibited across various aspects of film production (tellingly, while she hid behind a pseudonym to direct the hardcore *Anyone But My Husband*, she credited herself by name for photography, her true point of pride not authorial but craftsmanship), and her too-often overlooked narratives reflecting the conditions of women's lived experiences, including her own, that in some instances offered rigorous critiques of sexist and patriarchal cultures. It also gives space to recognize that she unquestionably *did* break new ground as a woman making adult films, despite her reluctance to accept such status. Accepting such decentering, however, doesn't preclude accounting for her anti-feminist and misogynistic rhetoric, on and off screen and in her production practices, much of which is detailed unsparingly throughout this collection. It is the complicated and contradictory fusion of all these things that ultimately defines Findlay's legacy; as many of the chapters that follow illustrate, that fusion reveals the ways in which conventional approaches can often fail to account for her unique and often paradoxical historical status. One thing, in the end, is certain, and hopefully captures our efforts with this collection: Roberta Findlay's own early description of the kinds of films she made as "all junk, different levels of junk," couldn't be further from the truth.[53]

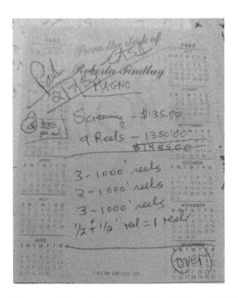 

Figure 1.5 Example of material from Roberta Findlay's files. Courtesy Roberta Findlay.

NOTES

1. J. R. Taylor, "The Curse of Her Filmography," *NY Post*, November 8–14, 2006, https://web.archive.org/web/20061108201842/www.newyorkpress.com/18/29/film/JRTaylor.cfm (accessed May 26, 2022).
2. Dennis Giles, "*Angel on Fire*: Three Texts of Desire," *Velvet Light Trap*, Fall 1976: 42, 44; Laura Helen Marks, "Re-Sexualizing Scrooge: Gender, Spectatorship, and the Subversion of Genre in Shaun Costello's *The Passions of Carol*," in Carolyn Bronstein and Whitney

Strub (eds), *Porno Chic and the Sex Wars: American Sexual Representation in the 1970s* (Amherst: University of Massachusetts Press, 2016), 58–9.

3. "'Angel Number 9' is No.1 in NY at 640," *Boxoffice*, December 2, 1974, E1.

4. Molly Haskell, "Are Women Directors Different?" *Village Voice*, February 3, 1975, 73.

5. Jill C. Nelson, "Roberta Findlay: New York City Woman," in *Golden Goddesses: 25 Legendary Women of Classic Erotic Cinema, 1968–1985* (Duncan, OK: BearManor Media, 2012), 182.

6. Michael Findlay and Roberta Hershkowitz, Certificate of Marriage Registration, license no. 1140, January 17, 1962, obtained from City Clerk of New York.

7. Nelson, *Golden Goddesses*, 168–73; Gerald Peary, "Woman in Porn: How Young Roberta Findlay Finally Grew Up and Made Snuff," *Take One*, September 1978, 28–30.

8. Ashley West and April Hall, "Roberta Findlay: A Respectable Woman—Podcast 53," August 16, 2015, *Rialto Report*, podcast, https://www.therialtoreport.com/2015/08/16/roberta-findlay/ (accessed July 28, 2021).

9. John Amero, *American Exxxtasy: My 30-Year Search for a Happy Ending* (Godalming: FAB Press, 2020), 44.

10. Elena Gorfinkel, "The Body's Failed Labor: Performance Work in Sexploitation Cinema," *Framework: The Journal of Cinema and Media* 53, no. 1 (Spring 2012): 86.

11. Taylor, "The Curse of Her Filmography."

12. Ads in *Detroit Free Press*, November 27, 1966; *Minneapolis Star-Tribune*, January 11, 1967.

13. Alexandra Heller-Nicholas, "What's Inside a Girl?: Porn, Horror, and the Films of Roberta Findlay," *Senses of Cinema* 80 (September 2016), https://www.sensesofcinema.com/2016/american-extreme/porn-horror-roberta-findlay/ (accessed May 26, 2022).

14. Ed Lusky post to Something Weird Video Fan Club, Facebook, September 17, 2015, https://www.facebook.com/photo?fbid=10156142116140455&set=gm.10153081421797681 (visible only to members, accessed June 6, 2022).

15. "Jack Bravman: 'Snuff', 'The Slaughter', and who was J. Angel Martine?," *Rialto Report*, March 25, 2018, https://www.therialtoreport.com/2018/03/25/jack-bravman/ (accessed May 26, 2022); Amero, *American Exxxtasy*, 94.

16. Peary, "Woman in Porn," 31.

17. "Customs Grab of Belgian 'Erotikon' to Trial March 18," *Variety*, March 13, 1968; "Judge's Cram Course on Film Sexsation," *Variety*, March 20, 1968; "Says 'Erotikon' Porno 55 of Its 90 Minutes," *Variety*, March 27, 1968; "Hung Jury for Belgian 'Erotikon'," *Variety*, April 3, 1968; "New Trial, New Judge on Belgian 'Erotikon'," *Variety*, April 24, 1968; Stuart Byron, "Swede Pic vs. U.S. Customs," *Variety*, May 15, 1968; Alison Nastasi, "Flavorwire Interview: Exploitation and Adult Cinema Icon Roberta Findlay on Making "Cheap" Movies, Getting Arrested with John Holmes, and Times Square's X-Rated Past," *Flavorwire*, December 30, 2017, https://www.flavorwire.com/609580/flavorwire-interview-exploitation-and-adult-cinema-icon-roberta-findlay-on-making-cheap-movies-getting-arrested-with-john-holmes-and-times-squares-x-rated-past (accessed May 26, 2022).

18. *American Film Institute Catalog: Feature Films 1961–1970* (New York: R. R. Bowker, 1976), 1063; Steven Puchalski, *Janie/Take My Head* review, *Shock Cinema* #13 (1998), 17. On *Erotikon*, "Customs Grab of Belgian 'Erotikon' to Trial March 18," *Variety*, March 13, 1968.

19. A. H. Weiler, "If I Were a Nell, I'd Be Singing," *New York Times*, March 18, 1973, 13, 26.

20. "'Make a Face' Screened at Cannes Festival," *Boxoffice*, March 29, 1971; "London Pic Fest Adds New Directors' Section," *Variety*, August 11, 1971; "New Yank Cinema Sidebar at Venice," *Variety*, August 11, 1971; "'Deliverance is Mostest of Bestest at Atlanta," *Variety*, August 23, 1972 (Karen Sperling, telephone interview, September 14, 2021).

21. Molly Haskell, "Moviemaking Without Men," *Village Voice*, May 10, 1973, 83.

22. "'Waiting Room' to Preview," *Los Angeles Times*, November 7, 1973, E16. Much more remains to be said about Karen Sperling and her important contributions to film history,

which were mostly dismissed or diminished at the time, in part because of her family legacy: she is the granddaughter of Harry Warner, co-founder of Warner Bros, and was able to self-finance her films. Neither of them has ever been released in any format; we are grateful for the copy of *The Waiting Room* she provided for us to view, and for her general recollections about the film's production.

23. Frank Fortunado, "Movies," *Hustler*, May 1977, 31–2.
24. "*Mystique*," *Adam Film World*, January 1980, 18–23; Scott Roberts, "A Sex Film Is a Sex Film Is a Sex Film," *Adam Film World*, May 1981, 50–2.
25. Roberts, "Sex Film," 52.
26. Nelson, *Golden Goddesses*, 189.
27. Alexander Auerbach, "Are Exhibitors Hurting X-Films?," *Boxoffice*, September 1983, 129.
28. This description is from the back cover of the DVD released by Shriek Show in 2005.
29. Timothy Green Beckley, "Female Porn Producer Roberta Findlay," *Sir*, September 1976, 11.
30. "Illinois Court Rules 2 Movies Obscene," [Moline, IL] *Dispatch*, September 29, 1967; "Judge Attends Movies; Shuts Theater Down," *San Bernardino County Sun*, January 5, 1968; "Charge New Orleans Exhibs in Hardcore Pic Crackdown," *Variety*, November 26, 1975; "Indiana Drive-In Beats Rap on a Technicality," *Boxoffice*, March 20, 1978; "Mounties to Erase Offending Cassettes," *Variety*, April 4, 1984; "Sex Movies Targeted by New Law," *Des Moines Register*, May 21, 1989; A. J. Carter, "D.A. Charges 12 with Obscenity," *Newsday*, April 30, 1974; "Judge Listens to Arguments On Alleged Obscene Movie," *Asbury Park Press*, September 7, 1978; "Pornographic Case Dropped," *Asbury Park Press*, May 18, 1979. The second arrest has often been attributed to the shoot for *Honeysuckle Rose*, after Findlay herself asserted that in the 2006 *New York Post* interview, but the contemporaneous news coverage makes clear that it was actually *Honey Throat*, which she shot for director Chris Covino ("John Christopher"). Performer Rob Everett confirmed this in response to a query to the Facebook Adult Films 1968–1988 group, November 24, 2021, https://www.facebook.com/groups/291177474238605/posts/4672482709441371/ (visible only to group members, accessed June 6, 2022).
31. See for example Peter Alilunas, "Ginger's Private Party Flyer (circa 1985)," *Film History: An International Journal* 26.3 (2014): 144–55; Whitney Strub, "Sex Wishes and Virgin Dreams: Zebedy Colt's Reactionary Queer Heterosmut and the Elusive Porn Archive," *GLQ: A Journal of Lesbian and Gay Studies* 23.3 (2017): 359–90.
32. *Banned*, never formally released theatrically or on home video (as outlined in Alexandra Heller-Nicholas's chapter in this collection), is set for a 4K release by MediaBlasters (John Sirabella, telephone interview, October 12, 2021). Findlay's profile on the Internet Movie Database (IMDB) is riddled with errors; as of this writing, it wrongly credits her with directing *Fringe Benefits* (1973) and *Slip-Up* (1974), both by Walter Sear, and with shooting the b-horror film *Invasion of the Blood Farmers* (1972), which its director denies. Meanwhile, having shot a succession of late-1970s films for director Chris Covino/John Christopher, she most likely also shot *Sweet Throat* (1977), a film without cinematographer credits, some footage of which recurs in both the Findlay-shot *Summertime Blue* (1979) and the Findlay-directed *Honeysuckle Rose* (1979). How many other uncredited Findlay efforts remain unacknowledged is an open question, one not even she can likely answer.
33. Taylor, "The Curse of Her Filmography."
34. Michelle Alexander, "For Michael and Roberta Findlay Fans: An Article from Their City College Days," *Chelle's Inferno*, 8 May 2016, http://chellehell.blogspot.com/2016/05/for-michael-and-roberta-findlay-fans.html (accessed May 26, 2022); "Coed Records Mood Music for Silent Film Program," *The Campus*, December 6, 1961, 5, http://digital-archives.ccny.cuny.edu/thecampus/1961/DECEMBER_109_18/00000149.PDF (accessed May 26, 2022).

35. Taylor, "The Curse of Her Filmography."
36. Linda Williams, *Hard Core: Power, Pleasure, and the "Frenzy of the Visible"* (Berkeley: University of California Press, 1989); Eithne Johnson and Eric Schaefer, "Soft Core/Hard Gore: *Snuff* as a Crisis in Meaning," *Journal of Film and Video* 45: 2, 3 (Summer-Fall 1993): 40–59; Joan Hawkins, *Cutting Edge: Art-Horror and the Horrific Avant-garde* (Minneapolis: University of Minnesota Press, 2000).
37. Elena Gorfinkel, *Lewd Looks: American Sexploitation Cinema in the 1960s* (Minneapolis: University of Minnesota Press, 2017); David Church, *Disposable Passions: Vintage Pornography and the Material Legacies of Adult Cinema* (New York: Bloomsbury Academic, 2016); Heller-Nicholas, "What's Inside a Girl?: Porn, Horror, and the Films of Roberta Findlay."
38. Alicia Kozma and Finley Feibert (eds), *ReFocus: The Films of Doris Wishman* (Edinburgh: Edinburgh University Press, 2021).
39. Kozma and Freibert, "Introduction: Making Films in Hell," *ReFocus: The Films of Doris Wishman*, 7.
40. Maya Montañez Smukler, *Liberating Hollywood: Women Directors and the Feminist Reform of 1970s American Cinema* (New Brunswick, NJ Rutgers University Press, 2018).
41. On the beaver film, a liminal and ephemeral form in the immediate pre-hardcore moment, see Eithne Johnson, "The 'Coloscopic' Film and the 'Beaver' Film: Scientific and Pornographic Scenes of Female Sexual Responsiveness," in Hilary Radner and Moya Luckett, *Swinging Single: Representing Sexuality in the 1960s* (Minneapolis: University of Minnesota Press, 1999), 301–24.
42. Kier-La Janisse, *House of Psychotic Women* (Godalming: FAB Press, 2012).
43. Diane Clapton, "Gal Porn Filmer Roberta Findlay: Men's Sex Trips are Her Meat," *Gallery*, March 1975, 136.
44. Nelson, *Golden Goddesses*, 193.
45. Nelson, *Golden Goddesses*, 169, 179.
46. Bill Wine, "Roberta Findlay's Love of Films is Hardcore." *Courier Post* (Camden, NJ), February 8, 1975, 26.
47. Nelson, *Golden Goddesses*, 180.
48. Bob Abel, "Roberta Findlay: She's No Angel," *Film International*, May 1975, 33.
49. Alexandra Heller-Nicholas, "Anti-auteur: The Films of Roberta Findlay," in Ernest Mathijs and Jamie Sexton (eds), *The Routledge Companion to Cult Cinema* (New York: Routledge, 2020), 402.
50. West and Hall, "Roberta Findlay: A Respectable Woman"; Peary, "Woman in Porn," 32.
51. Findlay's cinematographic skills (which were self-taught) have been highlighted even by mainstream critics; for example, Addison Verrill, in his *Variety* review of *Angel Number 9*, wrote that the film was "strikingly photographed." September 27, 1974, 16.
52. West and Hall, "Roberta Findlay: A Respectable Woman."; Nelson, *Golden Goddesses*, 192.
53. Abel, "Roberta Findlay: She's No Angel," 33.

CHAPTER 1

Singularity and Conformity: Feminism and Roberta Findlay's Strategic Marketing Communications

Finley Freibert

Attending the opening of her film *Angel Number 9* at New York's Lincoln Art theater on November 19, 1974, Roberta Findlay experienced a brief yet intense altercation. In a later interview, Findlay recalled that at the premiere two women—who she perceived as lesbians—confronted her about some press statements she had made to publicize the film; as Findlay put it in a derogatory manner, "these two women—and I use the term loosely—came in—real bulldykes—and started to rant and rave."[1] The two women took issue with Findlay's statement in the film's press materials that she would never hire a woman on her film crew for any reason, a statement reflecting both Findlay's extreme dislike for women and her past negative experiences on an all-woman film crew. As Findlay recalled, one of the two women was particularly furious, pointing her finger in Findlay's face and stating, "How the hell do you come off saying something like that? How're the rest of us going to get ahead?"[2] The two women reportedly left the theater as the film started.

This confrontation, which underscored gender inequity in relation to film industries, prefigures the more substantial feminist response to the Findlay-lensed *Snuff* (1976, dir. Michael Findlay), a film that instigated a large degree of feminist anti-pornography organizing.[3] Yet importantly, the main criticism Findlay received at the earlier *Angel* premiere was not focused on the film's pornographic content, but rather on Findlay's vocal commitment to sexist conditions of socio-economic inequality. This incident underscores the effectiveness of *Angel Number 9*'s marketing campaign at circulating Findlay's persona as an anti-feminist pornographer. In fact, the incident itself was recounted in press interviews with Findlay, in order to further promote her filmmaking enterprise and entrench her anti-feminist persona.

Roberta Findlay has repeatedly stated in interviews that she is not a feminist, through both direct refusal and explicit statements of her misogyny. Such statements circulate primarily in the contexts of male-dominated publics: male-oriented adult magazines, interviews with male journalists, and oral histories for cult cinema fandom venues.[4] While certainly Findlay's anti-feminist statements are an expression of an ideological perspective (often reiterated by Findlay in a sarcastic and comical tone), what if we take the various iterations of such statements in the contexts of Findlay's rise from contract employee (as primarily a cinematographer) to management as CEO of Reeltime Distributing? If we do so, such statements might be better understood as strategic communications generated to address both cultural and market contexts within which Findlay was working to position herself. This chapter examines numerous public communications with which Findlay was involved during her adult film career. It traces the contexts of Findlay's industrial advancement as a lens for understanding her public statements as strategic communications decisions.

Public communications of Findlay's position against the women's liberation movement served to assuage the anxieties against the perceived threat that a female director of pornography might antagonize her male-dominated customer base. The effectiveness of such public communications is reflected in the opening incident of this chapter, which instantiates that Roberta Findlay's public anti-feminism reached far beyond her perceived customer base to the women's movement itself, a movement that she associated with the two women who approached her at the *Angel* premiere. While perhaps she did not intend to incite feminists, the sheer repetition of her anti-women statements throughout her career suggest they were purposeful, in the mode of strategic communications.

The study of strategic communications is a sector of communication inquiry that aims to understand how individuals and groups craft and circulate messages to reach particular goals. Strategic communications are especially important to businesses because companies rely on a variety of communication methods to circulate perceived "values" of their products and services to certain stakeholders and customers. Such communications are understood as components of a company's marketing operations, which include advertising, publicity, and public relations, among other functions. Public relations and publicity are particularly advantageous forms of marketing communication than traditional advertising because they are usually more cost-effective and they are "generally considered to be more objective and therefore more believable in the perception of the target groups."[5] Strategic marketing communication involves more than message transmission; it is broadly concerned with providing a means to an end, whether that be selling a product or shifting a brand's image. Ultimately, strategic marketing communications construct a shared context of understanding between companies and their publics, aiming to situate the company, its stakeholders, and the public on the same page with regard to a given product or sentiment.[6]

While strategic communication studies are often future oriented, focusing on how effective strategies might be further developed and implemented from present insights, this chapter takes strategic communication as an analytic lens for understanding the past, and, specifically, how and why ideologies have circulated in previous periods of consumer capitalism. In the case of Findlay, a focus on strategic communications reveals how business interests operate by offsetting competing ideologies (entrepreneurial capitalism and anti-feminism, in this case) based on their profitability at the time. To this end, a media industry studies approach—indebted to the critical methods of cultural studies—is productive for framing a history of Roberta Findlay's public communication strategies. As John Thornton Caldwell has asserted, a key struggle of media industry research is the disentanglement of the intent and effects of certain strategic communications— what he calls "managed self-disclosures"—on publicly circulated information about a company and its products.[7] In the case of the marketing campaign for Roberta Findlay's *Angel Number 9*, the film was selectively singled out as "the first erotically explicit film made by a woman."[8] Yet just as this selective self-disclosure operates to differentiate the film in a market dominated by male directors, there is a simultaneous move to further manage this disclosure, for instance, by pulling back the reins on the disclosure's progressive potential through an assertion of Roberta Findlay's anti-feminism.

Findlay participated in a number of publicity events for the film—including press conferences, television appearances, radio conversations, and magazine interviews—to do just that.[9] In addition, rather than foreground laudatory comments from adult media personalities such as *Screw* publisher Al Goldstein, advertising copy for the film gave evidence of the film's media saturation strategy, featuring quotes from local New York radio personalities Bob Grant of WMCA and Bob Salmaggi of WINS.[10] Via this saturation campaign, which included numerous self-disclosures from Findlay, *Angel Number 9* could be transformed into a differentiated product through what Raymond Williams calls the "magical system" of marketing in which the products themselves "are not enough but must be validated, if only in fantasy, by association with social and personal meanings."[11] Perhaps a result of some of these marketing strategies, *Angel Number 9* led the box office in its New York premiere week, beating out both United Artists' *Lenny* (1974, dir. Bob Fosse) and John Cassavetes's *A Woman Under the Influence* (1974).[12] The film's promotion and box office success also likely contributed to its perception as significant in the academic sphere, instantiated by coverage in the French leftist film journal *Positif* and a lengthy psychoanalytic consideration in the early American film studies journal *Velvet Light Trap*.[13]

Jennifer Moorman has compellingly argued that even as "Findlay's work and persona mobilize troubling images toward potentially feminist ends," this is belied by the fact that Findlay's self-proclaimed pleasure in seeing violence against women represented an "internalized misogyny."[14] Extending from Moorman's observation, I argue that Findlay's misogyny is part of a larger communications strategy aimed at a male-dominated public for the purpose of product and personality differentiation. The communication of Findlay's industrial and cultural singularity entailed a number of associated components in the publicity campaign that focused on her gender as a marketing signifier.

By tracing Findlay's public reflections on her work in the adult film industry, this chapter argues that Findlay's marketing strategy evinces a complexity informed by both her personal views and her perception of market contexts. The chapter begins with a pre-history, recounting one of Findlay's initial involvements with publicity while she was a contract cinematographer. This publicity, for a film called *The Waiting Room* (1973, dir. Karen Sperling), emphasized the gender of the film's crew as the film's primary marketing component. The chapter then traces two main trends in Findlay's communication strategy around her adult filmmaking enterprises. As we will see, there are two genres of sentiment that Findlay's public communications aspire toward: singularity and conformity. The first genre conveys her singularity within a homogenizing industry, effectively differentiating her films from typical products in the market. The second genre asserts Findlay's conformity to dominant industrial and cultural values, dissuading fears that her market singularity might diverge from the status quo to the point of unmarketability. Findlay's strategic communications notably changed as a result of two key industrial shifts around 1980: Findlay's transition from partner in DFS Enterprises to CEO of Reeltime Distributing, and the rise of domestic consumption markets of cable and home video. Coinciding with these two shifts, Findlay began increasingly to target a female audience, a move contradicting her earlier statements, yet reflecting her strategy to expand her consumer base due to a perception of an overlooked viewer demographic.

FINDLAY ENTERS THE PUBLIC SPHERE

Before the development of a public communications strategy to promote her adult film enterprises, Findlay was involved with publicity events for an all-woman experimental film production, *The Waiting Room* (1973). The film was a pet project of Karen Sperling, heiress and granddaughter to Harry Warner (of Warner Brothers), and daughter of film producer-writer Milton Sperling. Despite its minimal public circulation, Karen Sperling's first feature, *Make a Face* (1971), was promoted substantially via coordinated press interviews and invitations for journalists to observe on-set operations, a harbinger of *The Waiting Room*'s later promotional strategy involving Findlay.[15] For example, *Show* magazine reporters were present at an on-set event when Sperling invited her parents and others to observe her non-conventional filmmaking style, which diverged sharply from her family's Hollywood sensibilities.[16] This coverage construed Sperling's film as a curiosity, effectively a vanity project of an upper-class Hollywood heiress.

For *The Waiting Room* Sperling cultivated even more press attention, this time emphasizing the film's all-female crew consisting of thirty-five women, with particular focus on Findlay. It is unclear how Findlay became acquainted with Sperling; however, Sperling did make connections in adult cinema when she appeared as a juror for *Screw* magazine's New York Erotic Film Festival of 1972 as part of a jury of high-profile figures including Gore Vidal, Andy Warhol, Betty Dodson, Miloš Forman, Sylvia Miles, and Al Goldstein.[17] Findlay's history in adult cinema was a key feature reiterated in the press coverage for *The Waiting Room*. Industry magazine *Boxoffice* asserted that Findlay was a figure "who has been successful in the sex film field," and the *New York Daily News* expressed in a parenthetical statement that Findlay had learned to make films via her husband, Michael, who "let her help out with his soft-core pornographic films."[18] Such statements of Findlay's pornographic connections combined with other details—the all-woman crew and Sperling's patina of Hollywood money— to promote the film's unique and unusual admixture of production personnel.

Notably, Findlay became a central visual fixture in the press coverage of the film. Reporting in the *New York Daily News* featured a photograph of her in the process of dollying the camera with assistance from Alexis Krasilovsky.[19] The Associated Press took several photos on set for a syndicated newspaper article by Eve Sharbutt. One photo was entitled "The Girls in the Crew" featuring Findlay pointing the camera at Sperling in a hospital hallway, and the second photo was a full shot of Findlay seated on the camera dolly sandwiched between two camera assistants.[20] These images were employed to emphasize a perceived affective distinction in women's filmmaking, and, specifically, the intense contemplation and psychological connections between the female crew members, underscored with a photo caption reading "Quiet Intensity—Cinematographer Roberta Findlay receives moral as well as technical support from her assistants."[21] Although the extent of the purposefulness of the staging within these press photographs is unclear, one historical audience member of a press screening alleged that Sperling had paid the prominent public relations firm Rogers, Cowan & Brennan to handle the film's media campaign.[22]

Press questions about the gender politics of hiring an all-woman crew reflect the fact that any divergence from the film industry's hegemonically masculine bias was understood as a challenge to male chauvinist hiring practices. Yet Sperling's refusal to align her film's all-woman production context with a feminist politics reflected a sort of product differentiation tactic, anticipating Findlay's later rejection of being perceived as a feminist pornographer. As conveyed in the photographs and captions of Findlay, Sperling argued that she hired an all-woman crew for atmosphere and affective charge rather than "any movement reason."[23] In this way, Sperling's employment practices were coded in the press commentary as marketable production decisions, construing the film not as a political statement but as a unique curiosity within a male-dominated market.

Figure 1.1 The premiere of *The Waiting Room* (*Los Angeles Times*, November 7, 1973).

COMMUNICATING SINGULARITY AS A GENDERED MARKETING SIGNIFIER

Recalling the gender-emphasizing publicity for *The Waiting Room*, Findlay returned to the public eye for the release of her film *Angel Number 9*. The advertising copy proclaimed the film to be "the first erotically explicit film ever made by a woman," and—as we will see—Findlay participated in a number of media events to promote the film that similarly emphasized her gender identity for marketing purposes.[24] Specifically, the topic of gender was marshaled to frame Findlay as exceptional in a homogeneous industry, and thereby her products could be singled out and differentiated within the adult film market. This focus on Findlay as a woman threw into relief at least two components of her marketable singularity. First, she represented one of the few exceptions to the male-dominated profession of adult film directing, and film directing in general for that matter. Second, Findlay's work in adult film was perceived as being in tension with her supposed alignment with the women's liberation movement, a notion that she dissuaded by rejecting feminist politics. The press's focus on whether Findlay and her work could be considered feminist resonates with fellow exploitation film director Stephanie Rothman's recollection that the press was obsessed with the lens of feminism as a "one-note interpretation" of her work.[25]

In the public communications accompanying *Angel* and her later adult films, Findlay subscribed to the seemingly paradoxical stance that despite her position as a woman in the adult film industry, she did not advocate for hiring women in non-screen roles (she would later specify that she meant crew roles other than wardrobe and makeup).[26] In interviews coinciding with the release of *Angel*, Findlay cited her negative experiences while making *The Waiting Room* the reason for her imperative not to hire women as crew members. For an interview with *Man to Man* magazine, Findlay recalled:

> The last one had a crew of 30 women and it taught me something, namely that women inexperienced in film making can turn out only one thing, a limping product. As of now, I wouldn't hire a woman because I wouldn't trust her to do the job.[27]

When an interviewer for *Sir* later asked her why the film industry was so male-dominated, Findlay injected her response with more of her trademark arch misogyny:

> Because most women are inept. That is to say, they have no skills in making a film. A few years ago I had the unfortunate opportunity to work on a project with thirty other women . . . Shit!—it was dreadful. The end results were catastrophic. For every three women we had at our disposal, it would have taken one man to do the job correctly.[28]

In such interviews, Findlay's display of misogyny and abhorrence for women workers dovetailed with her contemptuous stance toward feminism.

To Findlay, anti-pornography politics was an inextricable component to feminism. Yet notably, adult magazine reporters were inclined to read Findlay's films as feminist cultural productions, with one *Gallery* writer describing *Angel* as a "vicious, feminist, ball-busting, eunuch-making diatribe against men . . . the ultimate man-hating document," while an interviewer for *Adult Cinema Review* argued that with *The Tiffany Minx* Findlay was "making sex films from a feminist point of view."[29] Quick to contradict such readings, Findlay recalled being confronted by anti-pornography feminists at least twice, once following the release of *Angel* and then again after the release of *Snuff*. Given Findlay's viewpoint, it is important to note that not all feminists were against pornography. Anti-censorship feminist positions were asserted at this time by the sex worker collective COYOTE (Call Off Your Old Tired Ethics) and pioneering lesbian feminist activist Del Martin, yet the anti-pornography stance constituted a more vocal component of the feminist movement of the 1970s and 1980s.[30] Consequently, for Findlay, feminism represented a direct opposition to her profession. As Findlay put it, "many of these women who have called me and yelled at me have never seen a porn film, or if they have they've seen old pictures . . . They just assume that all X-rated movies are about degrading and humiliating women."[31]

Beyond the anti-pornography stance, Findlay's anti-feminism also stemmed from a staunch commitment to bootstrap ideology. Both the conservative "pull yourself up by your bootstraps" principle and a relentless individualism informed Findlay's communication of her industrial and cultural singularity. When asked about her stance on women's liberation, Findlay idealized a strong work ethic: "I'm mean and nasty, I guess, but I don't really have any sympathy for complaining women. I've worked pretty hard and I didn't rely on anybody else—women or men—to do anything for me, so I don't see why I should help anybody else."[32] The focus on herself was later clarified and reiterated throughout various interviews as a kind of libertarian politics of the individual. In 1975, for example, she stressed such self-determination:

> I really don't *care* about anybody else, you gotta understand that. I know I'm supposed to care about women's lib, but I know I'm not gonna be too popular on that front. When you talk sexual liberation, all I can think of is myself. And I don't have a single problem that I know of. I'm doing just fine![33]

In this way, an anti-collective personal form of liberation could be construed as Findlay's structural disruption of the status quo. Rather than a bellwether of industrial progress toward gender equality, she represented a singular exception to the gendered inequity of the adult film industry; an exceptional status attained through an investment in idealized American values of individuality and perpetual work ethic.

COMMUNICATING CONFORMITY AS AN INDUSTRIAL STRATEGY

In contrast to the cultivation of Findlay's singularity associated with her gender identity, a second strategy emerged in Findlay's public communications that situated her within the confines of industrial and cultural conformity. Such communications underscored Findlay's similarities—rather than her singularity and difference—to a number of cultural factors that constituted a status quo. Findlay increasingly conveyed her conformity in tandem with her ascent up the corporate ranks. After separating from her husband Michael by the early 1970s, Findlay effectively worked as a contract worker for Allan Shackleton, for whom she shot and directed several films for flat fees ranging from $2,000 to $4,000.[34] Physically abused by Shackleton, Findlay left to collaborate with acclaimed music producer Walter Sear.[35] With David Darby (aka Robert Michaels) they founded DFS (Darby Findlay Sear) Enterprises, a film company wherein Findlay and Sear coordinated production and Darby handled distribution, oftentimes on a states-rights basis.[36] Finally, Findlay and Sear broke from Darby to form their own company Reeltime Distributing in 1979.[37] Findlay's statements across this period employ an increasing amount of conformist rhetoric, balancing out the differentiation approach described in the previous section.

In public statements, Findlay positioned herself as comfortably assimilated into the industry of adult cinema. Akin to other producers of feature-length adult film, Findlay asserted the cultural cache of hardcore narrative features over non-narrative hardcore loops and "educational" features. In a 1975 interview, Findlay admitted to producing "fuck shorts" and white-coaters with her husband Michael, but denigrated their extremely low budgets and referred to such films as "depressing."[38] This class-inflected distinction between hardcore narrative features and the lower-tier products for storefront theaters and small gauge markets reflected the dominant position of adult film entrepreneurs that worked in the established 35mm feature industry, a position that—as Elena Gorfinkel asserts—was aimed at diminishing the competitive potential of the lower tier.[39] In contrast to lower-budget fare, Findlay aimed at approaching the zenith of porno chic. In *Adam Film World*, one writer described her as aspiring toward "excellence" in the production of *Mystique* (1979), and when asked how adult films could improve in "quality," Findlay argued that they needed a combination of high production value, character development, and narratives with seamlessly integrated sex sequences.[40]

If Findlay could be said to subscribe to an identity politics, it would be one centralizing her professional identity as an adult film cinematographer. Early in the 1970s, she attempted to join New York's Local 644, the first IATSE (International Alliance of Theatrical Stage Employees) union for cinematographers, founded in 1926. Findlay wanted to join the union "out of financial need rather than any compelling desire to go legit."[41] However, she was met with a number of barriers to entry into the union including an excessive membership fee, male chauvinist sentiments, and, ultimately, a refusal to tolerate her involvement in adult filmmaking.[42] Findlay's key moment of recognition of her identity as an adult filmmaker was her 1974 indictment on obscenity charges for shooting Jack Bravman's *All in the Sex Family* (1973). In interviews she criticized the trial's excessive length, the arbitrary enforcement of obscenity law (in this case, based on a filming location), and the absurdity of potential sentences (eight years). Speaking to the risk of obscenity prosecutions as part of her identification with an imagined community of adult filmmakers, Findlay estimated, "I guess during the course of our careers, we've all had run-ins with the law."[43] Findlay's obscenity indictment acted as an interpellation into this identity as a sex film

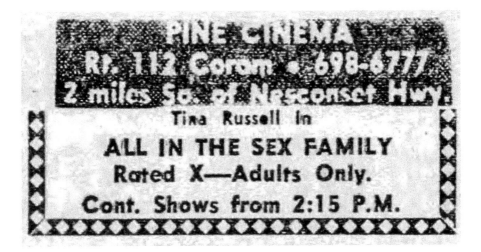

Figure 1.2 The screening of *All in the Sex Family* for which Findlay and Bravman were arrested (*Newsday*, January 28, 1974).

cinematographer because it differentiated her from the "legitimate" industry, both psychologically and legally. She attributed her exclusion from Local 644 to the obscenity indictment that functioned as a partitioning mechanism between unionized cinematographers and adult filmmakers, "So that's how I was thrown out of the union I was never in."[44]

In her public statements, Findlay would often call out the delegitimation of the pornography industry as an unjust cultural phenomenon, "people in the legit film field have a tendency to treat you shabbily as soon as they find out you do porn films. It's a mark against you."[45] Cultural contestations including Findlay's exclusion from Local 644 and the Bravman film bust entrenched Findlay's identification with her profession. In Illinois, even an interview with Findlay was deemed obscene due to its "patently offensive descriptions of sexual conduct."[46] As a rebuttal against obscenity enforcers, Findlay participated in a lawsuit against Point Pleasant and its police after she and several cast and crew members were detained without charge while filming *Honeysuckle Rose* (1979). Findlay's criticism and active opposition to the policing of her line of work aligned with her overall libertarian values, while offering an anomalous example of her alliance and identification with others within the same profession-based identity group.

Reflecting her dedication to an entrepreneurial profession, Findlay asserted an unwavering adherence to market circumstances; in some cases, that commitment contradicted her past misogynist rhetoric. Findlay's anti-feminism, discussed in the last section, catered to her primarily male consumer base, and she initially paid no mind to the possibility of female audiences. When asked in 1978 whether she would ever consider screening her films at a women's film festival, she declared that she would not, expressing her conformity to the formal conventions of a male-dominated industry: "I defy anybody to think that they are made by a woman."[47] However, this tone began to shift following the breakup of DFS and the founding of Reeltime Distributing in 1979. In strategic communication terms, Findlay shifted from an attempt to "create goodwill" with her imagined anti-feminist male audience, toward a new attempt at goodwill with her newly recognized female audience.[48]

With Findlay's ascent to CEO of Reeltime, her new responsibilities entailed not only film production but also, crucially, distribution—a role previously incarnated in DFS by partner David Darby. Findlay's distribution work, which entailed travel to exhibition spaces across the country, prompted her revelation that women comprised a significant portion of her viewership, both in the context of couples' audiences and as single viewers. She noted as much in 1981:

> In my travels through the country I stopped in many theatres that we deal with, just to see what was going on. And in addition to seeing a lot more couples in the audience, there were many women alone. In Chicago, I went to the big Flagship Theatre in the downtown area and there were an awful lot of unattached women.[49]

With this revelation in mind, rather than defy anyone to view her films as different than those made by men, Findlay underscored her different approach to filmmaking in comparison to male directors. She articulated a gender difference in directorial practices informed by a qualitative attention to detail: "I think I see more details then [sic] a man might. While working on a scene— sex scene or dialogue—I'm very interested in mannerisms and the personal interactions."[50] She further described *The Tiffany Minx* as specifically tailored to a female audience: "I think women like the idea of veils, sex cloaked in mystery. Women find the idea of two people being together, talking together, infinitely more erotic than the piston shot."[51] Findlay even began to openly use her name once again—rather than the numerous male pseudonyms she used in credits from 1975 to 1982—in credits and industry press coverage for later more romantic and less violent films like *Playgirl* (1982) and *Glitter* (1983). In a sense, Findlay was more inclined to claim female authorship and pursue what she perceived as a women's sensibility only as she discerned the specter of the female customer.

Findlay's vocal targeting of a female audience would become all the more important with the rise of distribution models geared toward home consumption, specifically home video, cable, and satellite television. Reflecting the home consumer market's particular association with female viewers, Findlay insisted to industry magazine *The Film Journal*, "the bottom line is that women have become an important segment of the home audience. Adult filmmakers, who before only had to concern themselves with a mostly male audience, are going to have to tailor their films to this reality."[52] Karen Jaehne, an employee of a cable station who reviewed and selected adult content for late night cable programming, viewed Findlay's *Playgirl* and dubbed Findlay's tactic of putting a veneer of female agency in pornographic films "feminismo," a cynical attempt to cash in on a newfound female audience rather than a sincere commitment to developing a feminist pornographic form.[53]

CONCLUSION: SELF-PROCLAIMED BOURGEOIS PORNOGRAPHER

Strategies of singularity and conformity can be understood as part of the construction of a bourgeois sensibility around Roberta Findlay's professional persona. The tactic of singling out Findlay's identity in an individualized manner worked in tandem with overall product differentiation strategies. In turn, so as not to threaten the industry in which she was ascending—from contract worker, to corporate partner, and eventually to chief administrator—a simultaneous strategy worked to convey Findlay's conformity to the industrial status quo. In this way, Findlay's public statements amounted to strategic communications, operating strategically in the sphere of marketing to position her both to adult film consumers and within the broader public sphere. With the chapter's focus in mind, it should be noted that Findlay was cognizant of her socially conservative bourgeois expressions to the point of witty self-deprecation.

Seemingly conveying her aspiration toward a higher position in the industrial hierarchy, a photo accompanying one of her earliest interviews features Findlay with accessories, holding a posture that connotes an ostentatious film producer.[54] In the photograph she wears a white turtleneck, her right hand resting against her temple in a relaxed pose as she seemingly glares at the interviewer, about to deliver one of her witty responses to a question. Sending the photo over the top is Findlay's left hand, which holds a gaudy cigarette holder of excessive length, a wisp of smoke visible against her dark hair. Findlay's self-presentation in this photograph embodies her bourgeois sensibility, a pretentious elitism tempered by a knowing irony.

More than once Findlay has described herself as bourgeois, often with a degree of sarcasm in the context of explaining her social conservatism.[55] Earlier interviews display a shift from Findlay's emphasis on narrative refinement as her tactic of elevating the genre, toward "quality" discourses (such as discussions of higher production value) employed after the founding of Reeltime and coinciding with the move to appeal to audiences of women.[56] Anticipating Linda Williams's famous description of the "narrative-number" dichotomy in adult film—yet in terms more oriented toward class distinction reflecting Findlay and Sear's avid operagoing—Findlay described the narrative structure of her hardcore films as equivalent to the structure of an opera with arias, soprano sections, and so on.[57] In more recent audio commentaries and interviews, Findlay often displays a more negative attitude toward her adult films, reiterating her bourgeois positionality, but in a more self-critical, yet still tongue-in-cheek, light. These tastes were long established, going back to Findlay's childhood training as a concert pianist, City College performances as an accompanist to silent film screenings, and arthouse moviegoing with Michael Findlay. Casey Scott's recent audio commentaries with Findlay are generative in revealing Findlay's filmic tastes, which amount to studio-era directors including William Wyler and Billy Wilder.[58] In this sense, Findlay institutes a new form of singularity, here a differentiation from the contemporary paracinematic reclamation of "low" culture (of which her work has been a part), and instead positions herself in alignment with conformity as a devotee to the finer popular cultural form of classical Hollywood cinema.[59]

For sake of comparison, numerous of Findlay's contemporaries have navigated their own public personas in a variety of ways. Vaulted into the porno-chic pantheon with the success of *Deep Throat* (1972) and *The Devil in Miss Jones* (1973), director Gerard Damiano cultivated a suave persona aspiring to the status of artist. Already culturally elevated with the urbane sensibility of his earlier softcore features, Radley Metzger retired to the pseudonymous shadows avoiding publicity (and perhaps obscenity charges) during the release of his hardcore features. Shaun Costello cranked out numerous one-day wonders, often working under pseudonyms or without directorial credit, yet has retrospectively gained name recognition and a cult fanbase following releases of his more notorious films *Forced Entry* (1973) and *Water Power* (1977) on DVD in the 2000s. On the west coast, Howard Ziehm was somewhat overshadowed by his producer and business partner Bill Osco, the "boy king of L.A. porno," until the 2010s when Ziehm re-emerged, granted interviews, and published his memoir.[60]

This chapter has focused on analyzing Roberta Findlay's public communications as strategic marketing decisions. If we consider Findlay's films alone, their sheer heterogeneity in form and content "resists orthodox auteurist frameworks," as Alexandra Heller-Nicholas has argued.[61] Yet considering Findlay's communication strategies within a market context, there are striking consistencies that might be best understood as an entrepreneurial signature. These communications amount to situating Findlay within a socially conservative bourgeois sphere, at once invested in the ethic of individuality that is entwined to her singular ascent up the corporate ladder, while also reflecting her conformity to the normative standards of a capitalist enterprise. Findlay's strategic communications positioned her for the industrial success that she ultimately attained, confirming

Raymond Williams's early observation that such communications go beyond sell-ing products in a market and instead function to "sell persons, in a particular kind of culture."[62] Findlay presents a representative case for the cultural implications accompanying the negotiated tension between differentiation and standardization within capitalist markets.

NOTES

1. Timothy Green Beckley, "Female Porn Producer Roberta Findlay," *Sir*, September 1976: 11.
2. Beckley, "Female Porn Producer Roberta Findlay," 11.
3. Carolyn Bronstein, *Battling Pornography: The American Feminist Anti-Pornography Movement, 1976–1986* (Cambridge: Cambridge University Press, 2011), 83–126; Whitney Strub, *Perversion for Profit: The Politics of Pornography and the Rise of the New Right* (New York: Columbia University Press, 2013), 230–6. Fascinatingly, famed gay pornographer Christopher Rage claimed that he was responsible for the title and advertising campaign for *Snuff*, see "An Afternoon with Christopher Rage at the Chateau Marmont," *Studflix* 6, no. 6 (October 1988): 9.
4. For examples from the 2010s, see "Roberta Findlay!," *Third Eye Cinema*, June 17, 2012, https://thirdeyecinema.podbean.com/e/third-eye-cinema-61712-with-roberta-findlay/ (accessed May 26, 2022); Ashley West and April Hall, "Roberta Findlay: A Respectable Woman—Podcast 53," *Rialto Report*, August 16, 2015, https://www.therialtoreport.com/2015/08/16/roberta-findlay/ (accessed July 28, 2021).
5. Patrick de Pelsmacker, Joeri van den Bergh, and Maggie Geuens, *Marketing Communications* (Harlow, UK: Financial Times Prentice Hall, 2001), 249.
6. Richard J. Varey, *Marketing Communication: Principles and Practice* (London, UK: Routledge, 2002), 27–30. Strategic marketing communication is sometimes used interchangeably with the closely related field of integrated marketing communication (often abbreviated as IMC); for overviews of these fields of study see the texts by Varey and Pelsmack et al.
7. John Thornton Caldwell, "Cultures of Production: Studying Industry's Deep Texts, Reflexive Rituals, and Managed Self-Disclosures," in Jennifer Holt and Alisa Perren (eds), *Media Industries: History, Theory, and Method* (Chichester: Wiley-Blackwell, 2009), 199–212.
8. *Angel Number 9* Advertisement for Lincoln Art, *New York Daily News*, November 20, 1974, 46.
9. For example, Findlay appeared at press conferences in New York and Philadelphia, on Ken Fairchild's WMCA show in New York, and on Tim Boxer's celebrity talk show *Traveling with the Stars* on Manhattan cable television. See respectively, "Philadelphia," *Boxoffice*, March 10, 1975, E5; "Radio Highlights," *New York Daily News*, November 16, 1974, 33; "Traveling with the Stars Advertisement," *Back Stage*, January 24, 1975, 7.
10. *Angel Number 9* Advertisement for Lincoln Art, *After Dark* 7, no. 9 (January 1975): 17.
11. Raymond Williams, "Advertising: The Magic System," 1961, reprint in Simon During (ed.), *The Cultural Studies Reader* (London and New York: Routledge, 1999), 335.
12. "'Angel Number 9' Is No. 1 in NY at 640," *Boxoffice*, December 2, 1974, E1.
13. Pisanus Fraxi, "Les Grandes chaleurs (Lo schermo di calore)," *Positif—Revue mensuelle de cinéma*, June 1976, 64; Dennis Giles, "Angel on Fire: Three Texts of Desire," *The Velvet Light Trap: A Critical Journal of Film and Television* 16 (Fall 1976): 41–5.

14. Jennifer Moorman, "'The Hardest of Hardcore': Locating Feminist Possibilities in Women's Extreme Pornography," *Signs: Journal of Women in Culture and Society* 42, no. 3 (2017): 708.

15. There was substantial high-profile newspaper coverage on Sperling and her film, as well as reporting in elevated cultural venues such as the gay-oriented magazine *After Dark*. See Roger Greenspun, "Screen: Karen Sperling's 'Make a Face' Arrives," *New York Times*, August 16, 1971, 34; Enid Nemy, "An Heiress Who Likes Doing Eight Jobs at Once," *New York Times*, August 28, 1971, 16; John Buchanan, "'I'll Keep on Persisting' Karen Sperling Is No Warner Brothers Debutante," *After Dark* 4, no. 8 (December 1971): 26–7.

16. Barbara Kevles, "Looking for Karen Sperling," *Show: The Magazine of Films and the Arts* 1, no. 6 (June 1970): 30–3, 86.

17. "NY Erotic Fete Prizes," *Gay Scene* 2, no. 8 (1972): 3.

18. "Broadway," *Boxoffice*, April 9, 1973, E-4; Kathleen Carroll, "A Film First By & About Women," *New York Daily News*, April 29, 1973, C24.

19. Carroll, "A Film First," C24.

20. "The Girls in the Crew," AP Newsfeatures Photo G3706, April 27, 1973, https://www.ebay.com/itm/1973-P...Sperling-actress-director-with-crew-of-Double-Circle-/303467258395 (accessed August 28, 2020); "Quiet! Intensity on the Set," AP Newsfeatures Photo G3705, April 27, 1973, https://www.ebay.com/itm/1973-Press-Photo-Roberta-Finley-films-...nd-New-York/372949214866 (accessed August 28, 2020).

21. Eve Sharbutt, "All-Woman Production Crew Puts Feeling on Film," *Press and Sun Bulletin [Binghamton, NY]*, May 12, 1973, 13.

22. sdiner82, "A Vanity Film, Barely Remembered and Best Forgotten," Review, IMDB, September 16, 2016, https://www.imdb.com/title/tt0243400/ (accessed May 26, 2022).

23. Carroll, "A Film First," C24. In another interview Sperling added, "None of us is really active in the women's movement, but all of us had done films before, and understood how an all-woman crew would contribute to the story," Sharbutt, "All-Woman Production Crew," 13.

24. *Angel Number 9* Advertisement for Lincoln Art, 46.

25. Alicia Kozma, "Stephanie Rothman Does Not Exist: Narrating a Lost History of Women in Film," *Camera Obscura: Feminism, Culture, and Media Studies* 94, 32, no. 1 (2017): 182.

26. For the later revision of this statement see Roberta Findlay interview by Casey Scott, Audio Commentary, *Mascara*, Blu-ray (Vinegar Syndrome, 2017).

27. Roberta Findlay, interview by Raoul MacFarlane, "Roberta Findlay: Queen of Porn," *Man to Man*, May 1975, 49.

28. Findlay, interview by Beckley, "Female Porn Producer Roberta Findlay," 9.

29. Roberta Findlay, interview by Diana Clapton, "Gal Porn Filmer Roberta Findlay: Men's Sex Trips Are Her Meat," *Gallery* 3, no. 2 (March 1975): 91; Roberta Findlay, interview by Gary Sheinfeld, "The Tiffany Minx," *Adult Cinema Review* 1, no. 5 (November 1981): 61.

30. Galloping Horse, "National Tattle," *COYOTE Howls* 4, no. 1 (1976): 3; Del Martin, "An Open Letter to Feminists about Anti-Pornography Laws," c. 1980, Folder 6, Box 27, Phyllis Lyon and Del Martin Papers, 1924–2000, Collection 1993–13, Gay, Lesbian, Bisexual, and Transgender Historical Society, San Francisco, CA, USA.

31. Findlay, interview by Sheinfeld, "The Tiffany Minx," 61.

32. Bill Wine, "Roberta Findlay's Love of Films Is Hardcore," *Courier Post [Camden, NJ]*, February 8, 1975, 26.

33. Findlay, interview by Clapton, "Gal Porn Filmer," 137.

34. Findlay, interview by West and Hall, "Roberta Findlay: A Respectable Woman."

35. Findlay, interview by West and Hall, "Roberta Findlay: A Respectable Woman."

36. For example, the Findlay-directed DFS films *A Woman's Torment* (1977), *Underage* (1977), and *From Holly with Love* (1978) all had distribution arrangements that involved subdistribution to certain territories on a states-rights basis. See "Maine," *Boxoffice*, October 17, 1977, NE-4; "Rhode Island," *Boxoffice*, May 1, 1978, NE-6; "New Bedford," *Boxoffice*, December 11, 1978, NE-4.

37. The founding date for Reeltime is listed as April 25, 1979 in the business filing records at the New York Secretary of State, "Entity Information: Reeltime Distributing Corp.," DOS ID #: 553604, NYS Department of State: Division of Corporations: Corporation and Business Entity Database, https://www.dos.ny.gov/corps/bus_entity_search.html (accessed August 28, 2020).

38. Findlay, interview by Beckley, "Female Porn Producer Roberta Findlay," 82.

39. Elena Gorfinkel, *Lewd Looks: American Sexploitation Cinema in the 1960s* (Minneapolis: University of Minnesota Press, 2017), 89–95.

40. Scott Roberts, "A Sex Film Is a Sex Film Is a Sex Film," *Adam Film World* (May 1981): 52.

41. Bob Abel, "Roberta Findlay: She's No Angel," *Film International* 1, no. 2 (May 1975): 85.

42. Bob Abel, "Roberta Findlay: She's No Angel," *Film International* 1, no. 2 (May 1975), 85, 95.

43. Findlay, interview by Beckley, "Female Porn Producer Roberta Findlay," 86. A discussion of the excessive length of the trial was also registered in a reported decision by the Supreme Court of Suffolk County, where the defendants' motions to dismiss were denied, *People v. Bravman*, 393 N.Y.S.2d 266 (1977).

44. Abel, "Roberta Findlay," 95. For reporting on the raid and its aftermath see, "'Movie' Shot in Great River Leads to Indictment of 12 on Porno Counts," *Islip Town Bulletin*, May 2, 1974, 7; "Porno Raid Grabs CBS Exec Producer," *Variety*, May 1, 1974, 3; "Teacher Is Arrested," *Suffolk County News*, May 2, 1974, 3; "12 Arrested in Porn Raid," *Long Island Advance*, May 2, 1974, 10-A.

45. Roberta Findlay, interview by Ken Gaul, "The Feminine *Mystique*," *Genesis* 7, no. 7 (February 1980): 58.

46. *City of Belleville v. Morgan*, 60 Ill. App. 3d 434 (1978), 442.

47. Roberta Findlay, interview by Gerald Peary, "Woman in Porn: How Young Roberta Findlay Finally Grew Up and Made Snuff," *Take One* 6, September 1978, 32.

48. On "creating goodwill" with audiences as a strategic communication method, see de Pelsmacker, van den Bergh, and Geuens, *Marketing Communications*, 247.

49. Findlay, interview by Sheinfeld, "The Tiffany Minx," 64.

50. Findlay, interview by Sheinfeld, "The Tiffany Minx," 62.

51. Findlay, interview by Sheinfeld, "The Tiffany Minx," 84.

52. Jeffrey Wells, "Sex in the Home (Where It Belongs)," *Film Journal*, June 28, 1982, 20, 22.

53. Karen Jaehne, "Confessions of a Feminist Porn Programmer," *Film Quarterly* 37, no. 1 (1983): 9–16.

54. Findlay interview by MacFarlane, "Roberta Findlay: Queen of Porn," 48.

55. "Roberta Findlay!," *Third Eye Cinema*; Findlay, interview by West and Hall, "Roberta Findlay: A Respectable Woman."

56. Findlay, interview by Beckley, "Female Porn Producer Roberta Findlay," 82; Findlay, interview by Sheinfeld, "The Tiffany Minx," 64; Roberta Findlay, "Female Porn Producer Counts Cum Shots," *Adult Cinema Review*, December 1983, 62.

57. Linda Williams, *Hard Core: Power, Pleasure, and the "Frenzy of the Visible"* (Berkeley: University of California Press, 1989), 120–52; Findlay, interview by Gaul, "The Feminine *Mystique*," 59.

58. Roberta Findlay interview by Casey Scott, Audio Commentary, *Liquid Assets*, DVD (Vinegar Syndrome, 2017); Roberta Findlay interview by Casey Scott, Audio Commentary, *A Woman's Torment*, DVD (Vinegar Syndrome, 2017).

59. Jeffrey Sconce coined the term "paracinema" to describe the taste culture associated with reclaiming cinematic "cultural detritus" such as vintage pornography, see Jeffrey Sconce, "'Trashing' the Academy: Taste, Excess, and an Emerging Politics of Cinematic Style," *Screen* 36, no. 4 (1995): 372.

60. Addison Verrill, "Bill Osco, Boy King of L.A. Porno, Grossing Over $2,000,000 Presently; 10-City Nucleus; 'Actors' A-Plenty," *Variety*, December 30, 1970, 5. Howard Ziehm, *Take Your Shame and Shove It: We Ain't in the Garden of Eden No More* (Township, NJ: BookBaby, 2015).

61. Alexandra Heller-Nicholas, "Anti-auteur: The Films of Roberta Findlay," in Ernest Mathijs and Jamie Sexton (eds), *The Routledge Companion to Cult Cinema* (London, UK: Routledge, 2020), 409.

62. Williams, "Advertising: The Magic System," 333.

CHAPTER 2

"Not Even a Lesbian," or Roberta Findlay's Ambivalently Queer/ Feminist Hardcore Cinema

Jennifer Moorman

"I don't like women."

Roberta Findlay[1]

"I like to see women raped on the screen . . . I get turned on by the beating of women. Of course, I don't do it in real life. I'm not even a lesbian."

Roberta Findlay[2]

As the quotations above suggest, Roberta Findlay is a self-professed hater of women. I will argue nonetheless that, as one of only a handful of women directors working in US adult film in the 1970s, her filmography and public persona mobilize troubling and even misogynistic images and ideas toward potentially—if unintentionally—queer and feminist ends. As such, her work contributes significantly to what I am calling the "minor cinema" of women's pornography.

The question of how to define a woman's film has been approached from many angles. Alison Butler argues:

Women's cinema is a notoriously difficult concept to define. It suggests, without clarity, films that might be made by, addressed to, or concerned with women, or all three. It is neither a genre nor a movement in film history, it has no single lineage of its own, no national boundaries, no filmic or aesthetic specificity, but traverses and negotiates cinematic and cultural traditions and critical and political debates.[3]

As such, Butler proposes that we conceive of women's cinema as a "minor cinema" rather than a counter-cinema. In so doing, she considers a range of cinematic genres, categories, and production cultures, from Hollywood to indie to experimental, but elides pornography. This is notable because, as I argue elsewhere, pornographic production cultures have consistently been far more accessible to women filmmakers than has Hollywood, and her innovative theoretical framework applies at least as well to their work.[4]

Feminist theorists in the 1970s and 1980s, such as Laura Mulvey, Claire Johnston, and Teresa de Lauretis, argued that women's cinema is a counter-cinema, offering different perspectives and foregrounding women's subjectivity in response to cinematic traditions dominated by the male gaze. Using Gilles Deleuze and Félix Guattari's concept of minor literature and drawing from the feminist film criticism of Meaghan Morris and B. Ruby Rich, Butler argues that women's cinema does not generate or employ a new cinematic language but rather could be seen as idiomatic or accented iterations of the dominant film language. Whereas in major cinemas, "the social milieu may serve as 'mere environment or a background' . . . for the individual concerns of the narrative," a minor cinema "emerges from a deterritorialized group," and therefore "its function is to conjure up collectivity, even in the absence of an active community."[5] This is what allows us to consider women's cinema without limiting definitions of womanhood to essentialist notions: "The communities imagined by women's cinema are as many and varied as the films it comprises, and each is involved in its own historical moment."[6] I appreciate this expansive definition, because although I insist that it is both appropriate and important to consider women's contributions to patriarchal film traditions, it is equally important to recognize that "women" is not a stable or coherent concept; it encompasses both transgender and cisgender women as well as some nonbinary femmes. For my purposes here, I am defining as "woman" anyone who identifies as such, including those—such as Findlay—who personally disavow any collective experience of womanhood.

Findlay, along with Charlene Webb and Doris Wishman, is one of the first in a long line of women to be elided from histories of pornography by cultural commentators, producers, and feminists alike. In some cases, this may be an intentional, politicized exclusion—like Linda Williams in *Hard Core*, for instance, the editors of *The Feminist Porn Book* list Candida Royalle as the first significant creator of porn made by and for women.[7] Before going on to become such, however, Royalle had appeared in Findlay's film *The Playgirl* (1982). A distinction should of course be made between the first woman pornographer and the first to make "porn for women," but Findlay's contributions as an early porn pioneer deserve a place in histories of feminist pornography as well as women's cinema more broadly.[8] In addition to being a prolific director, like Royalle, Findlay also founded her own production (Sendy Films) and distribution (Reeltime) companies.

This discussion of Findlay's pornographic filmography builds from my larger project on women, nonbinary, and queer filmmakers in pornographic production cultures.[9] I have found that, although they have changed dramatically in the last few decades, historically women's options for agency in the production of pornography have been contingent, restricted, and limited to on-camera roles. Women have, of course, always played a prominent role in the production of adult video as "talent," but actresses do not necessarily have much control over their cinematic representation unless they are also directing and/ or co-producing the movies in which they appear. Women filmmakers were few and far between in the 1970s—in addition to Findlay, Doris Wishman made two hardcore films during this period, Ann Perry directed three, and Charlene Webb was the first woman to direct a pornographic feature (*Goldenrod*, 1973). If we were to expand the definition of "pornographer" to encompass directors of experimental and underground film, we could include women such as Barbara Rubin, whose *Christmas on Earth* (1963) was arguably the first theatrically released film to include a money shot, and Honey Lee Cottrell, whose *Sweet Dreams* was released in 1979. But the landscape of women's filmmaking in the 1970s adult film industry was barren indeed. Only in the 1980s would women directors begin to rise to prominence, and their numbers would not be significant until the mid- to late 2000s.

In extending Butler's discussion of women's cinema as minor cinema to pornography, and arguing that it should encompass the work of Roberta Findlay specifically, I begin from the assumption that filmmakers' intentions should not limit our understanding of their work; it is enough for their films to expand avenues of access for filmmakers from underrepresented groups, create innovative gendered representation onscreen, and/or "conjure up collectivity."

Women pornographers have accomplished this in a range of ways. In the 1980s, for instance, Royalle founded Femme Productions to produce and distribute "porn for women" directed by herself and other women. Her films were made with an audience of straight women and couples in mind, with higher production values than the majority of contemporary video pornography, a dedication to narrative, safer sex practices, less of a focus on the genitals, more of a focus on women's pleasure, and a resistance to money shots. In the same period, women like Annie Sprinkle and Veronica Hart began directing films that prioritize women's pleasure, and filmmakers like Jackie Strano and Shar Rednour were making "dyke porn" by and primarily for queer women. In the mid-to-late 2000s, mainstream directors like Jessica Drake, working for Wicked Pictures, and Tasha Reign, working for a variety of production companies, would create porn "from a women's perspective," targeting straight men and women and couples alike.[10] Many women filmmakers working in the mainstream industry in this era cite specific twists on the formula that they employ in order to project their own vision: for instance, Reign professes to convey a "girl power" message of women working together in films like *Streaker Girls* (2013), and Drake intentionally creates images of strong women seeking their own pleasure in such titles as *What Girls Like* (2008). Beginning around 2008, the overtly politicized subgenres of queer and feminist porn began to flourish, with women and nonbinary filmmakers such as Tristan Taormino, Courtney Trouble, Madison Young, Shine Louise Houston, and Abiola Abrams developing a heterogeneous body of work produced with egalitarian production practices and diverse casts and crews.[11]

All of these filmmakers challenge societal gender and sexual norms and/ or gendered adult film conventions in disparate ways, but on the other end of the spectrum we can find women like Findlay, Mason, and Lizzie Borden, who challenge gender norms by disavowing femininity in their public personae and challenging the essentialist assumption that women prefer soft-lit, romantic erotica in their "extreme," and often violent, hardcore porn. Their tendency toward gender-neutral and/or masculine self-definition and cinematic address does not preclude conceptualizing their work as women's cinema. In defining women's cinema as a minor cinema, Butler notes that, "A female film-maker's body of work might intersect with women's cinema on occasion, but not consistently." She continues:

> Some of the most distinguished practitioners of women's cinema have deliberately distanced themselves from the notion, for professional and/ or political reasons, to avoid marginalization or ideological controversy . . . Their work, nevertheless, continues to be pulled into spaces of exhibition, criticism, and debate defined in terms of gender, such as women's festivals conferences, courses, and publications like this one.[12]

One such filmmaker is surely Roberta Findlay, who routinely disavows and even denigrates her gender in conversations about her work, and this is one such publication. Despite her general refusal of the designation "woman filmmaker"—let alone "feminist"—this chapter will explore the ambivalently queer and feminist potential of Findlay's hardcore cinema, and thereby argue for its inclusion in the minor cinema of women's pornography.

The vast majority of women directing in all of these eras have been—like Findlay—white, cisgender, and able-bodied. Unlike Findlay, most found opportunities to direct only after first building a brand as performers, meaning they are overwhelmingly gender conforming, thin, and conventionally attractive.[13] It is therefore unsurprising that anti-pornography feminists and political conservatives alike have been arguing since the 1970s that pornography is a genre created by and for men, and that it incites—and even instantiates—violence against women. Although it is a media industry with its own distinctions and peculiarities like any other, it has been framed through discourses of negative exceptionalism since its inception, partly because of its illicit origins as an underground, illegal media form, but surely also as a result of this singling out of pornography by groups that originated with a focus on media violence more broadly.[14] That is, unlike Hollywood or other cinematic traditions, pornography tends to be defined by its worst examples and dismissed wholesale rather than engaged critically on a text-by-text or production-by-production basis. This is true of certain feminists and anti-capitalists as well as conservative moral crusaders.[15] Beyond this political framework, in the context of pornographic production and consumption, "women" functions primarily as a discursive category, invoked for a variety of commercial and ideological purposes. ("Porn for women," for instance, is a near-meaningless marketing category on Pornhub.[16])

If we move beyond broad generalizations about pornography to assess women's creative contributions to it, a number of complexities and productive contradictions emerge. Through a series of interviews with directors and producers, I have learned that women enter into the role of director through different channels, and with a variety of motivations. Some seek more power, creative control, and higher salaries; others seek to challenge the status quo, eradicating labor hierarchies and bringing overlooked groups of people, sexualities, sex acts, or body types to light; some seek to prove that they can play the boys' game better than the boys, that not all women want softness and romance and flowers; others seek to fund their art-making through their porn or to break down the boundaries between art and porn; still others simply seek to take on a new role in the production of the same sort of porn they've enjoyed starring in. Despite their differences, collectively their work constitutes a minor cinema within US adult film, through which even anti-feminist, actively misogynistic women like Findlay—with avowedly apolitical and crassly economic motivations for making porn—contribute to opening up a space for women's authorship, sexual expression, and feminist praxis in one of the most masculinist of film genres and production cultures. Partly as a result of trailblazers like Findlay, as I have suggested, it has been increasingly and significantly more likely since the 1980s for women to find regular employment and widespread recognition as directors in the porn industry than in Hollywood.[17]

This is not an unproblematic phenomenon. It is precisely because they are so successful at being the objects in porn that so many women have been able to become its subjects and creators. Female performers routinely out-earn their male counterparts, and thus encounter paths of access to directing, but this could not be so without the corresponding phenomenon of industrial assumptions: that men are the primary viewers of porn and that women's bodies are what they will pay to watch. Findlay is a special case here, because unlike many of the filmmakers I have interviewed, she did not achieve star-level recognition as a performer on her path to becoming a director.

As Heather Berg has noted, when performers from marginalized groups succeed in taking on "management" roles such as directing or producing, they often reproduce the inequities that they were subject to as performers.[18] Directors may also find that they have less creative control than they might have hoped, depending on whether they are contracted to a studio, producing for a major distribution company, or self-producing and -distributing. In such a patriarchally organized industry, women's agency cannot but be restricted, but for that very reason we should seriously consider the feminist possibilities for women achieving any measure of creative control in pornographic filmmaking. In *A Taste for Brown Sugar: Black Women in American Pornography*, Mireille Miller-Young applies Saba Mahmood's conceptualization of agency as a way to consider the forms and amounts of power available to Black women working as porn actresses.[19] Using her ethnographic work on Egyptian women in the mosque movement as the basis for her analysis, Mahmood argues in *The Politics of Piety* that human agency is not limited to actions that overtly challenge social norms.[20] Instead, it is "entailed not only in those acts that resist norms but also in the multiple ways in which one inhabits norms."[21] Following Foucault, Butler, and other thinkers, Mahmood explores possibilities for agency beyond resistance to relations of domination, as a capacity for action that can be created and enabled within conditions of subordination. She argues that norms "are not only consolidated and/or subverted . . . but performed, inhabited, and experienced in a variety of ways," and as such envisions agency as more of a continuum than an absolute.[22] Following Miller-Young, I apply this concept in order to shift the frame for envisioning women in pornography: although women filmmakers in the porn industry must always function within a fundamentally patriarchal and often oppressive system, and all women filmmakers in the US function within the patriarchal and often oppressive society at large, they nonetheless can enact various forms of creative agency, even by inhabiting or replicating cultural norms. I begin from the assumption that all minoritarian media production can be read as "creativity within constraints" and that women filmmakers in pornography, as in any other media industry, should be read as both "creators of popular culture and as functionaries in the service of capitalism."[23] Following Berg, I embrace the labor contradictions of the adult film industry as "porno dialectics."[24]

Acknowledging these constraints, there are at least two ways in which work by women like Roberta Findlay—who enthusiastically inhabits and simultaneously rejects social norms—can be framed as "women's cinema" and even recuperated as feminist: on the level of production or that of representation. Her production practices can hardly be described as such; indeed, quite the opposite. Many self-identified feminist and/or queer pornographers—such as Tristan Taormino, Courtney Trouble, and Shine Louise Houston—and even some mainstream pornographers like Jessica Drake—have developed egalitarian labor practices, including informed and enthusiastic consent, which is often depicted on screen as well as obtained prior to filming; collaborating with performers to create sex scenes that they will enjoy participating in; safe working conditions; equitable compensation, including, for instance, a refusal to pay thin white women higher rates than Black or fat women; and hiring diverse casts and crews. Here again, though, Berg reminds us that the benefits of these supposedly egalitarian production practices are not necessarily straightforward.[25] Ethics and authenticity may or may not be integral to the political philosophies of any given feminist pornographer, but they do function as marketing tools for the subgenre. For some performers, the policies that facilitate these concepts are worthwhile and empowering, but for others they can be a burden. Some performers, for instance, believe that equitable pay rates for feminist porn simply result in lower compensation for performers across the board, and the imperative to generate "authentically" hot sex scenes with genuine chemistry can require additional hours and more energy on set. In this way, practices that are designed to promote a consensual, equitable workplace can in practice feel like an exhausting way to extract additional unpaid physical and emotional labor from performers.

Findlay has never hinted at considering or employing any such policies. Quite the contrary—in various interviews she has insisted that, far from using her position of power to create opportunities for other women on her crews, she would not even consider hiring women for any role other than "makeup artist," because she assumes women incapable of effectively making other contributions behind the camera.[26] It is curious, of course, that she excludes herself from the category of woman in this context; in addition to writing and directing, she routinely performed a variety of other above- and below-the-line crew roles, including editing, lighting, and cinematography. Beyond her refusal to hire women for her crews or enact egalitarian production practices, however, Findlay has acknowledged—largely without regret—exploiting a dead woman for her own personal gain. Porn star Shauna Grant had appeared in a few of Findlay's films before leaving the industry and eventually completing suicide. Findlay had some unused footage from these shoots lying around after Grant's death, and used it to make a pornographic "tribute" to the actress:

> I said, "She's in the news now. Let's take the outtakes and make a film out of it, and we'll pretend it's a documentary." I got Joyce James. She did the narration or interviews, I don't remember. I remember shooting her, though, and she thought it was a real documentary—a serious attempt at reconstructing Shauna's story.[27]

She released the resulting film as *Shauna: Every Man's Fantasy* (1984), and critics and audiences alike were almost universally disgusted.[28] Her adult film career likely ended as the result of this decision. She acknowledges that, "What I did was totally exploitative and pretty nasty, but I didn't see it that way at the time," but also says that she would "do it again."[29]

Despite these exploitative and even actively misogynistic production practices, if we shift our focus to the politics of representation, Findlay's films turned many gender and sexual stereotypes on their head before they had even been fully solidified. Before there was "porn for women" against which to define the rest of porn, there was Findlay making violent, often disturbing "porn with a woman's sensibilities."[30] Findlay's perspective about the need to depict female pleasure does align with that of many feminist pornographers: "I suppose women directors would shoot woman [*sic*] having orgasms in addition to shooting men having orgasms. Most male directors don't bother about showing women having orgasms."[31] She elaborates in another interview, with regard to depicting women's orgasms:

> Any "creator," if you will allow me to use that word, brings themselves to the project, whatever it may be—inevitably, subconsciously. Yes, but it was not done consciously. I guess I had feelings at the time, and they inevitably wind up in the film—but it's not a conscious attempt to change society or bond with my sisters, as they used to say to people.[32]

This is a rare instance in which Findlay seems to identify with the category of woman, and although she continues to reject participation in or concern for any collective experience of womanhood, let alone embrace a feminist politics, she implies having on some level an interest in validating women's right to sexual satisfaction.

Indeed, Findlay's films often prioritize women's pleasure in ways that tend to exceed depictions by her male contemporaries. Linda Williams and others have noted that 1970s porn is, at least on the surface, fixated on women's pleasure—many narratives, perhaps most famously that of *Deep Throat* (1972), center on a woman's journey toward achieving orgasm.[33] But as in that particular film, in which the woman protagonist's orgasm is conveniently achieved by performing the titular act on a man, understandings of women's pleasure and desires are often filtered—to the point of becoming unrecognizable—through the sensibilities of the films' cisgender, heterosexual (hereafter "cishet") male directors and their presumed cishet male audiences. These "golden age" films by male directors have been critiqued by Williams and others for their general ambivalence. Although they often feature women protagonists, the women's bodies are subject to the dictates of "maximum visibility," rendering them arguably more object than subject. And although most porn, unlike Hollywood and even most independent cinema, dedicates a significant amount of screen time to cunnilingus and manual stimulation of women's genitals, their orgasms are—if depicted at all—portrayed as secondary to men's, whose "money shot," or external ejaculation, nearly always constitutes the spectacular culmination of a mainstream hardcore sex scene.

Findlay's films tend to include at least a few notable tweaks to the gendered formula outlined above. For instance, a perusal of her adult filmography reveals the surprising inclusion of what we might call potential "boner-killers," like mentions of pregnancy (*Angel Number 9*, 1974), women killing men (*A Woman's Torment*, 1977; *The Tiffany Minx*, 1981), women bonding over men's mistreatment of and violence against women (*Mascara*, 1983), and women rejecting men altogether (*The Altar of Lust*, 1971). And, although most sex scenes are quite conventional in many ways, sex that is narratively framed as loving or meaningful—sex between couples in love—consistently does not end with a money shot (e.g. in *Angel Number 9* and *Fantasex*, 1976). These gestures to collectivity, unintentional though they may be, constitute one significant way that Findlay's work can provide a case for women's adult cinema as minor cinema.

As I have suggested above, however, hers is not the soft-lit, romantic couples' fare that popular accounts associate with women's porn. Findlay, rather, prides herself on making films that she perceives as gender-neutral; when asked by Gerald Peary if any of her films had ever played at a women's film festival, she said, "No, no. I never tried it. I defy anybody to think that they are made by a woman."[34] Most of Findlay's pornographic directing efforts are credited with male pseudonyms. *Angel Number 9* is one of the few films for which she is credited with her given name (see Figure 2.1), and Molly Haskell includes it among only a handful of examples of films that provide evidence of a

Figure 2.1 *New York Times*, November 21, 1974.

feminine sensibility in her celebrated essay, "Are Women Directors Different?"[35] Ironically, in a psychoanalytic reading of *Angel Number 9*, Dennis Giles suggests that "Roberta Findlay" was "possibly a pseudonym" for a male filmmaker.[36] This hypothesis would likely not have displeased Findlay. Whereas some women filmmakers like Royalle disavow the term "pornography" for its associations with misogyny and crass entertainment—preferring the more feminized term "erotica"—it is femininity itself that Findlay disavows, often referring to herself as a "cameraman" and speaking derisively of women.

This questioning of gendered authenticity illuminates a notable quirk of the US adult film industry. My research shows that, unlike in other patriarchal creative traditions—such as nineteenth- and early twentieth-century English and American literature, some twentieth-century genre fiction and Hollywood genre cinema, and US exploitation cinema—in which women would often adopt masculine or ambiguously gendered pseudonyms in order to be published as authors or hired as directors, women are more likely to be given *more* credit in porn as the result of a marketing strategy that first emerged in the 1970s but rose to prominence as a trend in the early 2000s. Seeking to reach new demographics, adult video producers began appealing to the "couples market" (for pornography, this demographic is understood to include straight women and couples) by releasing titles that were directed by women. This was designed to serve the dual purpose of making women viewers more comfortable—on the assumption that films with a "woman's sensibility" would be less offensive—and appealing to straight male viewers with promises of seeing their favorite porn stars' fantasies come to life. In some cases, this translated into women filmmakers developing prolific careers. In other cases, this led to women being credited with directing films in which they may only have performed. One such woman is Gail Parmentier, credited with directing three adult films as Gail Palmer in the 1970s. It has since been revealed that these credits were falsified in order to protect the real director, Harry Mohney, from potential obscenity charges. At the time of the release for *Hot Summer in the City* (1975), Mohney was already being prosecuted for other ventures, including the exhibition of *Deep Throat* at his Covington Cinema X location in Kentucky. But it seems that he also realized that a woman filmmaker could be a marketing tool. So Palmer was credited as director for *Hot Summer* and two subsequent films actually directed by Mohney. Prolific adult director Bob Chinn writes in his memoir *The Other Side of Paradise, Vol. 2* that "the true credit for the direction of these films should probably go to Harry . . . the powers-that-be [firmly] believed that a sexy, attractive female filmmaker and producer would [bring] in a larger audience to their films."[37]

This marketing strategy—selling women filmmakers' purported sexual fantasies to the couples market—would not be fully developed until decades later. But Findlay's career reveals that Mohney and company were not alone in thinking along these lines in the 1970s. Not only was Findlay credited as director with her given name for *Angel Number 9*, but she told Peary:

This time the distributor decided that it was time to declare that a woman was making erotic films. Not pornography. He hired two publicity guys to do whatever they do and I was on radio shows and in magazines . . . And so on the marquee, it opened at the Lincoln Art Theater in New York, it said "Roberta Findlay's Angel Number 9." And we thought it would make money.[38]

This marketing strategy is no doubt what led both Giles and Haskell to weigh in with their perceptions of the film's gendered sensibilities. Other women working at the time, such as Wishman and Webb, were both far less prolific pornographers and uninvested in branding themselves as such. In other words, theirs were marketed simply as pornographic films, rather than as porn with a woman's sensibility.

There continues to be a fair amount of confusion over which films Findlay did in fact direct. In interviews and director's commentaries on DVDs and Blu-ray releases of her films, she frequently forgets which films she actually directed and/or challenges a film's official credits. For instance, the cover of the Vinegar Syndrome Blu-ray for *Liquid A$$ets* lists Walter Sear as the director.[39] Meanwhile, in the film itself only Robert Walters (a Findlay pseudonym) is credited as director (whereas "Roberta Findlay" is credited as cinematographer), and online databases like Internet Movie Database (IMDB) and Internet Adult Film Database (IAFD) list Robert Walters as director with Walter Sear as an uncredited co-director. In the director's commentary she begins by saying, "I'm sorry to tell you that it's not mine [. . .] I let Walter write the script and direct it." A bit later she adds, "Now that I look at it, maybe I directed it," before finally concluding that, "Yeah, I did direct this."

This sort of confusion belies a lack of concern for recognition for her achievements as a director, as does her adoption of a range of male pseudonyms—in addition to Robert Walters, she used Robert Nelson, Robert W. Norman, Walter D. Roberts, Robert W. Brinar, and Bob W. Davis. We might attribute this lack of concern to her professed disdain for porn in general, but the confusion over credits and the adoption of male pseudonyms also demonstrate that Findlay and Palmer were the exceptions that proved the rule—it was not generally considered marketable for a woman to direct porn in the 1970s. If anything, it was assumed to be a liability. In other words, whereas many women film makers, beginning in the 1980s, would exploit their female personae in order to build and sell a brand, Findlay (and/or other industry players) apparently felt that she had to hide her femininity in order to produce and distribute her work. Possibly, the violent nature of much of her pornography contributed to her decision to use a male pseudonym, in which case we might read this choice as a concession to gendered expectations, and in particular the assumption that women prefer romance and dislike rough or violent sex.

Perhaps unsurprisingly for a woman working within a distinctly masculinist milieu, willing to hide or exploit her own name depending on what is deemed most profitable at any given moment, there is a notable tension in both her work and her public persona between what can be described as feminist potential and the lack thereof, sometimes verging on downright misogyny. In the handful of interviews to which she has consented over the years, as well as in director's commentaries on DVD and Blu-ray releases, she occasionally admits to feeling pride in what she managed to achieve with such meager budgets in this male-dominated industry. Yet she denies ever experiencing any obstacles as a result of her gender, and is as likely to be brutally self-deprecating as proud of any given film. Instead, she frames her accomplishments in terms of frugality, with frequent references to her and her compatriots' ingenuity in securing locations and otherwise getting the most bang (as it were) for their buck. It doesn't help that Findlay's statements in interviews are often contradictory, confusing, or inaccurate. She acknowledges her interest in depicting women's orgasms, but repeatedly asserts her disgust for women. Elsewhere she claims that she has "never made a lesbian film," but does acknowledge directing *The Altar of Lust*, a nearly unclassifiable film about a woman seeing a psychologist to "cure" her lesbianism.[40] It is difficult to deny that *Altar* is a lesbian film, including as it does several scenes of girl-on-girl action (to use the industry parlance), during and after which the protagonist favorably compares these experiences to her mostly horrifying sexual encounters with men. Ultimately, the film implies that there's nothing to cure. One could argue that Findlay is merely inconsistent, confused, or insincere. But I prefer to frame her as complicated—in addition to a woman-despising woman, she is also a Jewish filmmaker whose favorite film is *Triumph of the Will* (1935, dir. Leni Riefenstahl), with a complex creative vision.[41] Intentionally or otherwise, she has developed the public persona of a tough New York broad who prioritizes aesthetics over politics and doesn't want to be defined or limited by her gender.

Her adult filmography reflects this branding in several ways. With her then-husband, Michael, Findlay co-directed a series of softcore sexploitation features in the late 1960s about male serial killers, each of which delights in revealing and disarticulating women's bodies. She has since spoken critically of Michael, describing him as a "cowardly psychopath" who wanted to murder women but settled for cinematic depictions thereof: "Michael wanted to kill women, but I personally don't like them. I never did. I don't like women and children. They're an annoyance and generally in the way."[42] So it is not without interest that, in the films she went on to direct herself, she continued to utilize violent narratives but typically featured women in the role of killer. To explain her use of violence, Findlay reveals in an interview: "Maybe I shouldn't say this, but I seem to have a violent nature . . . I like to see women raped on the screen . . . I get turned on by the beating of women.

Of course, I don't do it in real life. I'm not even a lesbian."[43] Yet despite the internalized misogyny (and rather strange understanding of what it means to be a lesbian) implied by her expressed loathing for women and desires to see them raped and beaten, in *A Woman's Torment* and *The Tiffany Minx* Findlay repeatedly depicts the raped and beaten women as fighting back against and ultimately defeating their tormenters through murder. I read these tendencies as—intentionally or otherwise—an ambivalently feminist resistance to the proliferation of depictions of women as helpless victims in pre-1970s horror and sexploitation films.

On a small scale, each of her disturbed heroines strikes back against the patriarchy, be it with a knife, an ax, or even—akin to Chantal Akerman's sex worker-housewife heroine Jeanne Dielman[44]—a pair of scissors, as when the title character from *The Tiffany Minx* dispatches her rapist. As in Akerman's *Jeanne Dielman, 23 quai du Commerce, 1080 Bruxelles* (1975), the choice of murder weapon cannot be read as incidental. Primarily considered a woman's tool, for sewing and other domestic chores or for educational purposes, the scissors effectively teach the unfortunate male victims their final lesson, about the dangers of constraining and objectifying women. Unlike their male counterparts in the sexploitation films made by the Findlays, the heroines in Roberta's hardcore films do not murder out of hatred for another sex or a sheer joy in violence, but rather as a form of retribution or revenge for their own ill-treatment—a torturing of the men in response to the cultural dictate to "torture the women."[45]

In *A Woman's Torment* (1977), Karen, a mentally ill woman, is alternately neglected (quite literally as the woman in the attic) and infantilized by her sister and her sister's husband and, left alone one day, wanders away and into an empty beach house. A handyman arrives, perhaps in a nod to the stereotypical narrative formula for porn, and finds her to be easy prey. What starts out as a potentially consensual (to the extent that a woman in her condition is ever capable of consent) sexual encounter quickly progresses toward rape. The tables turn when Karen stabs the handyman-turned-rapist with a knife from the kitchen. As with so many rape revenge narratives, however, the potentially empowering image of a woman fighting back with a kitchen knife—a weapon symbolic of domesticity and "a woman's place"—can never quite erase the specter of the visual pleasure we are expected to have taken in watching her rape in the first place. This is perhaps even more true of adult video than of mainstream (non-adult) cinema, in that the sex scenes—including rape—are designed specifically and overtly to titillate.

Findlay would be only the first in a surprisingly long line of women directors known for making "extreme" pornography—that is, porn with "extreme" content and/or storylines in which women, and sometimes men, are murdered and/or violently raped. The women who create extreme porn raise some interesting questions about the gendered, and classed, assumptions surrounding conceptions of "women's porn." Filmmakers like Findlay can challenge conventional notions of femininity and broaden understandings of female desire in unexpected ways, by exploring edgy, dangerous, and/or crass pornographic fantasies.[46]

In light of the "extreme" content in films like *The Tiffany Minx* and *A Woman's Torment*, as well as Findlay's career trajectory from softcore to hardcore porn to horror cinema, it is productive to consider affinities between pornography and another "low" genre: the slasher film. (Findlay herself noted these affinities rather colorfully in an interview: "You know the money shots in porn films? Well, this was just a different substance: it was red."[47]) In her groundbreaking study of the slasher film, *Men, Women and Chainsaws*, Carol J. Clover describes the phenomenon of the Final Girl, a tough, masculinized "female victim-hero" who fights off the killer to become the last person standing.[48] The Final Girl, according to Clover, can only exist in a film economy in which women must perennially be the victims. "Abject terror," she writes,

> in short, is gendered feminine, and the more concerned a given film is with that condition—and it is the essence of modern horror—the more likely the femaleness of the victim. It is no accident that male victims in slasher films are killed swiftly or offscreen, and that prolonged struggles, in which the victim has time to contemplate her imminent destruction, inevitably figure females.[49]

Much as the gendered dictates of the slasher genre—"torture the women"—ironically allow for the existence of the potentially empowering "final girl" figure, so too do the dictates of industrial pornography—display the women—allow for the existence of more, better, and higher paid roles for female performers and ease of access for women filmmakers and in turn for those women to create more complex depictions of femininity on screen. Clover is ambivalent about the feminist potential of the final girl; I am equally ambivalent about the feminist potential of mainstream women's pornography. In each of these maligned "low genres," women's bodies act as a form of currency, yet in both cases, albeit in different ways, women nonetheless tend to end up on top. *The Tiffany Minx* and *A Woman's Torment* approach the status of "women's cinema" to the extent that they acknowledge patriarchal constraints on women and/or seem to celebrate women's resistance to them.

Even in the films that do not feature women as violent avengers, we can see hints of collective concerns. The aforementioned *Angel Number 9* is a particularly ambivalent case. To read a plot description of this film, in which a man dies and is punished by angels for his mistreatment of women by being returned to earth as a woman in order to be subjected to men's cruelty, one might assume a very straightforward feminist message. Yet the film's treatment of the subject matter ultimately conveys, as user Bondo suggests on the *Filmspotting* message board, roughly the opposite idea:

Billed as the first "erotically explicit" (read hardcore) film made by a woman, *Angel Number 9* makes the treatment of women its central theme, which is what one might hope for from a woman working in a medium typically dominated by the male gaze and frequent misogynistic plots. Steven is a cad and a heartbreaker and the angels see fit to have him killed and, as punishment for his behavior, sent back to earth as a woman in order to experience the pain that he gave others.

While there are some interesting uses of sex as debasement to show the ways these relational dynamics can strain the definition of consent as a form of emotional coercion, I have to admit the film's message is a pretty big failure. As someone inclined to be sympathetic on the general premise of men taking advantage, I found my response to the film was less a reaction to the caddishness of men but the craziness of the women.[50]

This was not the first hardcore film made by a woman, as I have suggested, though it was the first to be marketed as such. Otherwise, I found myself in complete agreement with Bondo's rather insightful assessment as I watched the film.

As Bondo notes, in line with Butler's definition of women's cinema as minor cinema, the film "makes the treatment of women its central theme." Beyond that, the film is patently queer, with scene after scene depicting the consciousness of a man in the body of a woman having sex with men and women.[51] On the other hand, the film also suggests that women are by nature pathetic and manipulative. The protagonist, who begins and ends the film as Steven, appears for most of the film as Stephanie. The film opens with Steven saying, "you're not here to think—just suck," in response to a question from his sexual partner.[52] The sex scene is otherwise banal and even occasionally charming, including a few moments of him happily performing cunnilingus, but afterwards when his partner professes her love and suggests that they get married and have kids, he says, "I'm not changing my life for you or any broad. Why do you have to get so fucking emotional?" Her reply to this verbal abuse is that she's already pregnant with his child, and he accuses her of lying about taking the birth control pill. All of this would be an appropriate setup for his later punishment, but in the course of their conversation she confirms that she had indeed been lying to him—she had stopped taking the pill in order to intentionally entrap him with a pregnancy! He kicks her out with some particularly cruel parting words, but ultimately one could argue that her actions are far more reprehensible.

As we will see, the film's ending is similarly problematic. But the majority of the film provides complex, interesting commentary on gendered embodiment and the fluidity of desire. Despite his initial protest to the angel that he'd "rather be dead than a woman," Steven/Stephanie actually adapts to his/her new body almost immediately. And rather than masturbate or seek out a woman to seduce—as is typically portrayed in popular media texts with similar premises—Stephanie's first action upon being returned to earth is to proposition the male driver of the car who had hit and killed him/her: "How would you like to try out my body? You'll be the first one, you know. It's brand new."[53] In the scene that follows, although technically we watch a cisgender woman performer and a cisgender male performer having sex, we are repeatedly reminded in the diegesis that Stephanie is in fact Steven. Stephanie is still wearing Steven's (now oversized) clothing at first, and in the course of the scene her/his lover repeatedly calls her/ him "weird" and "strange," perhaps most understandably when Stephanie responds to first seeing his penis with "mine was a little bigger." Lines like that ensure that the film does not entirely elide suggestions of queerness or gender fluidity.

In a shower scene that follows, Stephanie ecstatically explores her/his new body, with a poetic voice-over articulating her/his experience:

> Oh my hot liquid will mingle with the pulsating droplets of the shower. I've never known such excitement. I've never been so aroused! . . . Oh Steven, you can't know how this feels! I've forgotten already what it's like to be a man. Oh may I remain a woman forever! Oh it's a pleasure that's almost unbearable!

By having Stephanie talk to Steven in this way, the scene establishes a separation between the two, but ultimately it reaffirms that they are one and the same when, after orgasming, she/he thinks to her/himself, "That was nothing like being a man. Thank you Angel Number 9! I've never been so happy. Your punishment—it's like a reward." In this way, the film alternately and even simultaneously questions and reinforces the gender binary: establishing divisions through often essentialist characterizations of Steven vs. Stephanie, even as it emphasizes the character's fluid liminality. Steven/Stephanie is irreducible and ultimately undefinable.

Similarly, in the next scene, Stephanie sleeps with one of Steven's sexual partners, Linda. It takes only a little convincing for Linda to accept that Stephanie is in fact the reincarnation of her former partner. During the sex that follows, she rapturously cries out, "Oh Stephanie! I like you better as a woman. So gentle . . ." (The sex itself, like nearly all of the girl-on-girl scenes in Findlay's oeuvre, is lackluster verging on bizarre, making it clear enough that Findlay is indeed "not a lesbian" and is disgusted by the sex scenes that she repeatedly admits to not knowing how to direct.[54]) After they both apparently orgasm, Stephanie seems to agree, thinking aloud: "This is getting better and better!"

These scenes, in addition to emphasizing the character's gender and sexual fluidity, seem to reflect the contemporary understandings of sexual orientation and women's sexual pleasure, popularized by studies from Alfred Kinsey (*Sexual Behavior in the Human Male*, 1948, and *Sexual Behavior in the Human Female*, 1953) and William H. Masters and Virginia E. Johnson (*Human Sexual Response*, 1966). Kinsey's research proposed that sexual desire and behavior were far more fluid than they were popularly understood to be, with sexual orientation existing on a spectrum (the "Kinsey scale") rather than a homosexual/heterosexual binary, and that women were more likely to achieve sexual satisfaction from masturbation or oral or manual stimulation by a partner than from vaginal penetration alone. Masters and Johnson confirmed the last point, and found that women could have more and longer orgasms than men as well as experience multiple orgasms. Linda Williams notes in *Screening Sex* that this led feminist author and activist Barbara Seaman to conclude that "*The more a woman does, the more she can, and the more she can, the more she wants to.*"[55] Williams then applies this idea to a scene in *Barbarella* (1968), in which the villain attempts to pleasure the eponymous protagonist to death with his "Exsexive Machine":

> In this scene a finite, masculine concept of sexual pleasure as climax and crescendo—the quintessentially French and male concept of orgasm as a kind of finite *petite mort*—comes up against the lessons of Kinsey, Masters and Johnson, and feminist sexological revisions of female sexual pleasure as potentially infinite.[56]

In this way, Williams explains how these advances in sexology popularized the notion that women's sexual pleasure is uniquely boundless and uncontainable, which was in turn reflected in popular cultural depictions of women's sexuality. Similarly, Findlay's film portrays women's capacity for sexual satisfaction as more powerful and expansive than men's, but it goes further to suggest that women may be potentially superior lovers, an idea that might be as likely to inspire an inferiority complex than to titillate the target demographic of cishet men.

This sentiment is not entirely canceled out by the ending, in which Stephanie begs to be returned to her/his original form, the punishment having been fulfilled once Stephanie has fallen in love with a man, Jeff, who ultimately abuses and rejects her/him. Near the end of the film, Jeff tells Stephanie, "I'm bored with you, do you understand that? I had enough. I want you out of my life. You get the message?" She/he insists, pathetically, "But Jeff, I don't care how you feel about me—I love you. I just want to be married. Let me make love to you." He replies, heartlessly, "Is that what you want? You want to suck my cock? That make you happy, hm? Alright. Get down on your knees. But I want you out of here as soon as I'm finished, you understand?" The rough blow job scene that follows is punctuated with such niceties as "Go on, suck it, cunt," and "Love it baby because that's the last time you're gonna get it." After he ejaculates on her face and begins to kick her out, she/he begs to see him again, eventually convincing him to do so if she/he can organize a party at which other women will sexually service him. In the following scene, the party materializes, and Stephanie thinks to her/himself, "I have no pride left—nothing."

The final scene before Stephanie/Steven's return to heaven mirrors the opening scene. In this case, Stephanie makes a desperate attempt to get Jeff back, by showing up at his house and telling him she/he is pregnant. Again, it is revealed that the pregnancy resulted from a lie—Stephanie stopped taking the pill while telling Jeff she/he was still on it in order to prevent him from leaving her/him. Enraged (justifiably, for once), Jeff kicks her/him out, and she/he beseeches the angels to end her/his torment.

By having Stephanie automatically fall in love with a brutal man, and find her/himself in an identical situation to the one with which Steven's strange journey had begun, only with roles reversed, the film implies that women inevitably invite abuse and naturally respond with manipulation—a notion that is as misogynistic as it is inaccurate and essentialist. It would be easy to dismiss this implication as an expression of internalized misogyny—indeed this is what could lead someone like Giles to argue that "Roberta Findlay" must be a pseudonym for a male filmmaker—but the flipside of the suggestion that women are victims and manipulators in this film is the idea that men are brutes. Unlike Giles, I am not inclined to psychoanalyze, but it's not difficult to imagine why a woman who hates women might be inclined to portray the experience of womanhood as punishment. Although Findlay may personally misdirect those feelings of persecution toward other women rather than patriarchy, *Angel Number 9* nonetheless suggests that men like Steven should be punished for their mistreatment of women and invites us to consider whether and why women like Stephanie might be punished by individual men, and by extension patriarchy, for their boundless capacity for sexual pleasure. The emphasis on scenes that portray Stephanie enjoying her(/his) body, with sheer joy and without shame, could inspire us to reflect on the reasons for the kind of gendered brutality practiced by Steven earlier in the film. Someone who is inclined to psychoanalyze, for instance, might read Steven as an embodiment of a generalized male jealousy regarding women's perceived sexual and reproductive capabilities.[57]

Along with *Fantasex*, *Angel Number 9* is one of very few that Findlay recalls with any sense of pride, otherwise viewing her work primarily as a way to pay the bills. She told Peary:

> I have tried over and over to make one erotic scene. Not even erotic, but to make it even sexually realistic. There was only one scene in *Angel Number 9*, the blow job scene, that was actually powerful, I think. I just

let the camera run and I never cut or anything. Jamie Gillis played a bastard [Jeff]. The girl [Stephanie] was madly in love with him and he just accosts her and abuses her.[58]

When Peary asks how she feels about the fact that the scene shows a woman being abused, she replies:

> Women's groups protested this one scene because it looks real. It actually does. He's just abusing her. Slaps her around, hits her with his belt. Not hard, he just does it. And she's blowing him, and she is happy to do it because she is so madly in love with him. At the end of the scene, he comes and he throws her out of the room.[59]

She seems to avoid the question, but in suggesting that the "power" she perceives in the scene derives from its authenticity—that is, from its being "sexually realistic"—Findlay inadvertently implies a critique of gendered violence. This abuse, after all, is not portrayed as acceptable in the film; it is portrayed as punishment, treatment in kind for an abusive man. Although the person being abused appears to be a woman, Stephanie, she/he is actually also a man, Steven, as the film consistently reminds us. Beyond this, as I have argued, the opening and closing scenes do not entirely invalidate or overshadow the sexual fluidity and celebrations of femininity that comprise most of the film's run time.

I do not have the space here to consider all of her pornographic films, but I would be remiss to end without consideration of perhaps her most sophisticated take on women's subjectivity, *Mascara*. Ron Sullivan (credited as Henri Pachard) wrote the screenplay and directed the sex scenes, and Findlay directed the dialogue scenes. The narrative centers on a professional woman (Harriet) who, bored of office life, seeks out sexual knowledge from a sex worker (Lucy), who ultimately is happy to oblige. The premise may be flimsy, but ultimately it offers a surprisingly poignant depiction of female friendship. Along the way, it also makes room for Lucy to bluntly critique some of the distinctly unsexy aspects of life as a sex worker in a society that criminalizes her labor and therefore offers no protections against violence. After Lucy guides Harriet into a *ménage à trois* with two men they pick up at a bar, Harriet inadvertently snubs Lucy by rushing to turn off the lights and go to sleep.[60] Clearly hurt, Lucy says that Harriet shouldn't feel like a big shot for having a threesome:

> Try it some time when you don't expect it. Try it some time on a middle-class commuter and he's got a friend who's a little surprise, and you're so fuckin scared you can't even keep saliva in your mouth . . . Ever been fucked in the ass, tootsie? Try sucking one guy's cock while the other jams it up your ass, and you can't even make a whimper, not a sound, because you're a whore, sister—you're supposed to love abuse.

If Molly Haskell finds the mention of pregnancy surprising in *Angel Number 9*, as a "definite downer to Don Juan fantasies of quickie, no-fault sex" that could only have been devised by a woman, what can we say about this?[61] These lines would not seem out of place at a feminist consciousness-raising session, but—unlike pregnancy, which would in fact become a popular fetish in porn— they absolutely do in a porno film. Whether she and Sullivan intended the scene as a feminist critique, it absolutely reads as such.

On the whole, the women in this film are complex, fleshed-out characters in a way that is highly unusual in pornography and exploitation cinema alike. Their subjectivity is centered, many of their interactions with each other are tender, and they foreground—without sexualizing—difficult topics like violence against women. Indeed, one of the most notable things about this film within the context of 1970s US pornography is that BDSM is portrayed as overtly consensual, in contrast to the kind of nonconsensual roughing up perpetrated on Lucy by the pair of johns that she describes.

Despite some notable conflicts, in the end the film reestablishes the women's bond via a missed encounter that, through its suggestion of the women's mutual yearning to reach one another, leaves us with the impression that the central relationship in the film may in fact be a queer romance. The film is bookended by Harriet riding on a commuter train. In the opening scene, she looks exhausted, defeated by workaday life in capitalist patriarchy. In the end, having failed to find Lucy at her apartment, Harriet boards a train looking similarly dejected. This time, however, the line of action is intercut with Lucy rushing to a cab and then from the cab to the same train station from which Harriet departs. Lucy is a moment too late, but Harriet—on the train—turns around in time to see her friend rush up to the platform. Harriet smiles genuinely as Lucy manages a wave, and the final shot is a poetic close-up of Harriet's hand releasing the subway strap that she had been holding (see Figure 2.2). This ambiguous symbolism may suggest that Harriet is now ready to fly solo, having graduated from Lucy's mentorship, but to me it evokes relief that their relationship is on stable ground and suggests the pleasures of women's companionship as a respite from oppressive systems. In this way, through its queer suggestiveness and woman-centrism, *Mascara* is arguably the truest example from Findlay's filmography of women's cinema, despite the fact that it was written and co-directed by a man. It conveys something unique and meaningful about the milieu of working girls (in both senses of the word) rather than merely providing a backdrop and flimsy justification for a series of sexual numbers.

Although Findlay may deny the female/feminist inflection of her films, I have argued that they are nonetheless examples of women's cinema as minor cinema. She may be a misogynist, she may be avowedly apolitical, but we can recuperate Findlay as a feminist figure for being a trailblazer who—before Candida Royalle rose to prominence for founding Femme Productions—created

Figure 2.2 The final sequence in *Mascara*.

her own production and distribution companies in addition to directing around fifty films, pornographic and otherwise. Unlike Royalle, she was never concerned with opening avenues of access to other women or otherwise marginalized would-be filmmakers. Her casts, featuring overwhelmingly white, thin, able-bodied, cisgender women and men, do little to challenge industrial or social beauty norms or the associated labor hierarchies.[62] Her work itself may vary widely in terms of everything from aesthetic quality to political valence, but it does include some notable challenges to the conventions of 1970s pornography, including a focus on women's orgasms, the suggestion that women might prefer sex with women, women avenging male violence, and critiques of violence against women. Her professed motivations for directing adult film may be exclusively economic, and we might simply attribute her disavowal of the term "woman filmmaker" to internalized misogyny. Yet her refusal to be pinned down to a gendered category contributes, like the sense of gender and sexual fluidity explored in films like *Angel Number 9*, to revealing the limitations of an essentialist framework. In this way, we can recuperate her contradictory persona as feminist for challenging the very idea of a "woman's sensibility," much as the complexities of her films urge a redefinition of the category and the concept of "women's pornography."

NOTES

1. Quoted in "Roberta Findlay!," *Third Eye Cinema*, June 17, 2012, https://thirdeyecinema.podbean.com/e/third-eye-cinema-61712-with-roberta-findlay/ (accessed May 26, 2022).

2. Quoted in the "Bio/Interview" extra on the *Cult 70s Porno Director: Roberta Findlay* DVD (Alpha Blue Archives, 2006).

3. Alison Butler, *Women's Cinema: The Contested Screen* (New York: Wallflower, 2002), 1.

4. For more information, see Jennifer Moorman, "Women on Top: The Work of Female Pornographers and (S)experimental Filmmakers" (Dissertation, UCLA, 2014); Jennifer Moorman, "Selling a Rebellion: The Industrial Logic of Mainstream Alt-Porn," *Camera Obscura: Feminism, Culture, and Media Studies* 32, no. 2 (95) (September 2017): 29–61; Jennifer Moorman, "'The Hardest of Hardcore': Locating Feminist Possibilities in Women's Extreme Adult Film Production." *Signs: Journal of Women in Culture and Society* 42, no. 3 (Spring 2017): 693–716.

5. Butler, *Women's Cinema*, 20.

6. Butler, *Women's Cinema*, 21.

7. See, for instance, Linda Williams, *Hard Core: Power, Pleasure, and the "Frenzy of the Visible"* (Berkeley: UC Press, 1999 [1989]), 6 and 246–7, in which Findlay is described as the first person to take more than a "revisionist" approach to creating porn for women. See also: Tristan Taormino, Celine Pareñas Shimizu, Constance Penley, and Mireille Miller-Young, *The Feminist Porn Book: The Politics of Producing Pleasure* (New York: The Feminist Press at CUNY, 2013). On page 11 of the Introduction, the editors credit Candida Royalle with creating "a new genre: porn from a woman's point of view."

8. Williams does mention one of her films, *Angel on Fire*, in passing (*Hard Core*, 134), but never discusses her as a filmmaker. In the chapter in which she profiles Candida Royalle and other women filmmakers ("Sequels and Re-Visions: 'A Desire of One's Own'"), Williams's focus is on pornography that attempts to depict a woman's perspective, so perhaps she did not feel that Findlay's work would fall into that category.

9. Here I refer to my dissertation (Moorman, "Women on Top"), which forms the basis of my current book manuscript, entitled *The Softer Side of Hardcore? Women Filmmakers in Pornographic Production Cultures*. For more information on this topic, see Jennifer Moorman, "'Flows of Desire': 'The Pleasure Principle' (2019), *Shakedown* (2017), and Pornhub's Political/Libidinal Economy," *Synoptique* 9, no. 2 (Fall 2021): 97–123; Moorman, "Selling a Rebellion"; and Moorman, "The Hardest of Hardcore."

10. Here and elsewhere, I describe as "mainstream" any adult video that is marketed primarily to straight men and secondarily to straight women and couples, and theatrically released (in the 1970s) or disseminated (in the home video and digital eras) by one of the major distribution companies (like Pulse or Hustler) to online retailers and streaming sites, brick-and-mortar adult video stores, and/or cable channels and hotel networks.

11. To gain a richer understanding of women, nonbinary, and queer filmmakers' work and porn industry praxis—its norms and conventions, its gender, sexual, and racial dynamics, its ideological investments—I interviewed forty filmmakers and industry insiders, viewed approximately two hundred adult films, analyzed marketing materials and trade publications, observed on the set of productions, attended adult video conventions and awards shows, and was a participant–observer of retail sites as an employee of the "Oh My" sex shop in Northampton, MA, and as assistant manager of Babeland Los Angeles. For more information, see Moorman, "Women on Top"; Moorman, "Selling a Rebellion"; and Moorman, "The Hardest of Hardcore."

12. Butler, *Women's Cinema*, 1.

13. Findlay had worked as a performer prior to directing, but I would argue that she had not built up a brand in the way that women pornographers from the 1980s to the present generally do. In other words, she may have been a performer, but she was not a "porn star" prior to becoming a director. For more on the trend of women pornographers building a brand and

achieving stardom prior to accessing opportunities to direct, see Moorman, "Women on Top"; Moorman, "Selling a Rebellion"; and Moorman, "The Hardest of Hardcore."

14. For more information on the "feminist sex wars," see Carolyn Bronstein, *Battling Pornography: The American Feminist Anti-Pornography Movement, 1976–1986* (Cambridge: Cambridge University Press, 2011).

15. See, for instance, the work of Gail Dines, Andrea Dworkin, and Catharine MacKinnon, for arguments proposing that pornography both is and incites violence against women; and Stephen Maddison, "'Make Love Not Porn': Entrepreneurial Voyeurism, Agency, and Affect," in Ken Hillis, Susanna Paasonen, and Michael Petit (eds), *Networked Affect*, (Boston: MIT Press, 2015), 151–67, for a discussion of pornography's commodification of affect.

16. For more information, see Moorman, "Flows of Desire."

17. For more about women filmmakers in the US adult video industry, see Moorman, "Women on Top"; Moorman, "Selling a Rebellion"; and Moorman, "The Hardest of Hardcore."

18. See Heather Berg, *Porn Work: Sex, Labor, and Late Capitalism* (Chapel Hill: UNC Press, 2021).

19. Mireille Miller-Young, *A Taste for Brown Sugar: Black Women in American Pornography* (Durham, NC: Duke University Press, 2014).

20. Saba Mahmood, *The Politics of Piety: The Islamic Revival and the Feminist Subject* (Princeton: Princeton University Press, 2005). According to Mahmood, the mosque movement's primary objective is to recapture the pious sensibility that views Islam as integral to women's daily life through the re-integration of various forms of Islamic knowledge and practice.

21. Mahmood, *The Politics of Piety*, 15.

22. Mahmood, *The Politics of Piety*, 22.

23. Vicki Mayer, Miranda J. Banks, and John Thornton Caldwell, "Introduction: Production Studies; Roots and Routes," *Production Studies: Cultural Studies of Media Industries* (New York: Routledge, 2009), 2.

24. Berg, *Porn Work*. She begins her discussion of "porno dialectics" on page 3.

25. Berg, *Porn Work*. She begins her discussion of these production practices on page 65.

26. See for instance Ashley West and April Hall, "Roberta Findlay: A Respectable Woman— Podcast 53," August 16, 2015, in *Rialto Report*, podcast, https://www.therialtoreport. com/2015/08/16/roberta-findlay/ (accessed July 28, 2021).

27. Allison Nastasi, "Interview: Exploitation and Adult Cinema Icon Roberta Findlay on Making "Cheap" Movies, Getting Arrested with John Holmes, and Times Square's X-Rated Past," *Flavorwire*, December 30, 2017, https://www.flavorwire.com/609580/flavorwire-interview- exploitation-and-adult-cinema-icon-roberta-findlay-on-making-cheap-movies-getting- arrested-with-john-holmes-and-times-squares-x-rated-past (accessed May 26, 2022).

28. For more information on the film's popular and critical reception, see Alexandra Heller- Nichols, "What's Inside a Girl? Porn, Horror, and the Films of Roberta Findlay," *Senses of Cinema* 80 (September 2016), https://www.sensesofcinema.com/2016/american-extreme/ porn-horror-roberta-findlay/ (accessed May 26, 2022); and Alexandra Heller-Nichols, "Anti-auteur: The Films of Roberta Findlay," in Ernest Mathijs and Jamie Sexton (eds), *The Routledge Companion to Cult Cinema* (New York: Routledge, 2020), 402–10.

29. "Roberta Findlay!," *Third Eye Cinema*; West and Hall, "Roberta Findlay: A Respectable Woman."

30. "Bio/Interview," *Cult 70s Porno Director*.

31. "Bio/Interview," *Cult 70s Porno Director*.

32. Nastasi, "Flavorwire Interview."

33. Williams, *Hard Core*. Williams discusses this idea at length, but for instance on page 25 she notes that *Deep Throat* was "one of the first pornographic films to concentrate on the problem of a woman's pleasure."

34. Gerald Peary, "Woman in Porn: How Young Roberta Findlay Finally Grew Up and Made Snuff," *Take One*, September 1978, 32.

35. Molly Haskell, "Are Women Directors Different?" *The Village Voice*, February 3, 1975. Reprinted in Karyn Kay and Gerald Peary (eds), *Women and the Cinema: A Critical Anthology* (Dutton, 1977), 434. For more information on this minor controversy over who directed *Angel Number 9*, see the Introduction to this volume.

36. Dennis Giles, "*Angel on Fire*: Three Texts of Desire," *Velvet Light Trap*, Fall 1976. Giles writes: "*Angel on Fire* [aka *Angel Number 9*] is written, produced, directed and photographed by Roberta Findlay. Although this name is possibly a pseudonym, we are confronted with a feminine *persona* as a creator of a fantasy for a predominantly masculine audience" (42).

37. For more information on this, see Mark Edward Heuck, "Once Upon a Time . . . in the Hot Summer," *The Projector Has Been Drinking*, June 30, 2021, https://projectorhasbeendrinking. blogspot.com/2021/06/once-upon-timein-hot-summer.html (accessed May 26, 2022).

38. Peary, "Woman in Porn," 32.

39. I reached out to Joe Rubin, co-founder of Vinegar Syndrome, to inquire as to why only Walter Sear had been credited as director on the DVD packaging. In an email correspondence dated June 21, 2021, he understandably responded, "To be completely honest, it's probably just an error (or, equally likely, the result of confusion on her authorship claims), but I'd go with whatever she states in the commentary."

40. Quoted in "Roberta Findlay!," *Third Eye Cinema*. The film seems to have been marketed as a sexploitation roughie and most of the sex scenes are softcore, but Findlay refers to it in several interviews as "hardcore" and at least one scene does include hardcore content: an unsimulated blow job and cunnilingus.

41. She identifies her favorite film in Peary, "Woman in Porn," 34.

42. "Roberta Findlay!," *Third Eye Cinema*.

43. "Roberta Findlay!," *Third Eye Cinema*.

44. In *Jeanne Dielman, 23 Quai du Commerce, 1080 Bruxelles* (1975, dir. Chantal Akerman), the title character murders one of her johns with a pair of scissors near the end of the film.

45. Alfred Hitchcock famously said this, regarding how to keep film viewers entertained. Quoted in Carol J. Clover, *Men, Women, and Chain Saws: Gender in the Modern Horror Film* (Princeton: Princeton University Press, 1992), 43.

46. For more on women filmmakers of "extreme" hardcore, see Moorman, "The Hardest of Hardcore."

47. Quoted in the featurette *A Blood Sisters Reunion* on the 2004 Media Blasters home entertainment release of *Blood Sisters* (Roberta Findlay, 1987).

48. Clover, *Men, Women, and Chain Saws*, 53.

49. Clover, *Men, Women, and Chain Saws*, 51.

50. "Porno Marathon," *Filmspotting Forum*, September 4, 2009, http://forum.filmspotting. net/index.php?PHPSESSID=8dcf039f09419b77881d5739184d9102&topic=6463.0;nowap (accessed May 26, 2022).

51. I follow queer theorists such as Judith Butler, Jack Halberstam, Cathy J. Cohen, Eve Kosofky Sedgwick, and others in defining as "queer" sexualities and phenomena that are fluid, unstable, nonheteronormative and more broadly anti-normative, and resistant to categorization and easy understanding.

52. I use versions of "him/her" or "his/hers" for most references to Steven/Stephanie, because the majority of the film suggests a fluidity and/or dual consciousness. I use "his" in reference to Steven in the opening and closing scenes, in which Steven's status as a man is (re)affirmed.

53. In a variety of popular media texts, including *Some Like It Hot* (1959), *Scoobie-Doo* (2002), *Hot Chicks* (2006), the anime film *Kimi no na wa* (2016), and the pilot episode of *Legion*

(2017), a straight, cisgender man who is either dressed as or magically transformed into (whether actually or in a fantasy or a dream sequence) a woman begins by touching him/herself or attempting to seduce a woman. This happens perhaps most relevantly in *Switch* (1991), as the premise is nearly identical to that of *Angel Number 9*: as summarized on IMDB, "A sexist womanizer is killed by one of his former lovers and then reincarnated as a woman."

54. For instance, in the *Third Eye Cinema* interview, she admits that she would simply tell performers, "Alright, everybody screw" because she "didn't know how to direct sex scenes."

55. Quoted in Linda Williams, *Screening Sex* (Durham, NC: Duke University Press, 2008), 163; original emphasis.

56. Williams, *Screening Sex*, 267.

57. As these theories tend to have cisnormative and/or trans-exclusionary frameworks, I do not endorse them so much as cite them as continuous with the psychoanalytic framework of earlier feminist theories of women's cinema. For psychoanalytic perspectives on so-called "womb envy," "vagina envy," or "uterus envy" among cis men, see for instance, Karen Horney, "The Flight from Womanhood: The Masculinity-Complex in Women as Viewed by Men and by Women," *International Journal of Psychoanalysis* 7, 1926; Margaret Mead, *Male and Female* (Harper Perennial, 2001 [1949]); Barbara Engler, *Personality Theories*, 9th edn (Cengage Learning, 2013); Eva Kittay, "Rereading Freud on 'Femininity' or Why Not Womb Envy?," *Women's Studies Int. Forum* 7, no. 5, 1984; Harold Tarpley, "Vagina Envy in Men," *Psychodynamic Psychiatry* 21, no. 3, 1993.

58. Quoted in Peary, "Woman in Porn," 32.

59. Peary, "Woman in Porn," 32.

60. The guidance begins with helping Harriet to pick them up, and continues with Lucy watching and providing suggestions and other commentary while Harriet has sex with the men.

61. It must be said that Haskell, who admits in the same essay to not being a "blue-movie aficionado," could not have anticipated the fetishization of pregnancy that would later comprise a significant subgenre of porn. Belladonna, for instance, made several successful videos—including *Baby on Board* (*Evil Angel*, 2015)—in which she performed while pregnant.

62. For more about the racialized labor hierarchies in the mainstream porn industry, resulting in fewer job opportunities and lower pay rates for performers of color, see Miller-Young, *A Taste for Brown Sugar*, and Berg, *Porn Work*.

CHAPTER 3

Zero Girls and Lesbian Stylites: From Solar Sexuality to Camp in the Early Films of Roberta Findlay

Kevin John Bozelka

The sway of Roberta Findlay's career mirrors film history's general trajectory from a Cinema of Attractions to a mode of filmmaking centered on narrative. In such early sexploitation titles as *Take Me Naked* (1966) and *Mnasidika* (1969), Findlay created an oeuvre of extreme externality, showing bodies writhing in myriad combinations instead of telling stories driven by three-dimensional characters.[1] However, beginning with *Janie* (1970), *The Altar of Lust* (1971), and *Rosebud* (1972), she quickly accrued more narrative capabilities so that her hardcore features and later horror films, while decidedly low-budget and grungy, conveyed an ease with using film to invoke a consistent diegetic time and space.

Given that Findlay's early films are aligned as much with avant-garde practices as with sexploitation norms, they elicit different responses than her later, more narrative-driven work does. They point to a possible world, one where the women and lesbians who populate her films might flourish. Excruciatingly dull, obnoxious, and even flat-out unwatchable, they nevertheless become energizing when bearing down on them, built as they are on what Deleuze calls a "perverse structure" at odds with how cinema is traditionally supposed to work.[2] As such, they elicit confusion, boredom, even rage at each rule-flouting movement. By contrast, the later films evoke the world we know now and thus elicit a camp response, especially given how camp functions as a survival strategy for living in the world as it is. Where an aptitude for camp allows the viewer to decode the norms of cinema (as well as gender and sexuality) operative in the later films, the early films transmit an alien code that requires more active, even depletive, decoding on the part of the viewer.

To that end, after discussing precedents to the early films, I strive, borrowing Deleuze's words, to manifest their perverse structure[3] using Michel Tournier's

1967 philosophical novel *Friday, or, The Other Island* (French: *Vendredi ou les limbes du Pacifique*) with particular emphasis on *Mnasidika*.[4] A sensation among the French intelligentsia upon release, *Friday* retells the story of Daniel Defoe's *Robinson Crusoe* as a journey toward attaining a solar sexuality, an elemental, deindividuated jubilance free of language, categories, and rationalization. Through years spent alone, Tournier's Crusoe basks in his liberated sexuality and remains on the island at the novel's end in contradistinction to the original Crusoe's despair at being marooned.

The women in Roberta Findlay's films long for a similar transcendence. But they exist in a world that will not leave them alone. Where Tournier's Crusoe feels oppressed by mere communication with others, Findlay's heroines have much more threatening beasts to ward off. Pimps, psychiatrists, lecherous fathers, and all manner of derelicts subjugate them to sexual violence and/or attempt to correct their lesbian tendencies. Given how the later titles still lack a strong diegetic interiority, a viewer can take their horrors with a grain of camp. They seem to hail a self-actualized lesbian subject prepared to reject any oppressive realism. But *Take Me Naked* and *Mnasidika* seem to hail no one despite intimations in the latter of a lesbian Eden akin to Crusoe's island paradise of Speranza with an even more radical outcome than Tournier would allow.

PRECEDENTS

Despite the *sui generis* nature of Roberta Findlay's early films, they nevertheless have legible precedents. Most of the voices heard in *Take Me Naked* and *Mnasidika* are recitations from Pierre Louÿs's *The Songs of Bilitis*, a series of prose poems published in 1894 that Louÿs tried to pass off as a freshly unearthed work of Ancient Greece in the style of Sappho. For Stephen Broomer, the centrality of Louÿs to *Take Me Naked* places it within a tradition of beat cinema in both the aspirational and exploitative modes that characterize the film.[5] Quasi-fictional documents of beatnik life such as *Pull My Daisy* (1959, dir. Robert Frank and Alfred Leslie) and *Chappaqua* (1967, dir. Conrad Rooks) help contextualize Findlay's aspirations to high art, while gore classics featuring killer beatniks like *A Bucket of Blood* (1959, dir. Roger Corman) and *Color Me Blood Red* (1965, dir. Herschell Gordon Lewis) situate *Take Me Naked* on exploitation terra firma. But *The Songs of Bilitis*, in particular, has proven an enormously malleable text across a variety of contexts that places Findlay's use of Louÿs's work in a long, varied tradition.

The most immediate connection lies in the fact that many publications of *The Songs of Bilitis* featured illustrations by such artists as Louis Icart, Willy Pogany, Georges Barbier, Mariette Lydis, and Paul-Émile Bécat, all influenced by the ripe, Symbolist sexuality in Aubrey Beardsley's drawings. The poem's vivid erotic imagery seemed to beg for such visualization and Findlay's early films continue this tradition of rendering Louÿs's work flesh. Undoubtedly the most famous of Louÿs's adapters, Claude Debussy set three poems from *The Songs of Bilitis* to music and composed accompaniment for the recitation of twelve poems from the work. Several spoken-word recordings exist, often highlighting the more salacious aspects of the poems. For instance, in 1962, Fax Records, specialists in naughty stag party albums, released *Nights of Love in Lesbos*, a highly abridged version focusing on the lesbian sex and cooed in breathy tones to anonymous musical accompaniment. Finally, formed in 1955 as the first lesbian civil rights organization, Daughters of Bilitis took their name from Louÿs's epic. But like all of the instances above, they adapted it to their specific needs. As Gretchen Schultz notes, the group willfully ignored the more retrograde, voyeuristic aspects of *The Songs of Bilitis* and deemed it "a sensitive and searching picture of Lesbian love."[6] In Schultz's estimation, "they read it as affirming rather than exploitative and refashioned it into something closer in spirit to their own lives."[7] So however snugly Findlay fits into a sleazy exploitation profile, she was no less reverent in her borrowings from *The Songs of Bilitis* than the adapters outlined above.

FRIDAY AND THE CLICK

Since much of *Take Me Naked* and *Mnasidika* involves world making, it shall prove beneficial to outline the world as it is now, i.e. the patriarchal status quo that renders a woman (or women) alone an untenable proposition. The earliest surviving Michael Findlay title, *The Sin Syndicate* (1964), serves as a perfect portrait of this status quo. The film delineates the fate of several women who arrive in New York City via Greyhound and become Zero Girls, prostitutes for a mob syndicate. Each girl mourns their loss of individual identity and aches for even a moment away from their slavering clients. Such moments are rare indeed as when Candy (June Roberts) and Lorna (Judy Adler) towel each other off after a shower and confess, "I wish it could be like this all the time, just the two of us." But as the final monologue of fellow sex worker Dolores (Yolanda Moreno) makes clear, "These stories happened yesterday, are happening today, and will happen tomorrow. As long as there are men, you will find Zero Girls." *The Sin Syndicate* is the world to which *Take Me Naked* and, to a greater extent, *Mnasidika*, will provide a radical alternative.

Tournier's *Friday* offers a preliminary way of thinking about Findlay's extreme visions, given how much the novel is a meditation on the status quo. Equal parts philosophy and fiction, *Friday* features a Robinson Crusoe who comes off like a grad student in search of a seminar. He spends much of his solitude pondering the discrepancy between the norms of civilization from which he has been displaced and the absence of others as civilizing agents on the island where he is shipwrecked. His journal entries, which take up copious amounts of the novel, could be ripped from Freud's *The Future of an Illusion*, Lacan's *Écrits*, or de Saussure's *Course in General Linguistics*. One of these entries provides a convenient summary of the major theme of the novel.

As the activity of communicating with other people fades, Crusoe notes his more immediate and sensual relationship with the world around him. Objects seem to reveal their essences irrespective of Crusoe's ability to perceive them. This is a childlike state in which subject and object, perceiver and perceived, are one, and things vibrate in their unique "thingishness" with no meaning or function attached to them.

But then something happens, which Crusoe labels in his journal as "the click." The perceiver becomes aware of themselves perceiving and the object loses its sensuality: "The subject breaks away from the object, divesting it of a part of its color and substance. There is a rift in the scheme of things, and a whole range of objects crumbles in becoming *me*."[8] The click is Freud's ego, Lacan's Symbolic Order, de Saussure's sign, the world reordered to place the perceiving human subject at its center. From these points of existence, necessary to inhabit in order for one to take up their proper role in civilization, comes a system of exchange, not just of capitalist goods but of language and standardized identity. Every facet of life is then submitted to a process of efficiency and categorization. At the opposite end lies the Id, the Imaginary, and floating signifiers, the childlike mode outlined above. Much of the novel finds Crusoe teetering between these extremes.

Sometimes he will relinquish himself to this latter, more primeval state. Whether despairing or ecstatic, he forsakes progress, work, and any activity beyond the most elemental movements by submerging himself in a boggy, insect-ridden mire, depositing his body into the deepest, tightest womb of a cave, and plunging his penis into the mucky soil of a combe. When he emerges from these states, he tries to emulate the systems of exchange of the civilization now lost to him. His goal is to tame the island he has christened Speranza by rationalizing it down to its every grain of sand. He keeps time with a clepsydra, produces and stockpiles a variety of crops, and creates a byzantine skein of laws, titles, and departments. A typical to-do list gives an idea of the complexity of his endeavor: "Announce the results of the census of sea turtles, take the chair at the Drafting Committee of the Charter and Penal Code, and finally preside at the opening of a new bridge of lianas flung audaciously across a ravine a hundred feet deep in the heart of the forest."[9]

Crusoe also manages to reproduce the inequities of so-called civilization with the arrival on the island of Friday. Deeming him a savage and "not of pure blood,"[10] Crusoe immediately forces Friday into labor, eventually paying him a wage, although the gesture is born from a desire to simulate civilization, not to forge any kind of equity. Soon, however, Crusoe grows intrigued by this "body without a soul" who seems to live only for the present.[11] Unlike Crusoe, Friday appears uninterested in the deferral of gratification for some later payoff and enjoys an anti-productive, sensuality-oriented existence. He shoots arrows not to reach a target but to marvel at their heft in the air and the distance they travel. He befriends scores of rats and even encourages them to breed and multiply. He discovers jewels that Crusoe has rescued from the sunken ship and uses them to bedazzle the oddly shaped plants in the cactus garden that Crusoe has cultivated. Most strikingly, he sustains serious injuries while wrestling with goats and even manages to kill one in battle. He names this goat Andoar and to honor his majesty in battle, he fashions a kite and an Aeolian harp out of Andoar's entrails, the latter evoking an avant-garde drone composition.

Friday's activities impel Crusoe to finally and fully embrace the primeval state he has been wrestling with ever since his shipwreck. He abandons all pretense to civilization and opts to remain on the island instead of returning home on the schooner that has drifted off course to Speranza's shores. Under Friday's influence, Crusoe directs his sexuality toward Speranza and becomes flooded with sky-love, "a soft jubilation which exalts and pervades me from head to foot."[12] His decision to remain, diametrically opposed to the goals of Defoe's Crusoe, confirms his transformation from a genital to a solar sexuality, an auto-eroticized, elemental externality at one with the sun and its baking rays. He has acceded to the mode of existence predicted at the beginning of the novel in the Tarot reading given by the captain of the ship moments before it sinks. Speranza beckons as the City of the Sun depicted on one of the cards:

> the inhabitants are clothed with childlike innocence, having attained to solar sexuality, which is not merely androgynous but circular. A snake biting its tail is the symbol of that self-enclosed eroticism, in which there is no leak or flaw. It is the zenith of human perfectibility, infinitely difficult to achieve, more difficult still to sustain.[13]

At the end of the novel, then, Tournier leaves the strong suggestion that Crusoe might never again experience the click with which civilization burdens its inhabitants.

CLICKS AND CUTS

Take Me Naked is the Findlay film that most resembles *Friday* in that it oscillates between both sides of the click. But where Crusoe notes the click in his journal, Findlay simply cuts between gritty, realistic evocations of civilization and a topsy-turvy, confounding universe. A further difference is that *Take Me*

Naked concerns women who, on the supposed civilized side of the click, are subject to the murderous gaze of men. One could hardly conceive of a starker illustration of Laura Mulvey's fundamental feminist film theory that men look and women are looked at than the opening third of the film.[14] In a recognizable, grimy New York City, a derelict (Kevin Sullivan) looks out of his window at Elaine (Roberta Findlay) in a nearby apartment. She is unaware of his gaze as she undresses and caresses her body. The editing patterns and the derelict's voice-over organize the woman for his viewing. But subject and object become uncoupled via what Moya Luckett, in reference to the contemporary sexploitation films of Doris Wishman, calls "ludicrous visual juxtapositions."[15] The derelict remains fixed in his position as voyeur. But the woman moves freely throughout her apartment. For instance, she walks across the apartment and enters the bathroom to take a shower. There is a cut back to the derelict, but he has not moved. Therefore, he cannot possibly see her take a shower from his vantage point even though the editing wants us to believe he can.

It would be an overstatement to claim that the editing results in an unmooring of the derelict's vision such that he no longer dominates looking relations. But it seems equally preposterous to suggest that any viewer becomes sutured into this tattered diegetic space. We are left on the outside, which elicits, if not a camp response, then an inability to succumb to the film's illusions and/or subscribe to its patriarchal ideologies.

It is in the next sequence, however, where *Take Me Naked* becomes truly alien, and few standardized responses are available to help the viewer grasp it. The derelict comes away from the window and lies down in his bed. He reads a copy of *The Collected Tales of Pierre Louÿs* (illustrated by John Austen) and intones in voice-over, "In my dreams, dreams of poetry, I rise and seek to follow the sun of eternal love in poetry," before falling asleep and dropping the book to the floor (see Figure 3.1). The next ten minutes comprise a dream sequence that reconfirms the film as deriving from the derelict's perception. As he drops the book, there is a cut to a spatially baffling location with two women (Roberta Findlay and June Roberts) and a man cloaked in shadow. The high-contrast lighting offers few depth cues and the intricate scrim that fills the background makes the room feel like a theater set rather than Findlay's (or anyone else's) apartment. The fractured space does not immediately jar the viewer, since dream logic frames it. But an anonymous woman reading from *The Songs of Bilitis* takes over the narration. And while the poems recited vaguely mirror the images, they are random selections that make hay of the original narrative order.

For instance, at one point in this sequence, the disembodied voice recites "Regrets," which comes early in the *Songs* and depicts a young Bilitis rejecting the sexual advances of a man named Lykas. The accompanying footage shows a man (possibly the derelict) forcing himself on Roberts while both are shirtless

Figure 3.1 *The Collected Tales of Pierre Louÿs* in *Take Me Naked*.

in bed. But the next poem recited in the film is "The Warm Girdle," which comes toward the end of the *Songs* when Bilitis is a much older courtesan who teases Teleas, a client. She wraps her girdle around his head in an effort to make him intoxicated with her scent and then flees once he becomes aroused. This scene is played out in the film (with a towel instead of a girdle) by the same two characters who were just struggling together on the bed, severing any narrative connection between the two scenes, almost as if there are clicks within clicks. Even more baffling is the fact that the woman places her arms akimbo and starts to perform slight chicken-like motions, perhaps mocking the man's state of arousal. All of this bizarre activity could be chalked up to dream logic were it not for the fact that so much time has transpired since the dream has been attached to the derelict. The sequence goes on so long that it abandons any perceiving subject, an effect that will become exacerbated in the next sequence.

A cut brings the film back to clearer spatio-temporal relations as another derelict (Michael Findlay) comes into the room and wakes the sleeping man. Findlay makes a pass at him and the derelict bludgeons Findlay to death. He then falls asleep and dreams "of a goddess' love." Beginning with yet another cut, this dream sequence lasts over twenty minutes, a disproportionate amount of time for a film that runs only sixty-nine minutes. It opens with a gorgeous, soft-focus image of Roberta Findlay wrapped in veils and surrounded by candles. Another woman

(Darlene Bennett) joins her and they caress one another in frames so blurred as to become purely abstract. The anonymous woman again recites various poems from the *Songs* with no concern for their original narrative placement or their precise connection to the visuals. Even when she cries out "Mnasidika! Mnasidika!" there is no legible link to the later film. This entire lengthy oasis comes off as a respite not only from the derelict's deadly gaze but also from consistent time and space relations. It radiates sheer alien energy rather than the mere ineptitude at achieving continuity editing characteristic of most sexploitation films.[16]

The final sequence clicks back to the derelict with a cut to his apartment. Now clean-shaven and wearing a suit, he goes to Elaine's apartment and brings her flowers. For once, the moment feels sweet and gentle. But a jarring cut to the man in derelict form makes clear that he is hallucinating. The film cuts back and forth between the hallucination and the derelict beating and eventually murdering Findlay. As he mounts her dead body and the film comes to an end, his voice-over recites "Leves Amores," a poem written in 1895 by British poet Arthur Symons about a man watching over his lover as she sleeps.

On one level, the final sequence solidifies *Take Me Naked* as organized around the derelict's subjectivity. But on an even more palpable level, the sequences scored to Louÿs's poetry feel like de facto avant-garde shorts dropped into the film. As such, they seem attached to no subjectivity, a pure externality requiring potentially forthcoming categorization. Whether through excruciating boredom or delirious transport, we forget that the second sequence in particular is initially tied to the derelict's dream state. It bears no discernible relationship to the scenes of murder surrounding it apart from intimations of a world free from not only patriarchal violence but even basic, reassuring perceptual cues as well.

MNASIDIKA

The "self-enclosed eroticism . . . infinitely difficult to achieve, more difficult still to sustain"[17] that appears sporadically in *Take Me Naked* comes to near-full fruition in *Mnasidika*. Easily the most extreme title in Findlay's filmography, *Mnasidika* makes so few concessions to the viewer that it barely feels like an act of communication at all. If the later films elicit a camp response, then *Mnasidika* seems indifferent to response. The world it creates almost entirely erodes the sense of the click felt in *Take Me Naked* and a baffling perceptual field occupies most of the film's running time. Crusoe's description of Speranza as an island "steadily pursuing its course without me" applies just as well to *Mnasidika* and suggests the difficulties in watching it: "I must shrink to become that intimate phosphorescence which causes each thing to be known while no one is the knower, each to be aware while no one has awareness."[18]

Mnasidika takes place on an unknown isle as far away from any kind of recognizable civilization as Speranza.[19] A "smooth, unmarked, eternally present and unchanging utopia,"[20] this location hosts a tribe of women who have attained something akin to the solar sexuality to which Crusoe aspires. The difference is that Crusoe embarks on his trajectory toward the solar in the absence of others. For Deleuze, this absence results not just in a lack of other people but the collapse of what he calls, in a typical Deleuzian hyphenation, the structure-Other, a condition that organizes our perception.[21] Without the structure-Other, there are no longer any possible worlds mobilized by other people outside our immediate perception, and self fuses with object (and others) akin to the way an infant in Lacan's Imaginary cannot perceive difference or even exchange. This mode of existence results in a perverse structure, which Deleuze describes in a way that applies indelibly to *Mnasidika*: "Nothing subsists but insuperable depths, absolute distances and differences or, on the contrary, unbearable repetitions, looking like precisely superimposed lengths."[22]

However, the collapse of the structure-Other need not take place literally in the absence of other people as Deleuze's analysis of the works of de Sade makes clear.[23] A perverse structure obtains in *Mnasidika* despite the presence of a female populace. The women here have been emptied of interiority by a complete lack of synchronized dialogue. The soundtrack is constructed almost entirely of nineteenth-century poetry (including huge swaths of *The Songs of Bilitis*) and a hodgepodge of music from Ravel and twentieth-century Czech composer Bohuslav Martinů with vague effects of dreaminess and anxiety respectively. While the film's very title promises traditional character development (Mnasidika is the name of Bilitis's lover), none of the women function as goal-oriented, desiring individuals. They are, instead, dehumanized, undifferentiated concatenations of pleasure with no psychology and no history. Like Crusoe, they have attained, as a group, a self-contained sexuality that is "the symbol of both the non-reproductive aspect of solar sexuality and of its connection to elemental time, time unmarked and unjustified by production, whether sexual or economic."[24]

The de facto prologue to *Mnasidika* makes this aspect of solar sexuality clearer. The film opens with a series of shots of the sun as it sets (or possibly rises) over a shoreline. Each shot is repeated with such slight variations that they come across as jump cuts. It is impossible to determine if each shot is a new day or a different vantage point of the same day. Thus, the film initiates solar time, a circular, repetitive temporality that allows the film to swerve away from the forward-motion of a narrative drive. A woman's voice intones Paul Verlaine's "My Familiar Dream," a poem about loving a woman in a dream but marked by intimations of an inability to narrate (death, statues, stillness). An image of fire is superimposed over a forest. Two naked women enter the frame from opposite ends and kiss one another (see Figure 3.2). They join together

Figure 3.2 Superimpositions in *Mnasidika*.

several times in a row mirroring the repetitions in the opening shots. In this inaugural moment in the film, fire and forest and women flatten into one, corresponding to what Crusoe labels as the "primary, direct mode [in which] my awareness of an object is the object itself, the thing known and perceived without any person knowing and perceiving it."[25] The nameless women here lack not only psychological depth but pictorial depth as well. The images possess no interiority that could foster the illusion of diegetic space. We must attend to the images in all their externality rather than peering into them voyeuristically.

The next sequence offers the closest *Mnasidika* comes to the click. But whatever kind of reality (or structure-Other) it delineates rests on a much less sure footing than that portrayed in *Take Me Naked*. A fade-in reveals Michael Findlay standing on rocks by the seashore while a portion of Jules Laforgue's "For the Book of Love" is recited by the same woman who intoned the opening Verlaine poem. The bitter griping of an adult male virgin, "For the Book of Love" presumably represents Findlay's thoughts. But the disconnect between voice and image renders him a more fragmented subject than the derelict in *Take Me Naked*. He is dressed in contemporary garb but after a series of disconnected pillow shots, he suddenly appears in an ancient Greek tunic holding a straight razor to the back of his neck and crushing daisies with his bare foot, perhaps vague references to the flowers and knife in Laforgue's poem. A reverse-motion shot causes him to rise to his feet from a prostrate position. He then chases a woman in similar garb and catches up to her after a tree has fallen on her leg.

The apparent switch to ancient times and the fractured nature of the scene seem to suggest visions in a dream Findlay is having. But unlike *Take Me Naked*, there is no rigid demarcation cordoning off reality. Indeed, the dream logic gives way to a further hallucination, weakening the sense of any originating subjectivity. Findlay lifts the tree off the woman's leg and picks her up in his arms. But a cut reveals he is holding a bundle of sticks, and the woman remains pinned under the tree. He takes her immobility as an opportunity to rape her and beat her with a large stick at which point the disembodied woman's voice recites two poems from Charles Baudelaire's *Les Fleurs du mal*—"Heautontimoroumenos" and "Le Léthé." Both poems convey a sense of self-loathing and even self-annihilation rather than any outward violence, and again the woman's voice makes it difficult to pin the sentiments to Findlay. The scene ends with Findlay carrying the woman to another location and caressing her presumably dead body.

There is then a cut to footage of vegetation by a flowing river. A different woman's voice recites random chunks of "Lesbos," another poem from *Les Fleurs du mal*. No human figures appear until the voice starts to recite "Hymn to Astarte" from *The Songs of Bilitis*. And for the next approximately forty minutes in a sixty-eight-minute film, the voice will recite poems from Louÿs's work in random order over images possessed by an extreme discontinuity. This section of the film delineates a lesbian utopia with women radiating their sexuality in various groupings, couplings, and solo acts, all while Findlay radiates pride in utilizing radical film techniques. She places the women's activities into relief by indulging in her passion for cinematography with a parade of try-anything, *à la mode* film techniques: blurred edges, unmotivated dissolves and fades, superimpositions, slow motion, reverse motion, repeated shots, extreme close-ups abstracting nature, and so on.[26] Space does not permit a detailing of how nearly every scene and even shot presents a new externality rather than a link in a narrative chain. Like a soft-core *L'année dernière à Marienbad* (1961, dir. Alain Resnais), *Mnasidika* in these moments is all plot and no story, vectors of energy like Friday's directionless arrows. In this world of radical disconnection, there is a concomitant disconnection from the viewer. The film seems to occur with no regard for human perception, a phenomenon detected by Crusoe in his click off from civilization: "It was as though in ceasing to be related to each other according to their use—and their abuse—things had returned to their own essence, were flowering in their own right and existing simply for their own sakes, seeking no other warrant than their own fulfillment."[27]

As with *Take Me Naked*, only more pronounced, the click back to any kind of reality is muted by the lengthy amount of time it takes to arrive at that point. About ten minutes from the end of the film, there is a cut to the murdered woman whom we barely remember as even being murdered, especially since she has been unceremoniously resurrected in several subsequent scenes. Covered in blood, she opens her eyes, terrifying Findlay and causing him to flee. A retribution scene follows as a group of women capture Findlay and tie him to the ground. Yet even here, the film adheres to its own baffling logic. Reverse motion drops silver-painted squashes from the sky into the hands of the women. They place these around Findlay and proceed to smash them. The film color passes through various tints, finally resting on a bright yellow resembling, appropriately enough, solar photography, as the women stab Findlay with swords.

Unlike *Take Me Naked*, *Mnasidika* does not end with this click, however weakly it signifies a switch back to civilization (indeed, Findlay never returns to his contemporary garb). A brief coda reveals the women standing motionless on a rocky seaside cliff (see Figure 3.3). The woman's voice that opened the film returns and recites two poems by Paul Verlaine ("I Know Not Why" and "A Great Dark Sleep"), and the film's end mirrors the beginning with disconnected shots of the sun, presumably setting. The women of *Mnasidika* have thus dismantled the structure-Other while retaining the presence of other women. They have infused the concept of a Zero Girl with queer, productive energy, "a behavior unindexed to any broader characterological system" holding forth the possibility of a lesbianism without a subject.[28]

Figure 3.3 The women on the cliff in *Mnasidika*.

Their world is indeed ordered by a structure more perverse than any mode of existence in *Friday*. The coda comes closer to Tournier's original, more "rigorous" concept for the ending of the novel, which had Robinson becoming "a kind of stylite, immobilized standing on a column in the sun."[29] Instead, he ends it with Robinson mourning the loss of Friday (who has opted to leave Speranza on the schooner) before encountering a deck-boy who has escaped to Speranza from a life of servitude on the schooner. Robinson christens the boy Thursday and a new adventure together seems poised on the horizon.

Many scholars have written on this ending, no doubt because it posits such a stark contrast to Defoe's original. For Colin Davis, the ending "preserve[s] the possibility of narrative even at the expense of the internal coherence of [Tournier's] fiction."[30] The novel has been leading toward an eternally silent Robinson. His attainment of solar sexuality no longer requires language, the primary feature of Lacan's Symbolic Order that separates self from object. The novel relinquishes the first person in one final orgy of Robinson's journal writing, and the last two chapters return to the third person. But Tournier's original ending "suggests that the logical conclusion of his novel is a silence which excludes the possibility of further action and further narrative."[31]

This does not mean, however, that the novel must conclude here. As Dorothea Olkowski astutely notes, Robinson's solar sexuality is "an ontological rather than a narrative move"[32] and thus requires a non-narrative treatment to describe this new mode of being. *Friday* ends on a conventional note because Tournier's commitment to narrative "can give only an indirect account of the ineffable self-presence to which Crusoe begins to aspire."[33] By contrast, *Mnasidika* keeps with the spirit of the original ending for *Friday*. The film collapses first- and third-person modes of narration, and thus subject and object as well, for a more direct, presentational account of ineffable sexuality. Its closely miked voice-overs abolish spatial impressions and make it difficult for the viewer to enter into a voyeuristic relationship to the space represented.[34] And at the end of the film, the women maintain their silence even more rigorously. They stand motionless like stylites in the sun, and the last word (again uttered not by any of the characters but, rather, the disembodied woman's voice) is "silence." These are the Zero Girls free finally from patriarchy and a narrative chain of signification, "the detachment of an image which is vertical at last and without thickness."[35] In sum, where *Friday* "describe[s] the effect of an experience rather than the experience itself,"[36] *Mnasidika* gives full force to the experience of a perverse structure that can account for its defenseless position in film, and even sexploitation, history.

CAMP

In many ways, Findlay's next few films continue her commitment to an extreme externality. *Janie* (1970), *The Altar of Lust* (1971), and *Rosebud* (1972) feature dubbed dialogue, indifferent cutaways and inserts, a feeble diegesis, and so on. The viewer is kept at a distance, prey to no illusions of reality, resulting in a reception state conducive to camp readings. If, according to Susan Sontag's famous dictum, "camp introduce[d] a new standard [of] artifice as an ideal,"[37] then camp seems an appropriate description of looking in from the outside on a failed (or indifferent) attempt to create an artificial reality. In this respect, these Findlay titles resemble the sexploitation films of Doris Wishman, whose similarly tattered diegeses spark a distanced viewing position. As Moya Luckett writes,

[Wishman's] more brazen continuity violations appear intentional, designed to produce a dialectical separation of sound, image, and narrative that comment[s] on the diegesis, stimulating laughter and distraction that problematize the spectator's look at images of female degradation and softcore sexual material.[38]

The fact that Findlay's (and Wishman's) films often focus on lesbian characters provides a compelling opportunity for the viewer. They seem to elicit a lesbian camp response, one that does not seek any intrinsic authenticity to lesbian identity. The lack of any diegetic interiority speaks to a lack of any pretense to representing a "real" lesbian identity. As such, Findlay's films free the viewer from the expectations of confession, punishment, and tragic endings or, indeed, endings of any stripe that typically accompany more traditional, narrative-driven representations of lesbianism. They seem organized for a post-Stonewall lesbian subject in no need of validation, comfortable of remaining "outside" of representation, and perfectly capable of approaching texts with humor and distance.

For instance, in a flashback from *The Altar of Lust*, Viveca Hansen (Erotica Lantern) recounts a story to her psychiatrist Dr. Rogers (Fred J. Lincoln) concerning a three-way she had with her boyfriend Don (Harry Reems) and a girl named Marie (Suzy Mann). At first dismayed, Viveca grows so aroused by Marie's attentions that she voices no objection when Marie pushes Don away. Dejected, Don looks out of a window and over his close-up, Viveca says, "Doctor, I'm a lesbian. Can you cure me?" There is a glance-object cut to a pan across a rain-streaked window looking out on New York City over which the psychiatrist says, "Now just a minute, Viveca. There's nothing shameful in your confession." This is akin to the scene in Wishman's *The Sex Perils of Paulette* (1965) when Paulette (Anna Karol) confesses to her fiancé that they cannot marry owing to her past as a prostitute. As Luckett notes, "Wishman repeatedly cuts to out-of-focus close-ups of a squirrel running and eating acorns, deflating Paulette's confession."[39] Similarly, the cut to Don's point of view serves no narrative function and exists solely to provide MOS filler for non-synchronous dialogue. It deflates the imperative for psychiatric validation of homosexuality, and the lesbian viewer can treat the scenario as an occasion for humorous play.

She can, to borrow Sue-Ellen Case's words on lesbian camp, "move through a field of symbols . . . playfully inhabiting the camp space of irony and wit, free from biological determinism, elitist essentialism, and the heterosexist cleavage of sexual difference."[40]

But camp still wrestles with the known world. As Andrew Britton puts it, camp is "a means of bringing the world into one's scope, of accommodating it—not of changing it or conceptualizing its relations."[41] Despite (or because of) the fact that *Mnasidika* appears so dull and impossible, it tries to create a new world replete with heretofore unknown relations. By contrast, the sturdier narratives of the subsequent films engage the current world and feel like stops along the way to achieving the state of *Mnasidika*. Like the Zero Girls, the title heroine of *Rosebud* experiences only fleeting moments of freedom outside the purview of men. She wanders the streets and longs for a life-affirming zero status: "I belonged to no one. I guess I was seeking some sort of anonymity, a solace in being lost." But a woman alone on the streets becomes a kind of target and Rosebud is soon beaten and raped by a maniac who impregnates her.[42] She commits suicide in shame. Janie is locked in a padded cell. Dr. Rogers helps Viveca overcome her shameful lesbian drives by having sex with her. In these more conventional narratives, the women are caught in endless loops of exploitation, far removed from the freeing circularity of Crusoe's solar sexuality. But as with the concept of zero, one can view the final title of *The Sin Syndicate* with more hope: This is not the end. *Mnasidika* offers another end, a possible world outside of our present world, which too many films strive to accommodate.

GENERATIVE HAPHAZARDNESS

It may seem foolish to bring a text as lofty as Tournier's *Friday* to bear on a cinema as opportunistic as sexploitation. The outré structure of *Mnasidika* can be explained by a more earth-bound examination of its historical position as a 1969 American release featuring nudity and simulated sex scenes. Due to the softening of censorship laws in the late 1960s, sexploitation films started "moving away from elaborately plot-driven scenarios of dramatic action and toward a performative soft-core erotic tableau that maximizes the spectacle of nudity and simulated sex, becoming looser and more episodic, in an erotic picaresque mode."[43] And as the indefatigable IMDB porn reviewer lor_ suggests, Findlay's cinematography "comes just a silly millimeter short of penetration . . . cutting edge porn content for a film released in late '69, when 'split-beaver' shots were all the rage in stag/ arcade loops."[44]

Furthermore, there is a sense in which Findlay has created less an alternate world than a random stream of images with little aforethought. T. J. Clark's comments on the artist Cy Twombly serve well to evaluate Findlay's world-making capacities:

> My test of true, generative haphazardness, here as elsewhere, is whether the picture's handwriting does anything to the normal art-ness of picture space: to the kind of entry into an alternative world the picture offers, and the intimation of that world's shape, proximity and being-apart-from-us.[45]

Using this measurement, Findlay fails in that *Mnasidika* often feels like checking off a list of avant-garde cinematic techniques to throw at the screen. Such haphazardness lies in explicit contrast to the creative way of life Crusoe must mobilize in order to exist within the collapse of subject–object relations in solar sexuality, "otherwise the destructuring of the structure-Other is nothing but the disintegration of the world: chaos instead of objects, loss instead of plenitude."[46]

Nevertheless, *Mnasidika* remains one of the most uncompromising entries in all of sexploitation. The liminal space it occupies (too soft for porn, too avant-garde for sexploitation, too lacking in authorial enunciation for art cinema, too difficult for all but the most intrepid cinephiles) can place the viewer in an alien mindset. If we let go of intentionality and contemplate even the sleaziest, most opportunistic of films, we can meet *Mnasidika* in all its "virginity of things,"[47] its useless essence. And we can experience what Sasha Frere-Jones recently deemed "that click of knowing . . . that the proposed piece of art has established a new way of seeing."[48]

NOTES

1. The question of authorship with respect to Roberta Findlay's films is vexed at best owing to faulty memories and the relative lack of urgency in preserving porn history. In a *Rialto Report* podcast, Findlay states that while Michael Findlay's interest in Pierre Louÿs's *Songs of Bilitis* influenced *Mnasidika*, she shot the film although she remains uncertain about even this last point. Nevertheless, at the very least, her description of *Bilitis* as "little vignettes . . . tableaux vivants . . . women standing around" strongly suggests that she was well aware of the intent behind *Mnasidika*. Ashley West and April Hall, "Roberta Findlay: A Respectable Woman—Podcast 53," August 16, 2015, *Rialto Report*, podcast, https://www.therialtoreport.com/2015/08/16/roberta-findlay/ (accessed July 28, 2021).
2. Gilles Deleuze, *The Logic of Sense* (New York: Columbia University Press, 1990), 319.
3. Deleuze, *The Logic of Sense*, 319.
4. Michel Tournier, *Friday*, translated by Norman Denny (Baltimore: Johns Hopkins University Press, 1997).
5. Stephen Broomer, "Drunk on Poetry: Michael and Roberta Findlay's *Take Me Naked*," *Art & Trash*, episode 8, Vimeo video, 15:35, March 25, 2021, https://vimeo.com/528472333 (accessed August 11, 2021).

6. Gretchen Schultz, "Daughters of Bilitis: Literary Genealogy and Lesbian Authenticity," *GLQ: A Journal of Lesbian and Gay Studies* 7, no. 3, 2001: 381.
7. Schultz, "Daughters of Bilitis," 386.
8. Tournier, *Friday*, 93; original emphasis.
9. Tournier, *Friday*, 89.
10. Tournier, *Friday*, 138.
11. Tournier, *Friday*, 139. Or, as Roger Celestin makes clear, a "Deleuzian body without organs." Roger Celestin, "Can Robinson Crusoe Find True Happiness (Alone)? Beyond the Genitals and History on the Island of Hope," in Paula Bennett and Vernon A. Rosario II (eds), *Solitary Pleasures: The Historical, Literary, and Artistic Discourses of Autoeroticism* (London and New York: Routledge, 1995), 244.
12. Tournier, *Friday*, 212.
13. Tournier, *Friday*, 12.
14. Laura Mulvey, "Visual Pleasure and Narrative Cinema," *Screen* 16, no. 3 (1975): 6–18.
15. Moya Luckett, "Sexploitation as Feminine Territory: The Films of Doris Wishman," in Mark Jankovich et al. (eds), *Defining Cult Movies: The Cultural Politics of Oppositional Taste*, (Manchester: Manchester University Press, 2003), 145.
16. For more on the indifference to continuity editing in sexploitation films, see Elena Gorfinkel, *Lewd Looks: American Sexploitation Cinema in the 1960s* (Minneapolis: University of Minnesota Press, 2001), 102–3 and 172.
17. Tournier, *Friday*, 12.
18. Tournier, *Friday*, 95.
19. There are brief shots of boats and shoreline homes but they only add to the confusion since much of the film takes place in a location similar to Ancient Greece. Findlay claims the film was shot in Gloucester, presumably Massachusetts. West and Hall, "Roberta Findlay: A Respectable Woman."
20. Celestin, "Can Robinson Crusoe Find True Happiness (Alone)?" 246.
21. Deleuze, *The Logic of Sense*, 319.
22. Deleuze, *The Logic of Sense*, 307.
23. "[I]t is because [the Sadean pervert] is lacking the structure-Other and lives within a completely different structure, as a condition for his living world, that he apprehends Others sometimes as victims and sometimes as accomplices, but in neither case does he apprehend them as Others." Deleuze, *The Logic of Sense*, 320.
24. Celestin, "Can Robinson Crusoe Find True Happiness (Alone)?" 244–5.
25. Tournier, *Friday*, 93.
26. Michael Findlay appears briefly twice in this section but neither moment suggests it originates from his perspective, whether in a dream or reality.
27. Tournier, *Friday*, 90.
28. Annamarie Jagose, *Orgasmology*. (Durham, NC and London: Duke University Press, 2013), 134.
29. Celestin, "Can Robinson Crusoe Find True Happiness (Alone)?" 248.
30. Colin Davis, "Michel Tournier's *Vendredi ou les limbes du Pacifique*: A Novel of Beginnings," *Neophilologus* 73 (1989): 380.
31. Davis, "Michel Tournier's *Vendredi*," 380.
32. Dorothea Olkowski, *Gilles Deleuze and the Ruin of Representation* (Berkeley: University of California Press, 1999), 39.
33. Davis, "Michel Tournier's *Vendredi*," 377.
34. This insight is borrowed from Alan Williams's analysis of sound in Hollywood musical numbers. See "The Musical Film and Recorded Popular Music," in *Genre: The Musical*, edited by Rick Altman (London and Boston: Routledge, 1981), 151.

35. Deleuze, *The Logic of Sense*, 313.
36. Davis, "Michel Tournier's *Vendredi*," 377.
37. Susan Sontag, "Notes on 'Camp'," in *Against Interpretation and Other Essays* (New York: Picador, 19660), 288.
38. Luckett, "Sexploitation as Feminine Territory," 147.
39. Luckett, "Sexploitation as Feminine Territory," 145–6.
40. Sue Ellen Case, "Toward a Butch Femme Aesthetic," in Henry Ablelove, Michelle Aina Barale, and David Halperin (eds), *The Lesbian and Gay Studies Reader* (New York: Routledge, 1993), 305.
41. Andrew Britton, "For Interpretation: Notes Against Camp," *Gay Left* 7 (Winter 1978/1979): 12.
42. This is in keeping with the standard hardcore heterosexual pornography practice of the era whereby the city poses a constant threat for women as opposed to its conception as a queer oasis in gay male pornography. See Whitney Strub, "From Porno Chic to Porno Bleak: Representing the Urban Crisis in 1970s American Pornography," in *Porno Chic and the Sex Wars: American Sexual Representation in the 1970s*, edited by Carolyn Bronstein and Whitney Strub (Amherst and Boston: University of Massachusetts Press, 2016), 27–52.
43. Gorfinkel, *Lewd Looks*, 183–4.
44. lor_, "I liked the Findlays' experiment, so there!" *Internet Movie Database*, User Reviews, February 14, 2011 (accessed August 11, 2021). https://www.imdb.com/title/tt0064677/reviews?ref_=tt_urv (accessed May 26, 2022).
45. T. J. Clark, "At Dulwich: Poussin and Twombly," *London Review of Books* 33, no. 16 (August 25, 2011): 24.
46. Olkowski, *Gilles Deleuze and the Ruin of Representation*, 39.
47. Tournier, *Friday*, 93.
48. Sasha Frere-Jones, "Triple Double," *Bookforum* 28, Issue 2 (June/July/August 2021): 34.

CHAPTER 4

From *Slaughter* to *Snuff*: The Origins of a Cultural Myth

Giuseppe Previtali

INTRODUCTION—A DISCOMFORTING FEELING

I would like to start this chapter with a short personal memory. As someone who defined his cinephile identity in the first decade of the twenty-first century, I have a clear memory of the first time I saw Fred Vogel's *August Underground* (2001). I was expecting an extreme horror experience, but I had no clue about the content of the movie or its style. The first sequence of the film hit me in a very shocking way. As the reader may know, the movie starts *in media res*, without mentioning any title or providing initial credits. The first thing we see is a generic suburban exterior; we are given the point of view of a handheld camera that produces shaky and extremely lo-fi images. It is therefore extremely difficult for the viewer to have a clear idea of what is happening, of what he is actually seeing. After a few moments, we see a man walking toward us; we don't know who he is, while the man operating the camera seems to know him quite well.

The effect of the sequence is extremely perturbing: we can't figure out what is going to happen, but we progressively start to think that what we are watching is something that was not meant for us, a kind of amateur video content designed to circulate within a small group of people. In this sense, the movie betrays the expectation of a horror fan, adopting visual solutions that seem to derive rather from reality television.[1] The destabilizing aesthetic proposed by the movie is typical of an emerging subgenre, that Steve Jones rightly named "hardcore horror."[2] Its main feature, according to James Aston, has to do with its ability to produce a "multi-sensorial shock"[3] with explicit bodily connotations. In our example, this comes true when we discover the captive body of a young woman, tortured and covered in organic fluids. Apart from the extreme content of the images, the shocking value of *August Underground*'s incipit derives also from the fact that the spectator is left doubting the fictional nature of what is seen. Watching a horror movie is a potentially comforting experience because the spectator knows that every death he/she sees on the screen, no matter how realistic, is ultimately fake.[4] Vogel movie's has the ability to linguistically undermine this confidence, as if the film could possibly be an authentic snuff movie. Today it is of course quite easy to debunk this suspicion but in 2001 the mediasphere was far less interconnected and Vogel even hypothesized a specific distributive strategy to enhance the fear of having accidentally came across an authentic snuff.[5]

I perfectly remember the feeling of genuine discomfort that I felt the first time I watched *August Underground*. I found the same sensation of pain and unbearableness in very few other movies, such as the Italian *Mondo Cane* (1962, dir. Gualtiero Jacopetti, Franco Prosperi, Paolo Cavara), but maybe only the final sequence of Michael and Roberta Findlay's *Snuff* (1976) was capable of making me feel exactly the same sensation of guilt for what I had just seen. I believe that the sense of discomfort shared by these two movies is, far from being coincidental, something that needs to be acknowledged and that helps to understand the longevity of the cultural mythology of the snuff film.[6] In order to do so, it is worth remembering the complex and intriguing history of the Findlays' movie and to interrogate the ways in which its original 1971 core (titled *Slaughter*) has been resignified by the producer Allan Shackleton. As a matter of fact, the vast majority of the scholarship produced on *Snuff* is focused on the reception of the movie and on the legacy that it created in the following decades. My intention here is rather to focus on the original *Slaughter*, in order to promote a new understanding of this movie in the Findlays' filmography, taking into account the fascinating way in which the movie refers to its historical context (with specific attention to the cultural memory of the Manson Family's massacres).

EXPLOITATION AND EXPROPRIATION

Roberta Findlay, along with her husband, Michael, directed *Slaughter* (also known as *The Slaughter*) in 1971.[7] By that time, the couple had a vast experience in the market of exploitation cinema. Since the 1960s, Michael had directed very personal and often highly recognizable roughies films,[8] where morbid violence and eroticism merged together in unprecedented ways. *Satan's Bed* (1965) is already paradigmatic in this respect. Apart from the acting performance of a young Yoko Ono and the presence of Roberta Findlay (credited as Anna Riva) in the cast, the film is in fact a kaleidoscope of violence and depravity in a sordid and turbid urban background. The major themes of the Findlays' authorship are already defined and will be extensively scrutinized in all the following films of the couple. Another great example in this respect is offered by *Take Me Naked* (1966), where the connection between socio-economical desperation and sexual depravity is even more explicit, as exemplified by the drunk tramp who spies on his attractive neighbor. Subverting the campy aesthetic of the coeval erotic film, the Findlays depict an obscure and sick atmosphere, where sexuality is never experienced as something pleasant or attractive. This set of issues become even more crucial in the subsequent *A Thousand Pleasures* (1968), where realism and the grotesque merge together in a hopeless exhibition of misogyny and aggression toward the female subjects that will be further scrutinized in the so–called Flesh Trilogy.[9]

While Michael Findlay, alongside Roberta (who often served as actress or director of photography), was still exploring the possibilities offered by the formulaic nature of the roughies, the golden age of exploitation cinema was rapidly coming to an end. *Mnasidika* (1969), directed with Roberta, testifies to the search for new expressive directions: the sleazy figures of Findlay's maniacs are substituted by an apology of women's role in history and society. With this movie, Michael and Roberta become closer to a more conventional idea of cinema, with the consequence of losing part of their originality. It is precisely in this very specific moment of their career that they decided to go to Argentina. Here, with the help of another director (Horacio Fredrikkson) and a ridiculously low budget, they shot what will become their most famous movie: *Slaughter*. What is intriguing about the production history of the film is that it was never actually released in this initial form and was later bought by producer Allan Shackleton who, after a few years, released it with a new title: the Findlays' movie finally saw the light as *Snuff* (1976) but their role was obliterated. Shackleton commissioned a new ending from another director (Simon Nuchtern), who realized the infamous quasi-snuff coda.[10] Roberta Findlay herself has later dismissed part of this mysterious and fascinating history as fake,[11] but *Snuff* (along with the snuff movies on which it bases its disturbing nature) became something where reality and legend were bound to merge.

What Shackleton did was a true removal of the Findlays' authorship and the creation of something else. However, as the following pages will try to demonstrate, his operation has more than one common point with the original *Slaughter*. The new finale, far from being a betrayal of the original film, is probably its best possible completion. In order to understand in what sense this can be true, it is worth remembering the common cultural background that the Findlays' movie and the concept of snuff film (installed in *Slaughter* by Shackleton's coda) share.

IN THE SHADE OF MANSON

Slaughter's opening sequence is slightly reminiscent of the coeval cult movie *Easy Rider* (1969, dir. Dennis Hopper): in a female reenactment of the film, we see a group of women on their motorcycles riding to an abandoned industrial facility, where they meet another woman, smoking weed. They ask for a fourth girl named Ana, a "greedy bitch" that we immediately see sniffing cocaine and later falling asleep. When they finally find Ana they start chasing her with a gun, ultimately shooting her in the shoulder. This may seem the classical opening of a generic hippie exploitation movie that was common in those years: every element of this subgenre is apparently present, from the clothes of the protagonists to the crucial role of drugs.[12] Everything changes when an unidentified fourth figure appears in the scene: it is a young man who immediately clarifies his dominant position both from a visual (he looks at the wounded girl from above) and concrete perspective. As a matter of fact, he immediately starts to blame Ana for her behavior, condemning her to a physical punishment:

S: Ana, Ana! You disobeyed me!
A: Yes . . .
S: You will feel the pain!
A: Yes!
S: And you will not flinch from it.
A: No.
S: Susana. The feet!

After this short interchange between Ana and her mastermind (who will be named Satan shortly after this moment), one of the girls starts to cut Ana's feet open, with great blood perfusion. This sequence, which seems to anticipate some visual elements of the rape-and-revenge subgenre, is based on a very intriguing form of parallel montage, alternating between shots of Ana's face and of Satan's eyes. This solution not only intensifies the feeling of visual domination exerted by the man, but also implies the idea that what Ana is feeling is not just pain, but also some sort of sexual pleasure. This trait, highlighted in this inaugural sequence, is crucial in the mythology of the so-called snuff movie and is therefore relevant that it already marks the opening of *Slaughter*.[13] The specific contamination between pain and pleasure, two borderline feelings that always constituted taboo subjects for cinema,[14] becomes, in the urban legend of the snuff movies, one of its greatest visual attractions. Eroticism and death, as Bataille rightly pointed out in his visual history of these two feelings, have always been interconnected, to the point that they end up becoming almost indistinguishable.[15]

There is another trait that seems to connect the Findlays' *Slaughter* with the snuff mythology more deeply than one can imagine at a first glance. As a late example of a 1960s exploitation movie, *Slaughter* was made in order to capitalize from one specific event that was haunting America's collective consciousness during those years. Just two years before, in August 1969, a small group of Charles Manson's Family members killed six people in the hills of Bel Air. This shocking massacre, later followed by the LaBianca murders, imposed Manson's figure as a collective obsession, producing a vast media attention that is still relevant today.[16] If Manson's ghost is still haunting American film and popular culture, in the years immediately following the events, an enormous number of movies influenced by the case was released. They were mainly exploitation movies that tried to capitalize on the sense of anxiety and discomfort that the betrayal of the hippie ideal helped to produce, and *Slaughter* makes no exception.[17]

So, there exists a link that connects Charles Manson and *Slaughter*, but it is relevant to notice that Manson's figure is also deeply connected with the idea of snuff. Actually, one could even say that the snuff mythology was born thanks to Manson. The idea that homicidal madness could hide everywhere in the world was, of course, not uncommon in the cinema of the late 1960s and early 1970s, and it was precisely in this period that the idea of realist horror[18] was starting to be developed; but the idea that an actual death could possibly be filmed for the pleasure of paying viewers was something far more disturbing. It was precisely in the context of the Family's homicides that the term "snuff" was first used referring to cinema and the possibility of an actual filmed death. In his crucial book on the topic, Ed Sanders[19] depicted a very fascinating and accurate portrayal of Manson, as someone referring to whom it is ultimately impossible to discern legend, fantasy and reality. In one of the more intriguing parts of his book, Sanders analyzes the role of cinema and of moving images within the Family.

The use of cameras is attested since the beginning of 1968 and Sanders's investigation is permeated by vague and mysterious references to never-discovered porn films made by the Family. What emerges from these references is the image of a quite vast set of films that are impossible to actually find, since the Family destroyed or buried the vast majority of them. These films are said to exist, but no one has actually seen them or is willing to speak about them. In this ghostly filmography, one of Sanders's interviewees mentions one of Manson's filmic projects: a movie called *Easy Snuff*, with satanism, Armageddon, and a final and brutal carnage. This was the first time the term snuff was ever used in relation to cinema. Far from being an apex in Manson's film production, this mysterious *Easy Snuff* was just one of the gruesome creations of the Family: Sanders also mentions videos focused on animal blood drinking and on human sacrifices. What is relevant here is to notice that Manson somehow created the contemporary fascination for the concept of snuff, and it is therefore unsurprising that many of the movies connected with his figure were pervaded by the haunting presence of this concept. In this sense, I believe that Shackleton's reappropriation of Findlays' *Slaughter* had the (probably unintentional) merit of providing a stronger Mansonian link to the movie, making it the actualization of his dream to film death and sell it to a selected group of spectators.

BODIES OF VIOLENCE

It may sound obvious to state that the main visual attraction[20] of a movie called *Slaughter* lies in its violent sequences. We have already discussed the crucial role that the first display of violence has in the film. At a more general level, though, Findlay's work is deeply permeated by an interest toward violence, as if the act of killing was its real core. Immediately after the introductory sequence that we have described above, we see a young man arriving in a Chilean airport, where we follow him to the restrooms. Here he is immediately assaulted by a mysterious female figure that will be later revealed as one of Satan's acolytes. The victim is stabbed and subsequently slaughtered in a gruesome scene that directly quotes the tradition of Italian *giallo* both in the presentation of the killer and in the representation of the assault.[21] But if the homicide in the *giallo* is just the beginning of an investigative process that will later lead to the solution of the mystery, Michael and Roberta Findlay rapidly dismiss the whole concept of suspense and prefer to focus on the gory and brutal aspect of the killing.

The body of this victim (and, we can add, of every victim present in this movie) does not become a site of investigation, something to be inspected in a forensic way in order to extract knowledge from it in a quasi-Foucauldian way.[22] The corpse is immediately objectified, because the spectacularity of the killing moment is far greater than the desire to morbidly address the image of the dead body. This dynamic reappears later in the film, when a movie producer who plays a major role in the development of the plot is killed. Once again, the act is carried out with a knife; in this instance, the phallic nature of the weapon (widely explored by Carol J. Clover in her classic book on modern horror[23]) and the equivalence between death and orgasm is made immediately clear, since the parallel montage visually equates the act of killing and a sexual interchange. This connection is explored for the third time in a following sequence, when a young girl, tortured by the acolytes, is later freed and sexually possessed by Satan himself.

The body of the victims is therefore objectified and deprived of any form of human dignity (or identity, as in the case of the man stabbed in the toilet). For Satan and his group, what counts is the spectacular aspect of the open body, the pleasure involved in the act of torture. Adopting a very current term coined by the Italian philosopher Giorgio Agamben, the victims are reduced to a form of "bare life" and their function is precisely to be sacrificed in order to create something bigger (like the bond between Satan and his acolytes).[24] Violence is what brings and keeps together the members of this quasi-Mansonian "Family," and is repeatedly performed during the movie to reinforce the bonds that connect its members. As demonstrated in Elaine Scarry's pioneering work,[25] the violence performed on a human body acts as a form of *dispositif* that simultaneously deconstructs the victim's place in the world and performatively recreates the perpetrator's identity, producing new bounds and forms of belonging. This is exactly what happens in

Slaughter, where Satan's acolytes lose their identity as young women and, through the exertion of violence on the victims' bodies, become part of something new and bigger, a kind of collective being that depends directly on its leader.

If the body of the victims is reduced to a visual attraction, something to be explored in its being anatomically violated, the other body that emerges in the movie is the hypersexualized and ideal body of Satan himself (see Figure 4.1). Slightly reminiscent of a young Charles Manson but more overtly eroticized, Satan's body is the place where all the tensions of the movie converge and finally explode.

When he first appears, in the incipit of the film, Satan is reduced to a pure gaze, a scopic power that immediately points out the geometry of dominance that exists within his group. The sequence is visually centered on Satan's eyes, which become a vehicle of power and domination: one of his looks is more than enough to break the will of his followers, making them do unspeakably violent acts (see Figure 4.2). As in Manson's case, this sheds a very different light on the woman–on–woman violence depicted in the movie. The fact that Satan's faithful acolytes are almost exclusively women does not imply a form of female agency, since everything they do is ordered and wanted by their mastermind himself. It is possible to speculate that the particular way in which gendered relations are depicted in the movie derive from the clash of Michael and Roberta's personal creativities. As in *Mnasidika*, released in 1969 and co-directed by the couple, the focus on violence on eroticized female bodies clashes more than once with elements of progressiveness and female agency that will become more common in Roberta's later pornographic production.

Figure 4.1 Satan in *Slaughter*.

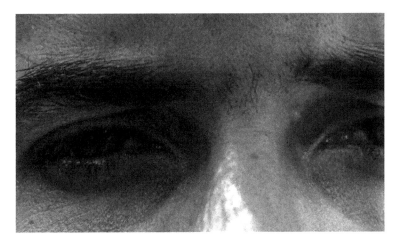

Figure 4.2 Satan's eyes in *Slaughter*.

EPILOGUE

A more in-depth analysis of *Slaughter* is crucial not just to return some historical and filmic value to a highly overlooked movie, but also to better understand
Shackleton's *Snuff* and the continued cultural importance inaugurated by its
mythology. As I have suggested, far from a process of betrayal, Shackleton's
operation offered a chance to the original movie to fulfill its own premises
despite the low budget and the complex production history. As Heller-Nicholas
acutely observed: "*The Slaughter* and the *Snuff* coda are so often viewed as separate entities because of their production history that is perhaps too easy to miss
how explicitly the coda relates to the film as a whole."[26] Shackleton's appropriation and elaboration process was surely guided by the desire to market a movie
touching on the morbid desires of the public, but (or precisely because) that was
also very timely and could capitalize on cultural anxieties that were common in
the late 1960s and early 1970s. Society was rapidly changing, and new cultural
forces were claiming their right to appear on the scene; this redefinition of the
field of the visual involved a new conceptualization of what could (and could
not) be seen on the screen, as the emergence of a more violent and grotesque
filmic imaginary testifies. In this climate, in both the US and the UK (where its
reception was intertwined with the wider phenomenon of the so-called video
nasties[27]) *Snuff* ended up incarnating the actual possibility that something so
brutal and extreme may actually exist, somewhere in the world.

From there, the cultural mythology of snuff as a concept and as a border
of the visible remained relevant to the present day. The possibility that actual
filmed deaths were recorded to be marketed has been, for instance, explored
from a media-archaeological perspective,[28] while various filmographies were

produced in order to map and classify the possible iterations of this idea on the screen.[29] All these attempts, while heuristically intriguing, are to some extent bound to fail, since the intrinsic quality of "real" snuff is its inaccessibility. In this sense, we may say that every attempt to partially visualize and give body to the haunting presence of snuff may be motivated by a desire to exorcise its disturbing nature. The real issue with the concept of snuff, maybe, is not that it is actually out there, but rather that it is connected with some of our most obscure and unavowable desires. And even before Shackleton's addition, this idea of an unmentionable fascination for pure and unmotivated violence was right there, at the heart of Michael and Roberta Findlay's most overlooked movie.

NOTES

1. The literature on this topic is extremely vast; still, for the purpose of this chapter, see at least: Amy West, "Caught on Tape: A Legacy of Low-tech Reality," in Geoff King (ed.), *The Spectacle of the Real: From Hollywood to Reality TV and Beyond* (Bristol: Intellect, 2005), 83–92; Aril Fetveit, "Reality TV in the Digital Era: A Paradox in Visual Culture?," in James Friedman (ed.), *Reality Square: Televisual Discourse on the Real* (New Brunswick, NJ and London: Rutgers University Press), 119–37; Alison Hearn, "Hoaxing the Real: On the Metanarrative of Reality Television," in Susan Murray and Laurie Oulette (eds), *Reality TV: Remaking Television Culture* (New York and London: New York University Press, 2009), 165–78.

2. Steve Jones, *Torture Porn: Popular Horror After Saw* (Basingstoke: Palgrave Macmillan, 2013). Besides *August Underground* and its sequels *August Underground's Mordum* (Fred Vogel, 2003) and *August Underground's Penance* (Fred Vogel, 2007), Jones mentioned the movies by Shane Ryan and Lucifer Valentine.

3. James Aston, "Nightmares Outside the Mainstream: August Underground and Real/Reel Horror," in Lynnie Blake and Xavier Aldana Reyes (eds), *Digital Horror: Haunted Technologies, Network Panic and the Found Footage Phenomenon* (London and New York: I. B. Tauris, 2016), 140.

4. Catherine Russell, *Narrative Mortality: Death, Closure and New Wave Cinemas* (Minneapolis: University of Minnesota Press, 1994).

5. "Vogel wanted to completely bypass the notion of an official release via legitimate channels and intended to leave VHS copies of the film in random public places such as playgrounds and airports. His purpose was to position the film as a type of found object to be picked up and played by curious passers-by." Aston, "Nightmares Outside the Mainstream," 143.

6. I have explored this hypothesis in Giuseppe Previtali, *L'ultimo tabù. Filmare la morte tra spettacolarizzazione e politica dello sguardo* (Milan: Meltemi, 2020).

7. It should be noted that, in an interview with *Rialto Report*, Jack Bravman took credit for the movie as well. See his interview: "Jack Bravman: 'Snuff', 'The Slaughter', and who was J. Angel Martine?" *Rialto Report*, March 25, 2018, https://www.therialtoreport.com/2018/03/25/jack-bravman/ (accessed May 26, 2022).

8. Elena Gorfinkel, *Lewd Looks: American Sexploitation Cinema in the 1960s* (Minneapolis: University of Minnesota Press, 2017).

9. The Flesh Trilogy is composed of three interrelated movies that tell the story of a misogynist psychopathic killer called Richard Jennings (played by Michael Findlay himself): *The Touch of Her Flesh* (1967), *The Curse of Her Flesh* (1968) and *The Kiss of Her Flesh* (1968).

10. For a more detailed exploration of *Snuff*'s production and release, see the still quintessential remarks by David Kerekes and David Slater, *Killing for Culture from Edison to ISIS: A New History of Death on Film* (London: Headpress, 2016), 4–25.

11. As Roberta Findlay told J. R. Taylor: "What really happened was that Paramount distributed a movie titled *The Slaughter*, if I'm not wrong, and to do so they bought the title from my husband and his partner. Paramount gave them a couple of hundred dollars, more or less. Then Shackleton found an article in the *Washington Post* about the 'snuff movies' imported in the US. He says, let's take that title. The only thing that I question, philosophically speaking, is that in the end no one was paid." It must be added that, years after her experiences with Michael in the film industry, Roberta dismissed her role in these productions as marginal, marking the beginning of her career precisely with Slaughter. The quote presented in this note is reported by Rudy Salvaggini, "Michael e Roberta Findlay: la coppia più kinky del mondo," *Segnocinema*, n. 153, a. XXVIII (September/ October 2008), 6. Translation from Italian by the author.

12. On this still overlooked topic, see Britton Stiles Rhuart, "Hippie Film, Hippiesploitation and the Emerging Counterculture 1955–1970," PhD dissertation submitted to the Graduate College of Bowling Green State University, August 2020, https://etd.ohiolink.edu/apexprod/rws_etd/send_file/send?accession=bgsu1590688651829o6&disposition=inline (accessed July 2, 2021).

13. Even if often overlooked or taken for granted, the importance of developing a correct definition of what a snuff movie should be is quintessential for the understanding of the phenomenon. As I have stressed elsewhere, studying the definition of snuff may help to realize that part of its cultural relevance and fascinating nature depends on the fact that it is doomed to remain an untraceable and haunting presence. Actually, no visual content that ever claimed to be an actual snuff (such as Luka Magnotta's viral video) actually fitted in the definition: the whole notion of snuff seems to depend directly on its "invisibility." See Giuseppe Previtali "Dimmi che non è vero. Lo snuff movie come limite del visivo," *Fata Morgana*, n. 34 (2018), 53–66.

14. André Bazin, "Death Every Afternoon," in Ivone Margulies (ed.), *Rites of Realism: Essays on Corporeal Cinema* (Durham, NC and London: Duke University Press, 2003), 27–31.

15. Georges Bataille, *The Tears of Eros* (San Francisco: City Light Books 1989), 285 ff. See also Georges Bataille, *Erotism: Death & Sensuality* (San Francisco: City Light Books 1986).

16. Between the most recent movies that contain more or less explicit references to Manson and the Cielo Drive's massacre, see at least: *Manson's Lost Girls* (Leslie Libman, 2016), *Wolves at the Door* (John R. Leonetti, 2016), *Charlie Says* (Mary Harron, 2018), *The Haunting of Sharon Tate* (Daniel Farrands, 2019) and *Once Upon a Time . . . in Hollywood* (Quentin Tarantino, 2019).

17. For an overview of Manson's presences in the media, see the useful guide by Ian Cooper, *The Manson Family on Film and Television* (Jefferson: McFarland, 2018). Between the most relevant exploitation movies focused on Manson's heritage, we can remember at least: *Beyond the Valley of the Dolls* (Russ Meyers, 1970), *I Drink Your Blood* (David E. Durston, 1970), *The Helter Skelter Murders* (Frank Howard, 1970), *Sweet Savior* (Robert L. Roberts, 1971) and *Wrong Way* (Ray Williams, 1972).

18. For the definition of realist horror see the quintessential study by Cynthia A. Freeland, "Realist Horror," in Id. (ed.), *Philosophy and Film* (London: Routledge, 1995), 126–42. On the possible link between horror cinema and snuff mythology, see Joel Black, "Real(ist) Horror: from Execution Videos to Snuff Films," in Xavier Mendik and Steven J. Schneider (eds), *Underground USA: Filming Beyond the Hollywood Canon* (New York: Wallflower Press, 2002), 63–75.

19. Ed Sanders, *The Family: The Story of Charles Manson's Dune Buggy Attack Battalion* (Boston: Da Capo Press, 2002). Another valuable source of information for Manson's Family is of course Vincent Bugliosi and Curt Gentry, *Helter Skelter: The True Story of the Manson Murders* (New York: Random House, 2014).

20. I use the term in the sense outlined by Tom Gunning, "The Cinema of Attraction: Early Film, Its Spectator and the Avant-Garde," *Wide Angle* 8 no. 3–4 (1986), 63–70.

21. In the vast literature devoted to the genre see, for the specific purposes of this chapter: Mikel J. Koven, *La dolce morte: Vernacular Cinema and the Italian Giallo Film* (Laham: Scarecrow Press, 2006) and Alexia Kannas, *Giallo! Genre, Modernity and Detection in Italian Horror Cinema* (Albany: State University of New York Press, 2020).

22. This issue has been explored in the crucial book by Michel Foucault, *The Birth of the Clinic: An Archaeology of Medical Perception* (London and New York: Routledge, 1989).

23. Carol J. Clover, *Men, Women and Chainsaws: Gender in the Modern Horror Film* (Princeton and Oxford: Princeton University Press, 1992).

24. Giorgio Agamben, *Homo Sacer: Sovereign Power and Bare Life* (Redwood: Stanford University Press, 1998).

25. Elaine Scarry, *The Body in Pain: The Making and Unmaking of the World* (New York and Oxford: Oxford University Press, 1985).

26. Alexandra Heller-Nicholas, "Snuff Boxing: Revisiting the Snuff Coda," *Cinephile* 5, no. 2 (2012). Available online: http://cinephile.ca/archives/volume-5-no-2-the-scene/snuff-boxing-revisiting-the-snuff-coda/ (accessed July 7, 2021).

27. Mark McKenna, "A Murder Mystery in Black and Blue: The Marketing, Distribution and Cult Mythology of Snuff in the UK," in Neil Jackson, Shaun Kimber, Johnny Walker and Thomas Joseph Watson (eds), *Snuff: Real Death and Screen Media* (New York and London: Bloomsbury, 2016), 121–36.

28. Akira Mizuta Lippit, "The Death of an Animal," *Film Quarterly* 56 no. 1 (2002), 9–22; Scott Combs, "Cut: Execution, Editing and Instant Death," *Spectator* 28 no. 2 (2008), 31–41.

29. See at least: Boaz Hagin, "Killed Because of Lousy Ratings: The Hollywood History of Snuff," *Journal of Popular Film and Television* 38 no. 1 (2010), 44–51; Steve Jones, "Dying to be Seen: Snuff-Fiction's Problematic Fantasies of 'Reality'," *Scope* 19 no. 1 (2011), 1–20; Shaun Kimber, "Why Would You Film It? Snuff, Sinister and Contemporary US Horror Cinema," in Jackson, Kimber, Walker, and Watson (eds), *Snuff: Real Death and Screen Media*, 225–40.

CHAPTER 5

"This is a Farce": Satire, Pseudonyms, and the Impact of Collaboration in Early Walter Sear/Roberta Findlay Films

Derek Gaskill

On November 21, 1974, an advertisement ran in the *New York Times* for Roberta Findlay's film *Angel Number 9* with the tagline "The first erotically explicit film ever made by a woman" (see Figure 3.1, Chapter 3).[1] But the next year, when her film *Anyone But My Husband*'s opening credits ran, Findlay appeared listed for photography but vanished behind pseudonymous writer-director "Robert Norman." In fact, *Angel* was not Findlay's first sexploitation film, nor was she the only woman working in the genre at the time. Findlay has been attributed many titles including Michael Findlay's wife, the first female cinematographer, the first female pornographer, a traitor to women, and the manager of Sear Sound recording studio. For most of my life I have known her as the partner of my late grandfather, Walter Sear. Findlay holds a curious place in the history of Times Square, pornography, and feminist cinema. This paper traces Findlay's work from the creation of her legacy as the supposed first female pornographer to the first films she made under pseudonyms and examines whether it retains the femininity her title implies, as well as examining the films she made alongside Sear and how they fit into those contexts.

Unlike Hollywood in the 1970s, there is an impressive list of women filmmakers who have worked in the production of exploitation films. Ann Perry-Rhine, for example, became the first female president of the Adult Film Association, starting her career as an actress during the "nudie cutie" era and then as producer of Evolution Enterprises. Other women who followed the career path of actress-turned-director/producer include Marilyn Chambers, Lina Romay, and, to some extent, Roberta Findlay (see Jennifer Moorman's chapter for more contemporary examples of this trajectory). Many began making exploitation films with hopes of becoming Hollywood directors but were unable to get their foot in the door. At the time, this was a viable career path for many male filmmakers (a very short list includes Francis Ford Coppola, Sam Raimi, James Cameron, and George A. Romero). However, not many women filmmakers were able to transcend the exploitation/Hollywood divide and most stayed within the exploitation genre. The prime example of this is Stephanie Rothman, who achieved notoriety when she became the first woman to win the Directors Guild of America Fellowship, an annual award given to the director of a student film, and continued on to work at Roger Corman's New World Pictures. In a 2007 interview with Henry Jenkins, she describes the struggle of being a female filmmaker. Her career, and the careers of most women working in this corner of the industry, can be summed up by her declaration that "I was never happy making exploitation films. I did it because it was the only way I could work."[2]

None of these women carry as much mystery and notoriety as Roberta Findlay, who capitalized on a changing marketplace to distinguish herself from the pack. A native New Yorker, Findlay married Michael Findlay—one of the most infamous and adored filmmakers of the "roughie" sexploitation sub-genre, and credited with directing more than twenty-four films—at eighteen. Though she is often credited with being involved in the production of many of Michael's early works, Findlay claims she was aware of the films, but that Michael shot everything himself. However, she's not the most reliable narrator. She makes cameo appearances in *Satan's Bed* (1965) and *The Ultimate Degenerate* (1969), and did voice-overs for the *Lusting Hours* (1966) and the Flesh Trilogy. Roberta has admitted to being involved with the making of *Take Me Naked* (1966), which she also starred in. Regardless of the depth of her involvement, Findlay was able to learn the ins and outs of filmmaking on the sets of these low-budget productions.

Despite working in film for a decade—at times under male pseudonyms including Robert Norman and Norman Roberts—it was during the porno-chic era of the 1970s that Findlay began to be marketed not as a director and producer, but as a female pornographer. She was not the first female pornographer, nor was she the only woman working behind a camera, yet even in current accounts she is cited as being both. Media interviews from the time reflect the press frenzy around her. In 1976, when Findlay was only twenty-eight, she was interviewed by *SIR! Magazine* for an eight-page article entitled "Female Porn Producer Roberta Findlay."[3] Two years later she appeared as the centerfold for a five-page article in *Take One* magazine entitled "Woman in Porn: How Roberta Findlay Finally Grew Up and Made Snuff."[4] However, if asked, Findlay is adamant that she is not a pioneer for women filmmakers, and she dares viewers to think a woman made her films. She explains in *Take One* that the distributors of her films thought marketing her as a female pornographer would make money. In her own words she recounts:

the distributor decided that it was time to declare that a woman was making 'erotic' films. Not pornography. He hired two publicity guys to do whatever they do and I was on radio shows and in magazines and he was going to try television but I refused.[5]

Her relationship with women in the film industry is complex and contentious. Throughout her career she used all-male crews, the exception being on-set makeup technicians and occasional help making sets. She defended this choice by pointing to the disparity in technical training: "[women] just don't have the opportunity—the background—to get involved other than in a very superficial level. Say, as maybe an editor or script writer."[6] She reiterated this view when asked about her work as the cinematographer for Karen Sperling's *The Waiting Room* (1973), which had a fifty-three-woman production crew; the only men on set were actors. While the filmmaker praised Findlay for being an especially good cinematographer, Findlay remembers the film as being a disaster: "for every three women we had at our disposal, it would have taken one man to do the job correctly."[7] Findlay was doggedly committed to creating the best films possible within the confines of her budget, which meant employing the best-trained people, and to her those people happened to be men.

The context in which Findlay found herself making movies was unique and contributed to her position in the annals of filmmaking history. Though unrecognizable today, Times Square was a sex district during the 1960s through 1980s. Movie houses, affectionately referred to as "grindhouses," played a major role in the makeup of Times Square. Clustered mainly on 42nd Street between 7th and 8th Avenues, the area became known as the Deuce. Film scholar David Church traces a concerted effort on the part of Hollywood, critical reception, and the press to link grindhouses and the movies screened there to low culture, thereby normalizing studio-based cinema and mainstream films. He notes in particular an article from 1969 entitled "Arts in the 60s: Coming to Terms with Society and Its Woes," in which theater critic Clive Barnes describes grindhouses as a "semi-pornographic theater not considered worth a critic's attention, at least not a critic on duty."[8] The attacks on grindhouses and exploitation films were aimed at audiences, but they also affected industry professionals, deterring filmmakers from entering the genre. Thus, exploitation was able to create its own production and exhibition norms. For instance, in Hollywood, white heterosexual men dominated filmmaking; exploitation filmmakers were able to employ anyone who could do the job for the lowest pay.

The coupling of the Deuce and exploitation film's warped sense of normalcy created a micro-society of film production and distribution with its own moral standards, social norms, use of spaces, and economy. While women were hardly treated as equal to men, the Deuce did allow women, and other marginalized people, to have agency. Though Findlay benefited from her connection to Michael, she earned her merit by continuously making films quickly and cheaply.

In the 1970s, the Deuce briefly saw an uptick in mainstream popularity. A 1973 *New York Times* spread by journalist and cultural historian Ralph Blumenthal heralded the arrival of the "porno-chic" era, detailing the phenomenal and unprecedented impact of the film *Deep Throat* (1972) on American culture and discourse. The policing of the film and accompanying media spectacle led to astronomically high viewership across barriers of gender and class. In January of 1973, the film was cited as drawing an average of "5,000 people weekly to the New Mature World Theater on West 49th Street" where it was seen by a diverse audience including "celebrities, diplomats, critics, businessmen, women alone and dating couples, few of whom, it might be presumed, would previously have gone to see a film of sexual intercourse, fellatio and cunnilingus."[9] The film's supposedly high production value and attempt at a plot line was also cited as "enough to persuade a lot of people that there is no harm or shame in indulging their curiosity—and perhaps even their frankly prurient interests—by going to see 'Deep Throat.'"[10] This combination of factors elevated pornography from a topic to be discussed in whispers into a more analytical, sophisticated, and mainstream context. Blumenthal recounts that pornography became a "premier topic of cocktail-party and dinner-table conversation in Manhattan drawing rooms, Long Island beach cottages and ski-country A frames."[11]

Women had previously been able to view softcore sexploitation films, but because of censorship laws, hardcore content had been limited to urban areas and skid row districts that were generally dangerous and unfriendly to women.[12] *Deep Throat*, and the porno-chic films that followed, represented the first time women were able to see hardcore pornography in a relatively safe environment that did not shame sexuality. Widespread public discourse around pornography led to more cavalier discussions of morality, subjectivity, and women in the genre. While *Deep Throat* was not marketed toward women, critics espoused the film for showing a woman's pursuit of pleasure and orgasm as well as Linda Lovelace's commanding performance.

Trying to exploit a new population of porn fans, pornography distributors attempted to create a new and intentional genre of pornography marketed toward women. Tropes of the genre were informed by both the successful elements of adult men's media content and larger cultural discourse around women's pleasure. Women's magazines *Viva* and *Playgirl*, which began circulation between 1973 and 1975, attempted to emulate men's magazines like *Playboy*, which at that point had been published for over a decade. Notably, *Viva* and *Playgirl* were both published by men. Bob Guccione, the publisher of *Penthouse Magazine*, started *Viva* with the intention of it becoming a *Penthouse* for women. Both magazines were housed in the same offices and shared editorial and art staff. With the exception of early issues, the women's magazines offered semi-nude or full male nudity and emulated the male magazine formulas of centerfolds and themed months. To transpose the formula of men's magazines for a female audience, content and marketing were influenced by a cultural shift in foregrounding women's sexuality and sexual satisfaction. Some of the women's liberation movement's most prominent activists wrote for *Viva*: a short list includes Maya Angelou, Molly Haskell, and Betty Friedan.[13]

Inspired by the emergence of these magazines and a window in an East 50th Street sex store that read "ADULTS ONLY: Women Also Welcome," Lois Gould wrote a six-page article for the *New York Times* in 1975 exploring the concept of film pornography for women.[14] She cites two 1974 films that appeared on the Deuce as trying to appeal to women's interests through advertising. *Emmanuelle* (1974, dir. Just Jaeckin) attached the tagline of "Lets you feel good without feeling bad," and *Wet Rainbow* (1974, dir. Duddy Kane) was advertised as "The first sex film about love." She claims that these taglines attempted to "soothe nagging female guilt feelings about voyeurism with the men folk," but, in reality, these films are "merely male sex fantasies warmed over."[15]

However, she writes, the reason there are not more female pornography fans is because the "typical porno flick" is missing "believable sexual tension between the man and woman. There is no seduction, virtually no romantic suspense, and only perfunctory foreplay (kissing, caressing, sensual interaction)."[16] By Gould's standards, then, the subgenre of porn made explicitly for women would include all these tropes—seduction, romantic suspense, and foreplay—and would be marketed in a way that made it approachable for a female audience. To mimic the success of *Deep Throat* with women audiences, porn for women would also, theoretically, put women's pleasure at the forefront. This would include emphasizing the importance of woman's satisfaction through authentic onscreen orgasms, featuring women as main characters, and showcasing women in pursuit of sexual pleasure.

Based on a close reading of films shown at the Deuce, as well as the women's magazine market at the time, the genre of porn for women can be defined as such: it emulates successful elements of men's porn and foregrounds female pleasure in response to cultural norms. It includes themes of seduction, romantic suspense, and foreplay. And it is marketed in a way that makes it approachable, i.e. not shameful, for women viewers. Through this lens, we will examine the work of Roberta Findlay, the Deuce's most prominent woman filmmaker, and determine whether her films fit within the subgenre.

Findlay left Michael in 1972, and both went on to have separate careers. Their friend and colleague John Amero recounts that after the divorce Findlay became "very assertive," and that she used her knowledge of the business to become a "hardcore director."[17] When Findlay approached Allan Shackleton, a successful producer and distributor whose movies were almost as sleazy as his reputation, and said "I can make you a film really cheap, and I'll make you a lot of money," he gave her $5,000 and she made *Altar of Lust*.[18] She followed that with four more films: *Rosebud*, *Teenage Milkmaid*, *The Clamdigger's Daughter*, and her first hardcore venture, *Angel Number 9*. Findlay's relationship with Shackleton ended when he refused to pay her for *Clamdigger*, she insisted, and he punched her in the eye.

After that incident, Findlay hooked up with Walter Sear, a recording engineer who made porn films on the side. Before teaming up with Findlay, Sear was best known for the hardcore film *Fringe Benefits*, released in 1974; the film is frequently misattributed to Roberta, reflecting both the intertwined nature of their work and the ambiguity around Roberta's oeuvre that persists to this day. Sear, who died in 2010, was an entrepreneur in the truest form; in the 1970s filmmaking happened to be his side endeavor. He was born in New Orleans and moved to Jackson Heights, Queens, when he was a year old. A trained tubist, he spent four years at the Curtis Institute of Music in Philadelphia and received a Bachelor's of Music from Catholic University. A short list of his musical accomplishments includes composing, creating a line of tubas, and performing with the Philadelphia Orchestra and in the Radio City Music Hall pit band. However, Sear was never not thinking and never not working; he also graduated with a chemistry degree from Temple University, a master's degree from American University, and pursued doctoral studies at Columbia University.

Like Findlay, Sear's entrance into pornography was unplanned. Sear's love of science and music materialized in the form of audio engineering. In 1970, Sear opened Sear Sound recording studio in the Paramount Hotel in Times Square. Prior to Sear Sound, Sear had dabbled in film as a composer for *Midnight Cowboy* (1969, dir. John Schlesinger) and with a small cameo as a judge in the exploitation film *Cool It Baby* (1967, dir. Lou Campa) (he was friends and colleagues with Lew Waldeck, a tubist who also filmed roughies). To compete with large commercial studios, Sear built a small film-mix facility with a board and transferring equipment. The small space lent itself to low rates, which attracted low-budget film producers. Upon recognizing the low cost and high returns for the films he was mixing, Sear decided to create films himself, and more cheaply.

His first project was *Fringe Benefits*, which was filmed partially in his studio; many of the props that are supposed to be medical devices are recording studio equipment. Sear wrote the script and produced the film, but as this was his first film endeavor, he paid a director to help. The music was produced in house from remixing and overdubbing tracks, and included original lyrics by his assistant, Steve Ziplow. Much to Sear's surprise, *Fringe Benefits* was a hit. It played for fourteen weeks at the Circus Cinema on Broadway, and generated so much revenue that Sear had a new problem: taxes. Another film provided the perfect tax shelter, and with his new business partner, Findlay, the couple began work on *Slip Up* (1975). The savings from using Sear Sound for recording and as a filming location, along with Findlay's industry experience and steadfast commitment to working as cheaply as possible, allowed the pair to spend more money on talent. Frequent stars in their early films include John Holmes, C. J. Laing, Eric Edwards, Tony Perez, Crystal Sync, and Marlene Willoughby. Together they made approximately twenty pornographic films from the mid-1970s to the mid-1980s. Observing the influence of VHS on the pornography industry, they pivoted briefly to cheap horror films in the mid-1980s and concluded their filmmaking careers in 1989 with the movie *Banned*.

As such, Findlay's films can be divided into four chronological categories, with sporadic exceptions. But broadly, they fall into the following groups: those she made with Michael Findlay; those she made on her own; porn films she created in collaboration with Sear; and horror films she and Sear worked on together. By isolating the time period after her divorce from Michael and before her collaborations with Sear—the time period in which she had complete control over her filmmaking process—Findlay can be examined as an auteur in the purest form. And by examining her early work with Sear, which she created under various male pseudonyms, we can see the way collaboration changes her filmmaking process.

Though the formatting of her films is like others in the sexploitation genre, her movies follow a specific formula and pacing that can be attributed to her background in music. The films from the early 1970s are feature length with ten to fifteen sex scenes per film. The sex scenes last approximately five minutes, after which there is a narrative sequence that pushes the story along just enough for there to be another sex scene. Findlay compares her formatting to that of an opera, though she thinks much more highly of opera. She explains: "You have the opera story, but then everything stops when the soprano has to sing an aria. It's the same thing in sex films. The story goes on, then it stops, then they have to screw. The script has stopped. Whatever the script might be."[19]

Additionally, there are motifs from this time period that are specific to Findlay. The recurring theme of the rotten father can be found throughout her career. Findlay's first film as a director-writer-producer, *Altar of Lust*, takes place in a psychologist's office where the main character, Vivica, is trying to figure out why she's a lesbian. She tells the story of how her father died when she was young, and her mother married an abusive man. After her mother dies, on a sunny day in a grassy field her stepfather rapes her. Though the sex in this scene is simulated (we see the stepfather viciously hump Vivica through their underwear; no genitals are shown), the effect of the rape is translated through point-of-view shots between the characters. Vivica moves on with her life and starts dating Don, played by Harry Reems. One day she comes home and catches Don cheating on her; they have a threesome. She develops feelings for the woman and eventually the threesome becomes a relationship between her and the woman. The film ends with the psychiatrist raping Vivica to fix her lesbian identity. The theme of the "rotten father" is shown here both literally in the stepfather as well as in the psychiatrist, taking the form of the trusting and protective father-figure, raping the main character. The next film featuring this theme is *Teenage Milkmaid*. The film has been lost, but Findlay describes it as being about a girl who lives on a farm with her hyper-religious father. Her next film, *The Clamdigger's Daughter*, was, in her words, "just like *Teenage Milkmaid* except her father was a clamdigger. He drank instead of reading the Bible."[20] She attributes the theme of rotten father to her strict upbringing and claims it would be impossible for her experiences not to bleed into her art. This theme is specific to her as a woman, as a daughter, and distinctly marks her films as made by a woman.

Angel Number 9, released in 1976, was the last film Findlay released through Allan Shackleton and it was specifically marketed as having a woman's touch, leading to the advertisement described in the opening of this chapter. In her own words, Findlay recounts that "on the marquee, it opened at the Lincoln Art Theatre in New York, it said 'Roberta Findlay's *Angel Number 9*.' And we thought it would make money."[21] Arguably her most advanced film of this period and the most critically acclaimed, *Angel Number 9* tells the story of a misogynist, abusive man named Steve, sent back to earth as a woman after his premature death. "I'd rather die than be a woman," Steve yells at his assigned angel, but, as Stephanie, s/he nonetheless must learn the suffering of women firsthand.

Angel Number 9 was met with mixed interpretations. The film is incredibly hostile toward men and treats women as humans with feelings—a rarity in grindhouse films, where women are usually devoid of authentic emotion. However, the men go relatively unpunished for their misbehavior. The driver who kills Steven is rewarded with sex with Stephanie. Another male character is rewarded for being an abusive lover when, instead of Stephanie breaking up with him, they decide to have a threesome. For this reason, Dennis Giles, a male psychoanalyst, concluded through an Orthodox Freudian approach that *Angel Number 9* was made by a man, and "Roberta Findlay" was a pseudonym.[22] However, Molly Haskell, a critic for the *Village Voice*, found conclusively that the film was made by a woman. She writes that this is not because of the trope of having a man return to earth as a woman, but because "two women greet their lovers with the unwelcome news that they are pregnant." She continues, "pregnancy is a no-no in sexploitation movies, a definite down to Don Juan fantasies of quickie, no-fault sex."[23] The hostility toward men and interruption of the fantasy of sex without consequence marks Findlay's femininity in the film.

The next year Findlay released *Anyone But My Husband* under a male pseudonym. The title credits appear in the same fashion as her previous films, but on the title slide of "writer-director-producer" she's listed as Robert Norman. Findlay lists herself by name as Director of Photography. It is curious that following the success of *Angel* and the marketing campaign around her as a female auteur she would choose anonymity. In 1976 in a *Sir!* interview she is asked about her confrontation with members of the women's liberation movement and recounts that at the last *Angel* premiere, "These two women . . . came in . . . and started to rant and rave. They had seen a press release which quotes me as saying I would never under any circumstance hire a woman on my crew."[24] In the same interview, Findlay, who has never been fond of her fans, is asked, "Do you get a lot of weird phone freaks calling you and trying to engage you in conversation while they jerk themselves off?" She replied, "Certainly—and at all hours. I've just had my number changed and it's unlisted now."[25] There were surely perks to cultivating a fan base in the porno-chic era, but for Findlay, the cons may have outweighed the pros.

Ironically, *Anyone But My Husband* is Findlay's most feminist film. The film follows the sexual awakening of Nora Pelham, played by C. J. Laing, a housewife who has become fed up with her adulterous husband, Sam, played by Robert Kerman. The opening scene cuts between Nora stuffing a chicken and Sam, a high school history teacher, having sex with a student. When Sam returns home, Nora has set the table for a romantic dinner, including a bottle of champagne. Sam, who is worn out from his escapade, shuts her down, explaining that he is too tired from his job as a teacher and implying that Nora is nagging him. In a high-angle shot with shadowed lighting, highlighting her feelings of isolation, Nora asks Sam, "Have I gotten too old for you?" We find out later that Nora was sixteen when they were married, and she is now twenty-two. Sam replies, "Yes, too old in all the wrong places," and berates her for spending money on caviar and champagne. Despondent, Nora slips away into the bathroom with the champagne, which she uses to masturbate.

Nora seeks the advice of a psychologist, played by Robert Combs, who suggests she should have an affair to let out her pent-up desires. However, Nora, who has only been with her husband, doesn't know how to have an affair. Enter the comic relief of her best friend, Sylvia, played by Jennifer Jordan, to guide her through her journey of self-discovery. The first sex scene Nora engages in is a nonconsensual BDSM whipping scene with an artist, played by Beerbohm Tree, whom she meets at an erotic art exhibit. Nora's disposition to Sam immediately changes after the encounter; as he is getting ready to leave for yet another teacher's convention, he says, "The least you could do is say that you'll miss me, maybe even ask me what hotel I'll be staying at." The disinterested Nora replies, "I'll miss you, but must I know which hotel you'll be staying at?" The scene cuts between the bickering couple and Sylvia, who is eavesdropping outside of their door. After Sam leaves, Nora recounts her encounter with the artist to Sylvia, who asks if Nora will see him again. Nora replies, "I wanted to go to bed, not to the hospital; that man should be locked up," acknowledging the violence of their interaction. This leads her to the opposite extreme, a poet, played by Eric Edwards, who takes Nora on a picnic and reads her poetry. Humorously and satirically for Findlay, who claims not to have been able to shoot a romantic scene, Nora wonders aloud, "Is all this necessary?" before engaging in oral and then penetrative sex with the poet. In a first for Findlay, Nora breaks the fourth wall after the poet suggests marriage to say, "Oh fuck off, aren't there any sane men left in this world that just want a good lay?"

Dissuaded by the "freaks" she has encountered, Nora contemplates her love for her husband. Sylvia, the optimist, takes Nora to a fortune teller to see if her luck with men will change. Gazing into her (obviously plastic) crystal ball, the fortune teller predicts a man for Sylvia who is thirteen and a half inches tall. "No that can't be . . . a man 13½ inches long," the fortune teller corrects. Then "The Hook," played by Tony Perez, is led out by the fortune teller for Sylvia's enjoyment. "He speaks no English," the fortune teller acknowledges, but actually he doesn't speak at all. In his scene with Sylvia, and in the following scene where he interrupts Nora and the fortune teller in a jacuzzi, "The Hook" doesn't say a word. Following their encounters with "The Hook," and in the funniest scene Findlay has written thus far, the two disheveled women limp down the street; Sylvia is walking bow-legged, and Nora has developed laryngitis.

Nora returns to the psychiatrist to report on her exploits. She is excited and says, "I've never felt so alive in years!" The physiatrist shoots down her feeling of liberation, ranting about an Oedipus complex, and concludes that her laryngitis is psychosomatic. Nora replies that he doesn't know what he's talking about: "If you'd just given head to 13½ inches, you'd be a little hoarse too!" The doctor suggests she return to her husband now that she is cured and continues to rant about her Oedipus complex, while Nora walks out angrily. The story then cuts to a scene of Nora's husband hooking up with a woman after a party; he is feeling guilty about his adultery and refers to the woman as Nora. Sam returns home to Nora, acknowledging that he has been neglectful and offering her wine and sex. Nora is already in bed asleep, and she ends with a speech for frustrated housewives everywhere:

> What did you think? Did you think you had a rough day? Well, I have it tough. Washing and cleaning, and then trying to look beautiful. I've never been so worn out. Sure, Nora will be there, her body waiting for her lord and master. Sure, buy wine, but nobody even asked me if I want wine!

Mirroring the beginning of the film, Nora rolls over and says, "and Sam, turn off the damn light!" Sam then slinks into the bathroom and closes the door.

Anyone But My Husband has many eccentricities that make it an outlier from the rest of Findlay's work. Following a fight between Findlay and Allan

Shackleton, this film was released by Anonymous Releasing (*American Sex Fantasies* [1975, dir. Beau Buchanan], *My Master My Love* [1975, dir. Ralph Ell], *Captain Lust* [1977, dir. Beau Buchanan]). The most unique aspect of the film is the subversion of male gaze. While Findlay's previous films delve into the topic of women's sexual exploration, Nora, encouraged by Sylvia, is on an active mission to find a man who fits her specific needs. Their friendship aligns with the buddy comedy troupe of two best friends on a sexual bender, but instead of two men, the storyline features two women. Men, especially "The Hook," are reduced to their ability to fit the needs of Nora and Sylvia. When we are introduced to "The Hook," he is naked and being led to meet Sylvia by the fortune teller, who is using his penis as a leash. He has no lines; the only thing the viewer learns about him is that he has a thirteen and a half-inch penis. Like the men in other hardcore films, the women do not face consequences for their actions; in fact, the only person who does face consequences is the husband, Sam. The interaction between Nora and the psychologist adds a layer of social commentary about how women are treated in the male-dominated field of psychology. The doctor rants about Nora's relationship with her father, ignoring her reality. When looked at in the context of the rest of her work, *Anyone But My Husband* represents an in-between stage for Findlay: she continued to hone in on characteristic elements of her filmmaking, but she attempted to disguise her fingerprints on the film with a false name. She would continue the practice in partnership with Sear, in which she would also loosen her hold on certain hallmarks that distinguished the films as hers.

Fringe Benefits and *Slip Up*, the two films written and directed by Walter Sear, contrast heavily with Findlay's 1972–4 films. *Fringe Benefits* opens with a secretary sitting naked at a typewriter, typing the credits of the film. The second scene is a panning establishing shot of Manhattan. The camera lands on an office building window—the supposed headquarters of the Tighttwat Institute for Sexual Research. (The company placard is displayed with their logo: a vulva.) The film follows the woes of Harry Flatout, played by Eric Edwards, who had served as the executive director of the personnel department of the Spurtover Oil Company (their logo is symbolic of a penis). He enters the Institute following a shock that has led him to be impotent. Told in flashback format, which is also typical of Findlay's early films, Harry recounts his time at Spurtover where, to combat the high turnover rate of stenographers, he instituted the Sex Hour. There are, of course, many issues with this new fringe benefit, but mainly the logistics of when and where the Sex Hour will occur. After a few scenes of Harry with the stenographers, he sets his eyes on his boss's secretary. He is caught by his boss who fires everyone in the office, causing Harry's impotency. Harry recounts his story to Dr. Tessy, played by Georgina Spelvin, who tries to get him back into condition by testing his impotence on herself. When that fails, he is sent to Dr. Cherrypopper and his assistant, Miss Sissy Motormouth, to try the experimental Electrotesticular Cockerector. Unfortunately for Harry, the doctor and his assistant have sex during the process, distracting them from the fact that the device is overloading. Harry is cured of his problem but has a new one: his erection won't go down. His permanent erection drives him crazy; we learn through a call to Motormouth from hospital security that Harry has raped "three nurses, two dogs, one old lady, and topped it off by raping Dr. Tighttwat." Dr. Tessy declares, "My god, I've created a fucking monster!" Harry returns to Spurtover to find his boss's secretary overjoyed that his impotence is cured. His boss walks in on the scene, but this time he is happy to see Harry back. The stenographers have revolted and are threatening to unionize if they don't get their fringe benefits back. Harry is offered his job back, and with a promotion! The film ends with the stenographers undressing and then a close-up of Harry's penis covered in a cloth with fringe. The ending credits show the secretary back at her typewriter; she puts on clothes to sit down and then takes them off.

Slip Up is the sequel to *Fringe Benefits* and made with a much higher budget. Dr. Cherrypopper, now played by Jamie Gillis, has a plan to take over the country by building a machine capable of giving every man in America an unrelievable erection. Penelope Juiceslit, played by Darby Lloyd Rains, has kinky fantasies and a libido that has sent her boyfriend to the hospital twice. Her boyfriend insists that she gets help from Dr. Cherrypopper and she heads to the institute, where incompetence seems to be as widespread as sexual energy. A telephone repairman crosses the phone lines while getting a blowjob, and Juiceslit is able to eavesdrop on Dr. Cherrypopper's evil plan. To stop him, Juiceslit calls the Federal Undercover Counterintelligence Agency, the FUC, but Mr. Ballbust, the head of the agency, ignores her and calls her a crackpot—until his secretary undresses Juiceslit and gives her head. Afterward, Ballbust directs Juiceslit to the Washington office. When Juiceslit finally arrives, the chief of FUC, Mr. Quimtwiddle, takes Juiceslit to dinner where he and his secretary dine on her. More incompetence ensues at the company's primary energy-producing power plant, Polutem, Pecker, Power, & Light. The main engineer has become distracted by the woman who brings him lunch. He is not allowed to take a lunch break let alone a sex break, but that doesn't stop them from having sex on the control panel. Signs that say "screw up" and "big fuckin' screw up" flash and blare, smoke starts to come out of the machines, but all are ignored by the engineer (see Figure 5.1). Meanwhile at the institute, the conditions are just right to switch on Dr. Cherrypopper's erection machine. As the countdown begins there are flashes of light, jump cuts, and loud blaring. Due to the engineer's incompetence, the power has gone out, and Dr. Cherrypopper's plot is foiled. The film ends with Dr. Cherrypopper breaking the fourth wall and manically asking the audience, "Is everybody fucking off?!"

From the first scene of *Fringe Benefits*, the difference between Sear's and Findlay's filmmaking is evident. The scene cuts between a medium close-up of

Figure 5.1 Jamie Gillis as Dr. Cherrypopper, breaking the fourth wall in *Slip Up*.

a secretary sitting at the desk, to the credits rolling on the typewriter paper, to a close-up of her breasts dangling over the typewriter. This is exaggerated by the character of Miss Sissy Motormouth, who is never fully dressed. Women are constantly gaslighted in the films. During a sex scene on a plane in *Slip Up*, Juiceslit points out that there is a gorilla in the seat behind her and Clitsplit, who replies, "Ok ok, I need you to shut up and fuck." A similar dynamic occurs when Juiceslit is called a crackpot by the head of the FUC and ignored by its chief until he begins groping her. Frustrated at dinner she says, "I just can't get him to pay any attention to me, I can't get anyone to listen to me, they always seem to get distracted!"

There's also a marked difference in the flow of the sex scenes in Findlay's and Sears's movies. Findlay's films are not known for their foreplay, but at least there is an attempt at progression from kissing to oral sex to penetrative sex. In *Fringe Benefits* and *Slip Up* there is no caressing or foreplay, and there are very few kissing scenes. In the dinner scene in *Slip Up*, when the waiter asks Juiceslit, who's being eaten out under the table, if there is anything he can get her, she says, "Yes, a kiss!" and he screams and runs away. Many sex scenes are instigated by a man arranging a woman to be penetrated or pushing a woman's head in place to give a blowjob.

Sear also is incredibly funny, self-referential, and satirical; his films are advertised as social commentaries and belong to a raunchy vernacular sex culture that runs from the folk wisdom of the seventeenth-century anatomical manual *Aristotle's Masterpiece* through the crass humor of Larry Flynt's *Hustler*.[26] In addition to the names listed, above other notable names are Miss Fartblow, Alan Clitsplit, and Miss Muff Puff. In a scene at the FUC, Mr. Ballbust requests that his secretary help him with his erection. In response she picks up a book and reads aloud, "It says right here in the civil service guide that my classification is a G.S.7 subheading cunt lapper, now if you want a cocksucker what you have to do is file . . ." she continues to the bureaucratic process while Mr. Ballbuster and Juiceslit have sex on the couch in his office. In *Slip Up*, during the airplane scene, Alan Clitsplit, played by Eric Edwards, gets turned on while helping Juiceslit clean up. She says "Mr. Clitsplit, we can't do it here" to which he replies "why not? I'm the fastest strip in the west." In three snap cuts he goes from fully dressed to naked. Juiceslit replies "that's pretty good but you ain't seen nothing yet," and strips naked in one cut.

Findlay and Sear came together as true partners on their first film, *Love in Strange Places*, in 1976 and made three more films that year. The films fall into the category of "the three-day wonder." The phrase, coined by Steve Ziplow in his 1977 book *The Film Maker's Guide to Pornography*, refers to the creation of an entire picture, or even two, in just three to five days. The art, he notes, is not in what is projected on the screen, but in how all the elements are assembled together with "a minimal amount of mistakes for a minimal amount of money." The defining features are "just enough plot to pass as a motion picture and enough sex to satisfy any customer."[27] Sear and Findlay were masters of this craft, often churning out two or three movies at a time and reusing scenes from one movie in another. Presumably to appeal to the largest market, all of the films from this year are heterosexual (though they do include at least one lesbian sex scene), and show no kinks or fetish sex acts. Sear, who had a family and a reputation as a musician and an audio engineer, only appears in the credits under pseudonyms, notably Harold Hindgrind. Findlay also appears in the credits of these films under the pseudonyms Robert D. Walters, Robert Norman, and Anna Riva. The cast of all of the 1976 films includes John Holmes, Tony Perez, Eric Edwards, Marlene Willoughby, C. J. Laing, and Crystal Sync. Other notable actresses who appear are Jennifer Jordan and Marlow Ferguson.

Sear and Findlay made two films based around hospitals with the same cast, who played different characters in vastly different styles. The first film, *Love in Strange Places*, follows Nurse Nancy Blue's first day on the job at the Hospital for the Sexually Insane, which has been taken over by the patients. Headed by Dr. Hook, played by John Holmes, who is pretending to be a brain surgeon, and Dr. Fraud, played by Don Peterson, who is pretending to be a therapist, the hospital provides sex as therapy. There is very little plot progression; rather, the film contains various vignettes of the patients. During scenes where the plot is forming, sex regularly begins and is interrupted by a loudspeaker announcing that it is time for therapy or medication; music then comes on and the films cut to interspersed scenes of couples having sex that last between five and seven minutes. The film takes a psychological horror turn, ironically on psychodrama night, where they "tear each other apart and then screw," when Nurse Blue can't escape the hospital. During the orgy, Nurse Blue sneaks out and sets the staff free, including the head of the hospital, who rapes her. The film ends in a giant orgy with staff and patients. The orgy scene is reused at the end of the next film.

Sweet Sweet Freedom is a social commentary on the medical industrial complex. The hospital is facing a crisis: they are killing patients too quickly, before they can pay their bills. The problem stems from them admitting too many sick patients, mostly middle-aged men whose blood pressure is too high from stress and whose desire to live is too low from ambivalence. The head of the hospital, Dr. Mangle, played by Don Peterson, comes up with the Early Admission Policy, a rest and rehabilitation plan that they can charge to Blue Cross. Of course, as the tagline "a treat instead of a treatment" suggests, sex is the primary offering. The film is supposed to be a comedy, but many of the gags are repetitive. For example, the pharmacist has five scenes in which the janitor comes by to pick up Spanish Fly for the water supply and is ambivalent about the fact that she is having sex doggy style behind the counter. There are scenes cut in throughout the film of a frazzled and crude dietician, played by Findlay, her back to the camera, doing increasingly gross acts, like making mashed potatoes with her feet and defecating in them when she gets fired (see Figure 5.2). The final twenty minutes of the film are of an orgy in the hospital solarium.

Figure 5.2 Roberta Findlay as the hospital dietician in *Sweet Sweet Freedom*.

Dear Pam is a high camp porn parody. Pam Sanders, played by Crystal Sync, is nominated by the Decency and Morality League for the "Most Moral Woman of the Year" award for her advice column. To secure the award, Pam reads the judges a letter she's just received detailing the depraved sexual antics of Harry Phallis, played by Eric Edwards, which are conveyed to the audience through vignettes. His problem is that, sometime during his sexual antics, he lost his necklace. The letter causes so much outrage among Pam and the League that they must investigate its authenticity by meeting with the women Harry describes. But, as the film's tagline "do as she says, not as she does" suggests, Pam and the League are anything but moral. Each woman investigated by the League ends up having sex with a member. John Holmes plays a member of the League, and upon his return to Pam's office they have sex on her desk. This turns prudish Pam sex crazy; she insists that they have sex at the party where she is to be presented with her award. As the Chairwoman of the League is announcing the merits of Pam, the curtain rises to reveal Pam's mouth around Holmes's penis, and she can't get it out. The party ends in an orgy scene typical of the previous films.

Dear Pam is highly self-referential, which adds to its parody and camp elements. In the first sex scene, Harry recounts interviewing a new secretary at a restaurant during his lunch break. He asks her for her qualifications, to which she replies with her secretarial qualifications, Harry interrupts her to say, "No no no, I don't mean those qualifications, I mean height, bust size . . ." as if asking her for her qualifications on being cast as a secretary in a porn film. After they have sex and sit back down for lunch, they are still naked, but the waiter is unbothered and delivers Harry's meal. The heightened absurdity is a nod to the formulaic "get down to business" writing in porn scripts. Further, Harry's lost necklace, which gets passed around from one person's genitals to another as they have sex, symbolically ties the characters together, but is also a joke about how most of the cast members have already had sex with each other in other films, including Sear and Findlay's.

Sweet Punkin' I Love You stands apart from the previous three films. As *Flick* magazine notes in their review, "the plot is minimal at best."[28] C. J. Laing plays the character of Punkin', a hillbilly who works as a maid to an elderly millionaire, and who maintains a career as a porn star on the side. She marries her boss, who soon dies of a heart attack. The rest of the plot surrounds her inability to fit in with the high society that now surrounds her. Critical reception of the film praised Laing for her sexual performance and condemned the dialogue and plot. The film is incredibly slow paced. With the exception of the ending orgy scene, the rock music of Sears's and Findlay's previous film is replaced with pseudo-classical music played on a synthesizer. The dialogue is monotone, rambling, and uninteresting. There is an attempt at a romantic sex scene between Laing and Eric Edwards; they are in front of a fireplace with

Spanish guitar playing. In contrast to other sex scenes, there are cuts to kissing and caressing. The couple is shot in multiple full-body scenes and there are no extreme close-ups of genitals. *High Society*'s review of the film sums it up well: "your cock will erupt—that is if the rest of the film doesn't put you to sleep."[29]

Taken as a body of work, the four earliest films in the Sear/Findlay canon show elements of both of their distinctive styles. Findlay's mark on the films is in the camera work. Compared to *Fringe*, there is an increase in variation of shots; of particular note is the tracking shot in the orgy scene of *Punkin'*, and an attempt at using more varied angles to convey plot points. Sear's contribution is evident in the films' humor, absurdity, and camp. While *Anyone But My Husband* shows that Findlay was capable of conveying humor, their collaborations, as epitomized in *Dear Pam*, allowed the duo to do parody without over-parodying, even if the jokes didn't always land. As both are musicians, music is used to advance plots in the film, and cuts are often to the beat. Findlay's musical instincts were enhanced by Sear, whose connection to musicians and his studio gave them access to original music, as compared to Findlay's films, which often used whatever she could steal. Their collaboration muted negative aspects of both of their work—Findlay's monotone diatribes and Sear's social commentary—which allowed for the real focus of their films, sex, to take center stage.

While Findlay's influence can be discerned in the 1976 films, much of her voice vanished along with her name in her early partnerships with Sear. For example, though the theme of the rotten father occurs in early Findlay/Sear collaborations, it's incorporated through vignettes that have little effect on the overall plot. This contrasts with Findlay's first three solo films, which forefront the main characters' relationships with their fathers. The female character development present in Findlay's solo films gets lost in the Findlay/Sear collaborations. Though three of the four films made in 1976 have a woman as the supposed main character, their growth and depth are subverted by the seemingly random sex scenes between supporting characters and the absurdity of the plots.

In part, the disappearance of Findlay's distinctive touch was due to the process by which her films with Sear were made. By speeding up production, Findlay and Sear had to churn out scripts; there was little time to explore nuance in plot or theme. To keep budgets as low as possible, they could not do reshoots, meaning they were stuck with their original takes, regardless of quality. While the quality of Findlay's filmmaking declined, she and Sear hit a different kind of stride under pressure. As Ziplow notes, their speed and resourcefulness became an asset; the team was able to shoot *Strange Places* and *Freedom* simultaneously and interspersed orgy scenes in both films. Plot continuity was sacrificed in favor of sheer volume and absurdity. Ziplow's book contains interviews with Sear, coded as Mr. Blue, which give us an insight into his script-writing process and his point of view on sexploitation as a genre at this point in his career. When asked about novelty in the genre he laments, "I wish I could think of something totally new in this field, but it's been around a long time . . . I mean, you can try different props, different sets, different situations . . . But the basic idea is that the whole thing is ridiculous to begin with."[30] Sear's creative process prioritized profit and trivialized plot, as he noted: "The whole concept of making a film on the budget that we're making them on is ridiculous. If you go for serious acting or realism, it becomes a farce, so you might as well start off and say this is a farce."[31]

For the rest of Findlay's career, she would work in collaboration with Sear and others, never again making a solo project. The consequence of her decision to act as a collaborator, rather than an auteur, was that her distinct point of view as a woman pornographer was subsumed. Findlay's early work is exceptional in part because it can be distinguished as made by a woman. The critical success of *Angel Number 9* and *Anyone But My Husband*, which depict men as maladroit misogynists, demonstrates Findlay's mastery of her subject matter. She employed the tropes of the porn industry to capture her unique perspective, rather than participating in the subgenre—porn for women—that was forming around her. Unlike the women's porn magazines, Findlay did not transpose her films for women viewers. She proclaims in *SIR! Magazine* that she believes women have just as much of a sex drive as men but says they perhaps have different viewing desires. In the same interview, Findlay echoes the principles of porn for women that Lois Gould outlined in the *New York Times*: "Most women—and I'd include myself—want their sex heavily veiled and kind of mysterious."[32] She grieves to the interviewer in *Take One* magazine that she has "tried over and over and over to make one erotic scene. Not even erotic, but to make it even sexually realistic."[33] While she acknowledges the differences, Findlay does not make her films any more erotic or sensual than her male counterparts do. She is more interested in appealing to her pre-set audience: businessmen and tourists. Findlay's editing in both her solo films and her collaborations heavily contributes to foregrounding sex over eroticism. The sex scenes in both sets of films feature extreme close-ups of genital stimulation (done through penetration, oral stimulation, or by other means), which eliminates any semblance of foreplay or suspense. Orgasms and pleasure are shown through medium close-ups of faces, effectively detaching the actor from their body. The shot-reverse-shot technique is often used in sex scenes, which implies the act's continuation but interrupts the connectivity between characters. Thanks to the combination of editing and camera angles, the sex sequences effectively prevent any intimacy or sexual tension from developing between characters, placing Findlay's films firmly outside the subgenre of porn for women.

Ultimately, Findlay's adherence to form made her very financially success-ful, which was her goal both as a solo filmmaker and as a partner to Sear. In his interview with Ziplow, Sear essentially offered the adage: if it ain't broke, don't fix it. "Some people have come in and spent a lot of money and do fancy productions, but I think the market is fairly set," he said. "I don't think people today are going to any type of entertainment for a message. I think they're going to kill a few hours, to have a little fun and get away from their own inter-nal problems and troubles. If they get a laugh out of it, fine."[34]

NOTES

1. Display ad, *New York Times*, November 21, 1974, 56.
2. Henry Jenkins, "Exploiting Feminism: An Interview with Stephanie Rothman (Part One)," *Confessions of an AcaFan*, October 16, 2007, http://henryjenkins.org/2007/10/stephanie_rothman.html (accessed May 26, 2022).
3. Timothy Green Beckley, "Female Porn Producer Roberta Findlay," *Sir*, September 1976, 8, 11, 80–4.
4. Gerald Peary, "Woman in Porn: How Young Roberta Findlay Finally Grew Up and Made 'Snuff'," *Take One*, September 1978, 28–32.
5. Peary, "Woman in Porn," 32.
6. Peary, "Woman in Porn," 32.
7. Peary, "Woman in Porn," 32.
8. David Church, "From Exhibition to Genre: The Case of Grind-House Films," *Cinema Journal* 50, no. 4 (2011): 16.
9. Richard Blumenthal, "'Hard-Core' Grows Fashionable—and Very Profitable," *New York Times*, January 21, 1973, 28.
10. Blumenthal, "'Hard-Core' Grows Fashionable," 28.
11. Blumenthal, "'Hard-Core' Grows Fashionable," 28.
12. On more background on sexploitation films and women's access see Bret Wood and Felicia Feaster, *Forbidden Fruit: The Golden Age of the Exploitation Film* (Baltimore, MD: Midnight Marquee Press, 1999), 173–90.
13. On the rise of women's adult magazines and marketing see Carolyn Bronstein, "Mass-Market Pornography for Women: Bob Guccione's Viva Magazine and the New Woman of the 1970s," in Carolyn Bronstein and Whitney Strub (eds), *Porno Chic and the Sex Wars: American Sexual Representation in the 1970s* (Amherst, MA: University of Massachusetts Press, 2016), 125–53.
14. Lois Gould, "Pornography for Women," *New York* Times, March 2, 1975: 209.
15. Gould, "Pornography for Women," 209.
16. Gould, "Pornography for Women," 209.
17. Bill Landis and Michelle Clifford, *Sleazoid Express* (New York: Simon & Schuster, 2002), 43.
18. "Week 19: Roberta Findlay," *Third Eye Cinema*, podcast audio, June 17, 2012, https://thirdeyecinema.podbean.com/e/third-eye-cinema-61712-with-roberta-findlay/? (accessed May 26, 2022).
19. Peary, "Woman in Porn," 32.
20. Beckley, "Female Porn Producer Roberta Findlay," 82.
21. Beckley, "Female Porn Producer Roberta Findlay," 82.
22. Dennis Giles, "Angel on Fire: Three Texts of Desire," *The Velvet Light Trap* 16 (Fall 1976): 42.

23. Molly Haskell, "Are Women Directors Different?" *Village Voice*, February 3, 1975, 73.
24. Beckley, "Female Porn Producer Roberta Findlay," 11.
25. Beckley, "Female Porn Producer Roberta Findlay," 82.
26. See Helen Lefkowitz Horowitz, *Re-reading Sex: Battles over Sexual Knowledge and Suppression in Nineteenth-Century America* (New York: Vintage, 2003); Laura Kipnis, *Bound and Gagged: Pornography and the Politics of Fantasy in America* (Durham, NC: Duke University Press, 1999).
27. Steven Ziplow, *The Film Maker's Guide to Pornography* (New York: Drake, 1977), 14.
28. Review, *Flick Magazine*, September 1976, 10–11.
29. Reggie Danzig, "Film On Exhibit," *High Society*, September 1976, 29.
30. Ziplow, *The Film Maker's Guide*, 143.
31. Ziplow, *The Film Maker's Guide*, 143.
32. Beckley, "Female Porn Producer Roberta Findlay," 11.
33. Peary, "Woman in Porn," 32.
34. Ziplow, *The Film Maker's Guide*, 140.

CHAPTER 6

Fragments of a Porn Star: Hybrid Documentary and Avant-garde Impulses in *Shauna: Every Man's Fantasy*

Kier-La Janisse

"Only a sociopath could have made this movie." It was my first thought on viewing *Shauna: Every Man's Fantasy* (1985), Roberta Findlay's hardcore documentary about the suicide of porn star Shauna Grant. And it was a reaction that begged further investigation, prompting this chapter—which considers the film from a range of methodological and critical approaches, beginning with production history which contextualizes the film within Findlay's adult canon, and intersects with both first-person interviews and archival research concerning Grant's suicide.

Positioning the film from this perspective, I then approach *Shauna: Every Man's Fantasy* as a hybrid documentary, examining the ways that Findlay's juxtaposition of repurposed footage with interviews about the star's suicide and additional scripted/staged sex scenes places the film in a surprising conversation with avant-garde tradition, and looks at the ways this dialogue is also apparent in Findlay's earlier films. In drawing upon the image bank of hardcore pornography itself, Findlay creates a document that constantly questions its own objectivity.

Inescapable are Findlay's complex (and perhaps performative) sexual politics: she is on the record for her dislike of women, and this translates into the unique layering and compartmentalization of exploitation inherent in *Shauna: Every Man's Fantasy*. This allows the chapter to map out how Findlay's film simultaneously transgresses accepted ethical guidelines of documentary, and questions long-standing assumptions that this perceived lack of empathy resulted in her alienation from the hardcore industry.

"I KNEW SHAUNA GRANT. I CRIED WHEN SHE DIED."

Before Shauna Grant became one of the best known stars of the adult film industry, her name was Colleen Applegate, a teenager from Farmington, Minnesota, who left home at eighteen to seek fame and fortune in Hollywood with her high school boyfriend in tow. They parted ways not long after she answered an ad for Jim South's World Modeling. South was the gateway for many golden age west coast adult stars, and Applegate soon went from nude modeling to doing films.

Within a few short years, she had starred in thirty hardcore films and been featured on the covers of *Hustler, Oui, Erotica, Club, Velvet* and more. But while she was undeniably photogenic, Grant was never comfortable performing sex acts onscreen; the films became a way to fund her increasingly debilitating cocaine habit, which as writer John David Ebert has pointed out, became "a way of creating an artificial membrane between the two personae" of Colleen Applegate and Shauna Grant.[1] Rumors spread back in her hometown that caused shame to Shauna's strict family. She desperately sought to make her parents proud—misguidedly thinking that the industry wages she was raking in would do the trick—and struggled to reconcile these conflicting aspects of her life.

In 1983 she quit the films and moved out to Palm Springs with her then boyfriend Jake Erhlich, a cocaine dealer who also owned a local leather goods store where Shauna would work. Shauna reveled in what she perceived to be a newfound domesticity and stability, unaware that her boyfriend's drug trade was about to catch up with them. After he was arrested in February 1984, Shauna found herself the frazzled custodian of his piling debts. She resolved to go back to work. She was nominated for multiple acting awards at the March 1984 Erotic Film Awards—she sat at a table with Francis Ford Coppola—and planned to shoot a comeback film up in San Francisco for Henri Pachard, aka Ron Sullivan, eight days later. The film, *Matinee Idol*—produced by exploitation godfather David F. Friedman and an updated riff on his 1969 softcore film *Starlet*—was eventually made . . . but without Shauna Grant.

The night before she was to arrive on set, Sullivan says Shauna called him to ask if everyone would be disappointed in her if she didn't show up. He reassured her that they were all really looking forward to working with her. But she didn't show up. Instead, she was found in the back bedroom of Jake Erhlich's Palm Springs pad, dead of a gunshot to the head that was ruled to be self-inflicted. It was March 21, 1984.

While investigating Shauna Grant's death is outside the purview of this chapter, let it be said that some in the adult industry did not actually believe she killed herself. As Roberta Findlay tells it, her longtime partner Walter Sear

> opined to everyone that no young, pretty girl would shoot herself in the head with a shotgun. So, how should I put it? I didn't know that much about her, but she seemed to have *bad friends* in California. We never met any of these people, but we heard tell of such things. So I don't know that it was a great surprise.[2]

Nevertheless, when Roberta Findlay made her paean to Shauna Grant, *Shauna: Every Man's Fantasy* in 1985, these suspicions were not part of the narrative.

Grant's death was seized upon by the media—both industry and main-stream—in various ways. Findlay had brought Shauna to New York to direct her in a pair of films back-to-back in 1983, *Glitter* and *Private School Girls*, the latter co-directed with her longtime collaborator Jack Bravman,[3] and had outtakes from the two films. "So, we took the outtake negative from the other films and made a narrative around this," she explains. "And it was a practically a free picture. This is no 'memorial' to Shauna Grant or anything . . . I guess we learned of her death and then time went by and I said, look, we can cash in on her name. Isn't that awful? [laughs] And so we did."[4]

The resulting film, *Shauna: Every Man's Fantasy*, released in August 1985, is not quite a documentary. And it did more than cannibalize these two films; the footage forms part of a complex patchwork that borrows a variety of structural techniques from Findlay's past oeuvre, including recycled footage and elements of the white-coater, the diary film and the epistolary tradition. In this unique hybrid film, characters step in and out of fictional scenarios without clearly delineated margins. Ultimately this transgression of structural and generic boundaries would contribute to the film's persistent status as a shocking work.

But what many viewers find equally confounding about the film is the role of other women—namely Findlay and the film's onscreen host, *Cinema Blue* editor Joyce James—in exploring Grant's tragic suicide in a manner that jarringly juxta-poses it with hardcore sex. "I knew Shauna Grant," James assures us onscreen. "I cried when she died." James's darting eyes betray that she is reading her lines—written in part by her soon-to-be husband and creative partner, the late John Fasano, who also contributed writing to Findlay's *Blood Sisters* (1987)—which pose the film's central hypothesis. With a pensive expression mimicking the Olympian television reporter, she asks: "DID pornography KILL Shauna Grant?"

Joyce James was in reality Cynthia Cirile, a university-educated, recently divorced single mom with a toddler, who lived in Westchester County and taught English at a local college. Through odd and somewhat comical cir-cumstances, she was initiated into her career as a porn journalist through her connections at the La Leche League, a society of nursing mothers. Someone knew someone who knew someone, and soon Cindy Cirile was on her way to a job interview at *Oui Magazine*. Or so she thought: it was actually *Adult Film Review*, and she quickly found herself on the frontlines of New York's vibrant porn scene, which is how she came into the orbit of Roberta Findlay.

In an interview, Cirile explained how her job as editor was essentially to operate as public relations for the industry:

> In my job as editor of a slew of different erotic film guides, my job was
> to publicize porn movies, and especially east coast porn movies. And so

Figure 6.1 Cynthia Cirile interviewing Shauna Grant, with performer Sharon Mitchell. Photo courtesy of Cynthia Cirile.

I was encouraged, I mean, basically *told* not to write anything real about the movies and to just make them sound hot. And to use a lot of pictures and basically that was it. So I took it on myself to try to make the east coast pornographic scene sound like an exciting place, like a forum of creative eroticism—which it most certainly was not![5]

She went on to describe the origins of *Shauna*:

It's possible that I came up with the idea for *Shauna*, in the most typical "Joyce James" way possible, in that this would be a great opportunity to share that the life of this girl was a lot more than just, "Wow, look at her. She's so gorgeous and blonde and she didn't mind taking it up the ass on film. Oh, and she's dead." So, you know, which would be basically what that movie is . . . And I thought this would be a great opportunity to get people to actually watch a documentary. And for Roberta to make a documentary, because John was trying basically to take over Roberta and Walter's place. Like, become the person who decides what movies they make, what their schedule is and become their primary writer and director.[6]

Cirile and Fasano needed the gig because Fasano had just gotten them both fired from *Cinema Blue*; nevertheless, that remains Cirile's onscreen industry credit in *Shauna: Every Man's Fantasy*. Findlay claims to have cuckolded Cirile, who was under the impression that it was a serious documentary examining Grant's life and tragic death.[7] This is only half true; while the film's genesis was likely in Cirile's urging for an earnest documentary on Grant, it was apparent pretty quickly that this was not the direction it was taking. Cirile recalls how the production changed:

> Every step of the way I'm like, no, no, no, no, no, you can't do this. This is terrible! I'm like Jiminy Cricket on this film. And I'm talking to John, because after all he's writing the script. So, I figured what's the point of talking to Roberta, I'll talk to John. And also John's 22. He's certainly going to listen to me! No! He doesn't listen to anything I say, he's just full of hubris! And I say, you have to tell this to Roberta. She can't do this, this particular thing, this is going to be awful. People are going to rebel. There's actually going to be people up in arms over this.[8]

In the end, for Cirile it was one day on set and a memory best shelved in the recesses of her mind, stirred only occasionally by a phone call such as my own.

Joyce James will not only be our guide through the film's sordid interrogation of Shauna's death, but she will also be a surrogate for Findlay herself. The two women are not dissimilar in appearance, and Findlay's voice will stand in for James's frequently throughout the film, although she leaves the hard questions for James. "Do you think Shauna ever felt degraded by what she did on film?" James asks actress Karen Summers, as the latter licks an erect penis. Cutting to a seated interview in which Findlay takes over as offscreen interviewer, Summers describes Grant as a sweet girl who "got pushed and shoved, and I feel sorry for her," a statement abruptly curtailed by a suspiciously placed splice. And though James will ultimately reassure audiences that they are not responsible for a twenty-year-old girl's suicide, the probing and the ironic juxtaposition make for uneasy compartmentalization, violating the contract between industry provider and customer that promises erotic escape.

But James's role here as a character-within-a-character will be in keeping with the film's overall mode of disruptive hybridity, artifice, and roleplay. At the core of Shauna Grant's internal distress was her inability to meet expectations, and her messy construction of personas through which she, too hoped to compartmentalize. And this film's inability to meet expectations—artistically, socially, ethically—is the reason we are still talking about it today.

"WHAT ARE YOU, A DIALOGUE FREAK?" LOGORRHEIC PASSION AND THE EPISTOLARY TRADITION

The investigative framework of *Shauna: Every Man's Fantasy* aims to structure the hardcore film's obligatory sex scenes around what is being offered as a real-life mystery. In doing so there is direct address to the camera, there are in-situ interviews, formal seated interviews, and voice-over.

What this means is that cumulatively there is quite a bit of dialogue in the film, which has been credited to John Fasano, though Cindy Cirile vaguely recalls writing her own dialogue—albeit through the camp lens of her adult industry persona, Joyce James:

> It was like "here you ask about this, and then, you know, go off." There's no, no script. I mean the whole script was maybe 40 pages? Which is not unusual. But a lot of it would be, "this is where we put the footage from this movie."[9]

As for the dialogue itself, she cringes, responding in exaggerated, cartoonish fashion:

> Oh, what did you think when you heard that Shauna was killed? I thought that was really SAD. And it made me really MAD. Because I thought, maybe I could have TALKED to Shauna. Maybe that would've HELPED. She probably had some psychological problems. I think she was a TROUBLED GIRL.[10]

Dialogue in adult films is often considered an afterthought, and it's worth noting that Findlay's scripts—often self-penned—are deliberately over-wrought, humorous or camp. But she is clearly an educated writer, often calling back to earlier literary styles and modes of storytelling. Additionally, based on interviews, she was much more interested in writing and directing dialogue scenes than the sex scenes. "She could never encourage people to be erotic," says Cirile. "She'd say, 'Okay, fuck for like three and a half minutes while I have a smoke.'"[11] The privileged position of dialogue and voice-over in Findlay's films is not just something later academic analysis pointed out; while filming the epistolary framing device for *New York City Woman* (1977)—in which John Holmes recites his inner thoughts to a reel-to-reel tape recorder as transitions to sex scenes inserted from other films—he asked Findlay, "What are you, a dialogue freak?"

In *Shauna: Every Man's Fantasy* the sex scenes are not even separated from the dialogue scenes; in some cases, as with the first interview subject, Karen Summer, the interview takes place simultaneously with fellatio, penetration, and orgasm. Findlay's logocentric approach stems from her earlier period of roughie filmmaking with then-husband Michael Findlay; take, for example, the Findlays' *Take Me Naked* (1966), wherein the poetry of Pierre Louÿs is read salaciously aloud while visual perversities play out onscreen. But exploitation films were in a conversation with other kinds of cinema; as with many avant-garde and experimental films in the 1960s and 1970s, the period Findlay was most active, budgets often limited the use of sync sound, and so the two modes of filmmaking share a reliance on voice-over. There is an important difference, however: whether that dialogue is meant to add colorful poetic abstraction, or to clarify something that can't be depicted for budgetary reasons.

In Susan Sontag's 1967 essay "The Aesthetics of Silence" she writes about the tendency of mid-century modern art toward obfuscation, something that frequently frustrated audiences who found the deliberate abstraction of communication "an aggression against them."[12] If highbrow cinema was "withholding," then exploitation cinema countered this with a directness and accessibility that appealed to audiences who felt snubbed by the methods of "intellectual" art. The Findlays' films lay somewhere in between, birthed in the landscape of exploitation but with apparent literary and artistic ambitions. That these films reached for "legitimacy" through such artistic choices remains a notion met with derision by Roberta Findlay—in one interview she dismissed Louÿs as a "French hack writer" that Michael was obsessed with[13]— but these films were clearly susceptible to the cultural conversations happening around them, and like many underground and experimental films of the time, they blended sensationalism with criticism and poetry.

Though she pinned Louÿs on Michael, these literary pretensions continue into Roberta Findlay's solo hardcore work. Her film *Mystique* (1980), a surrealistic film about a terminally ill woman in a power struggle with a sadistic shadow-spirit, opens with the last two verses of French poet Paul Valéry's 1922 sonnet "Le Vin Perdu":

> One day into the sea I cast
> (But where I cannot now divine)
> As offering to oblivion,
> My small store of precious wine . . .
>
> What, oh rare liquor, willed your loss?
> Some oracle half understood?
> Some hidden impulse of the heart
> That made the poured wine seem like blood?
>
> From this infusion of smoky rose
> The sea regained its purity,
> Its usual transparency . . .
>
> Lost was the wine, and drunk the waves!
> I saw high in the briny air
> Forms unfathomed leaping there.

Though less obvious in *Mystique*'s truncated version, the sonnet is a fitting prelude to a film about a woman who goes to the sea to die, and aligns with the images of suicidal women that haunt Findlay's work (she recalled Walter Sear saying of the script, "Man, nothing sexier than a woman dying of cancer").[14] Though penned by Roger Watkins (under the name Richard Mahler), Findlay cited *Mystique* as tapping into many of her personal fantasies and anxieties, and admitted to interviewer Jill C. Lewis that she got "carried away with a poem by Paul Valéry,"[15] revealing that the poem itself was brought to the project by Findlay.

Likewise, Findlay's tendency to include voice-over persisted in her work beyond the limitations of sync sound; it may well have been a technique first tapped out of necessity, but it became an aesthetic stamp. Immediately before the Valéry poem is inscribed across the screen, *Mystique* opens with a voice-over. Like Joyce James in *Shauna: Every Man's Fantasy*, the voice is authoritative and didactic, drawing from the tradition of square-ups, those moralistic preambles in exploitation films masked as instructional aids.[16] Similarly, the narration signposts for the audience that they are about to embark on a mystery about the secret passions of a woman. "Together, let us explore what is true, and what is ambiguity," the voice implores. "Is it all an illusion in the mind's eye?"

In Findlay's films, she would often perform this voice-over herself. Whether playing an offscreen mom in *Anyone But My Husband* or a dramatic narrator in *The Clamdigger's Daughter*, Findlay's voice is present in her films in more ways than one. When her voice stands in for interviewer Joyce James, in *Shauna: Every Man's Fantasy*—neither could recall which lines were said by whom—it blurs the lines of performance and accountability. Are the questions being asked those of the concerned interviewer or the exploitive director?

Further, this logocentricity and the mediating presence of the director's voice connects Findlay's work to the essay film—which, as André Bazin wrote, "privileges language over image"[17]—and in the case of *Shauna: Every Man's Fantasy*, the argument could be made that the film is more essay film than documentary. But the essay film is deeply entwined with the epistolary film—scholar Laura Rascaroli wrote that "the letter is at the heart of the tradition of essay filmmaking"[18] film—a form that Findlay has overtly referenced in interviews, specifically regarding her 1972 film, *Rosebud*.

"Have you ever read *Clarissa*?" she asked Ashley West of *The Rialto Report*, referring to *Clarissa; or, The History of a Young Lady: Comprehending the Most Important Concerns of Private Life. And Particularly Shewing, the Distresses that May Attend the Misconduct Both of Parents and Children, In Relation to Marriage*, an eighteenth-century epistolary novel by the English writer Samuel Richardson. "I don't know why that one stuck in my mind, but I adored it!" Findlay laughs when I ask her about it (before excitedly adding that she is obsessed with the nineteenth-century English writer Anthony Trollope and has read every one of his fifty-odd novels). References like these belie Findlay's attempts to downplay the impact of her education on her films, but also help to explain the innate hybridity of her work. An epistolary novel is one that is comprised of various texts and documents, letters, diary entries, newspaper clippings and so on. Other famous epistolary novels include *Letters of a Portuguese Nun* (1669), which would later be adapted by exploitation filmmaker Jess Franco—well known for a cultural literacy that sometimes belied the "cheap" genres he worked in—*Fanny Hill* (1748), also an exploitation film staple, and *Les Liaisons dangereuses* (1782). Even *Dracula* is an epistolary novel, entirely comprised of letters, ship's logs, diary entries, and telegrams.

Such autobiographical and/or literary devices are common textual tools in Findlay's films. "Well, that's a good format," she concedes. "In the very, very beginning with Allan Shackleton, he wouldn't give me enough money for live sound. So, I have to make special devices, a diary, voice-over or whatever to get around the fact that there was no sound, I couldn't afford it. So, you can't have people talking to each other, you have to do something, put a frame on the darn thing. But yes, epistolary novels are great fun."[19]

Rosebud, in particular, stands as an important key here.

Like *Shauna: Every Man's Fantasy*, *Rosebud* begins with a suicide. In particular, it begins with a suicide note, in the form of a reel-to-reel tape, creating a diegetic logic for *Rosebud*'s voice-over (a voice-over that is again performed by Roberta Findlay herself). Rosebud is in love with her playboy father, with whom she has a sexual relationship. "I realized as I was dying that I had a sickness. I loved too much and too well. I loved the wrong person. I loved Daddy . . ." she begins. "This is a story of a searching for forgetfulness, the only way I knew how—through sex." Distraught by his refusal to give up other women, she runs away from home, and here we see the film's second instance of the epistolary address in the form of her runaway letter, where she writes of living as a vagrant, seeking anonymity.

What makes the epistolary tradition enticing for a filmmaker like Roberta Findlay, especially in the service of sex films, is the implied intimacy of the letter, the diary, and the oral storyteller. "The letter is, like the diary, a form that radically mixes and merges private notations and commentary on public matters," notes Rascaroli, "the record of both everyday life and momentous events, thus lending to the epistolary essay film its hybrid approach."[20]

While it's easy to see Findlay's use of the epistolary form as a gimmick common among sexploitation filmmakers, it becomes another way Roberta Findlay is a pioneer in her field. For, while the epistolary film was not uncommon prior to the 1970s, the "women's epistolary film"—which has been defined as an epistolary film made by a woman and centering the female experience—has been credited to Chantal Akerman and Agnès Varda, for films such as Akerman's *Je, tu, il, elle* (1974) and *News From Home* (1977) and Varda's *L'une chante, l'autre pas*, also 1977—all of which materialized several years after Findlay's *Rosebud*. While *Rosebud* follows a clear exploitation formula (girl runs away from home, loses herself in empty sex, dies tragically), its depiction of female alterity is clearly in line with Akerman's, despite being taken less seriously given its lack of an arthouse pedigree.

As scholar Lourdes Monterrubio Ibanez muses in her 2021 journal piece on women's epistolary cinema, "women's epistolary practices delve into the exploration of intimate space, authorial vindication, epistolary materiality, intersubjectivity, and cinematic thinking to create diverse experiences of female alterity, developing this postmodern paradigm inherent to epistolary device."[21] While Ibanez's essay is focused on francophone filmmakers—to Akerman and Varda she also adds Marguerite Duras's *Aurelia Steiner* (1979) as a key film—these women were working in a milieu that included Chris Marker and Jean-Luc Godard, who had made epistolary films previously with *Letter from Siberia* (1958) and *Letters to Jane* (1972) respectively, and so if one argues that Findlay was mining a familiar format adopted by male filmmakers via things like *Fanny Hill*, the same could be said about the lineage from Marker and Godard to Akerman, Varda, and Duras. There is an artistic continuity in both instances. *Rosebud* even stands up to an argument that women's epistolary cinema often stars the directors themselves as performers; it is Findlay, after all, who provides Rosebud's voice in the film.

Rosebud is not the only time Findlay used the epistolary format; *New York City Woman* (1977) is framed as a replay of events described in John Holmes's diary, and like *Shauna: Every Man's Fantasy* is comprised of footage from other films. These films, as well as Findlay's films that are framed by therapy sessions, such as *Altar of Lust* (1971) or *Anyone But My Husband* (1975), enunciate a means of "recall" and preservation of memory. In all cases there is the implication of an addressee: a recipient of the letter, a hearer of the tape, an ultimate audience for the story. The format creates a sense of intimacy while also emphasizing the distance between the writer and the receiver. While from a practical perspective the epistolary form allows Findlay to fill in gaps for anything she doesn't have the budget to shoot, it also allows for a narrative that sometimes runs counter to the imagery and its context of a hardcore sex film, which is something that certainly comes into play with *Shauna: Every Man's Fantasy*. And as scholar Rebecca Ann Sheehan points out, the use of the epistolary form often accompanies a displacement of the subject—they are away from home, traveling, lost.[22]

HYBRID FORMS AND UNSAFE SPACES

In addition to a textual layering, there is also a layering of film genres. Many modes of filmmaking—from exploitation ballyhoo, to strategic television formula to avant-garde and experimental cinema—converge in Findlay's work.

Recycling footage from other films is a tradition that goes back to the exploitation cinema of the 1920s, as historian Eric Schaefer has pointed out, using examples such as Samuel Cummins's *The Naked Truth* (1924), S. S. Millard's *Is Your Daughter Safe?* (1927), and Dale Sonney's *Hell-A-Vision* (1936).[23] It was a tradition that Roberta Findlay gleefully seized upon. Footage is shared between *Kinky Tricks* (1977), *From Holly with Love* (1978), and *Mystique* (1979); footage from *Sweet, Sweet Freedom* (1976) was edited into *Underage* (1977), and the list goes on. Sometimes she could shave enough recycled footage and outtakes to emerge with what she called "a free film," a composite stitched together with the slightest of added framing devices. Two such films predated *Shauna*: the aforementioned *New York City Woman* (1977) features footage from *Fringe Benefits* (1974) and *Anyone But My Husband* (1975), while *Beach House* (1980) recycles footage from *Anyone But My Husband* (1975), *Underage* (1977), *A Woman's Torment* (1977), and *From Holly with Love* (1978). All of this repurposed footage is held together with an establishing shot of the house and a single setup of the women seated in the living room around a fire.

What distinguishes the exploitation film usage of recycled footage from the higher aspirations of the compilation film pioneered by Soviet filmmaker/editor Esther Schub with something like *The Fall of the Romanov Dynasty* (1927) is that in the latter, the archival nature of the footage is never obscured, and is in fact often announced, whereas in the exploitation tradition its origin and prior usage is disguised. There is often no discernible temporal disparity and the films are marketed and sold as entirely new films. According to scholar Jay Leyda, whose 1964 book *Films Beget Films* remains the seminal work on compilation films, to disguise the origin of the footage is to neutralize much of its ironic power.

Such irony, absent in Findlay's earlier "free films," would be restored in *Shauna: Every Man's Fantasy*, which has a more ambitious structure that goes beyond her usual mashup of outtakes. Clips of Shauna Grant are acknowledged openly as artifacts from the past, but while the film is presented as a documentary (Findlay seemed surprised by this: "I didn't realize it was a documentary, but I guess that's what you'd call it. Okay"[24]), its questionable verisimilitude places it in more direct conversation with archival fabrications such as mock-documentary or Mondo, where audiences are "tricked" into understanding the footage as "real."

There are many exploitation/documentary hybrid films predating *Shauna*: Shaun Costello's *Forced Entry* (1973) features real Vietnam footage intercut with New York Street scenes; Alex de Renzy's *Animal Lover* (1972), with Bodil Joensen, combined hardcore bestiality with documentary; Bonnie Sherr Klein's documentary *Not A Love Story* (1981) contained so much transgressive sexual material that its anti-porn message notoriously backfired; and Shauna Grant herself had starred in Bobby Hollander's *Paper Dolls* (1984), a documentary about the sex industry that combined interviews with staged pornographic scenes. Most significant for comparison here is Andrzej Kostenko and Karl Martine's *Confessions of a Blue Movie Star* aka *The Evolution of Snuff* (1978), a documentary about the sex industry in Germany that features several staged sequences, most notably a "snuff" coda at the end, which repurposes footage from Wes Craven's *Last House on the Left*. Adult performer Claudia Fielers committed suicide during the shooting of the film, and tabloid news coverage of her death and photos of her grave and her family are juxtaposed with moralistic voice-over not unlike that of *Shauna: Every Man's Fantasy*. This hybrid structure was a staple of the mid-century exploitation era, with square-ups and white-coaters galore, and notably the aforementioned Mondo cycle, most with a contrived "social purpose" attributed to the salacious material under investigation.

The proliferation of the Mondo film was indebted to changes in the portability of television news camera gear that allowed greater mobility for ethnographically minded filmmakers (although it still wasn't *that* portable, ask Roberta Findlay), and other changes in television news formatting throughout the 1970s would also prove an influence on *Shauna: Every Man's Fantasy*, however unconscious.

In the wake of the Watergate scandal, journalists reasserted their commitment to journalistic integrity and began a stream of Special Reports, such as "The Selling of the Pentagon" (1971) and "You and the Commercial" (1973), a CBS exposé on how commercials—which basically paid for the news to exist—were engineered to manipulate consumers (perhaps not unlike a triple-X film that asks the question "Can porn kill?").[25] At the local news level there was the rise of *Eyewitness News*, with sensationalist crusaders like Geraldo Rivera, who won a Peabody Award for his WABC report on patient abuse at the Willowbrook Sanitarium. Joyce James's line of questioning into the dangers of the porn industry, and even her manner and delivery, align with Rivera's persona in the 1970s—which would only get even more exaggerated and abrasive as he reached his peak in the 1980s talk show era.

But while the television news—especially the confronting vox pop immediacy of its 1970s incarnation—would prove an aesthetic influence on Mondo-type documentaries, what separated Mondo from real reporting was the staging. And this it shares with *Shauna: Every Man's Fantasy*: contrived scenarios, scripted dialogue, dramatizations, and a confusing blend of truth and fabrication. At one point in the film, actress Karen Summers is interviewed about her first experience in the industry. She then recalls the tale through flashback, playing a "younger" version of herself, and is accompanied by a friend (played by Amber Lynn) to an audition with an established producer that quickly escalates to a threesome. But then the "producer" from the flashback does a seated interview about his experience directing Shauna Grant before her death; "I loved her," he says, summoning false reticence. "When Shauna and I first met, she came on the set—no makeup, her hair hanging straight down her back, blue denim jacket—she was the All-American girl gone hardcore." Except the role is played by an actor (Jay Serling), and his character is entirely fictional. And yet the staging and framing for his interview is identical to that of the other seated interviews in the film; the film breaks its own rules of authenticity. There are several moments like this in the film that destabilize our perception of which aspects of the film are real and what insights have bearing on the real Shauna Grant.

This incorporation of re-enactments in which real-life participants step into a fictional context to examine traumatic past events is not unique to *Shauna: Every Man's Fantasy*, but it is the one I've encountered in which the lines between reality and fabrication are the most frustratingly obfuscated. The year before *Shauna*'s release saw the television debut of *Victims for Victims: The Theresa Saldana Story*, in which actress Theresa Saldana herself reenacts her horrific multiple-stabbing by a crazed fan. Earlier, Martha Coolidge's hybrid documentary *Not a Pretty Picture* (1976) depicts her onscreen staging a reen-actment of her own rape in high school by a classmate. The film combines drama with scenes of Coolidge and her actors examining the motives of the "characters," together with straight interview footage. As Coolidge herself asserted, "the breaking up of the story between narrative and documentary allows the audience to examine the motives, ramifications and the effects of the event without turning the rape into an 'action scene.'"[26] Coolidge also points out that at the time of release her film was referred to as a "Brechtian" exercise, and this critical reference becomes interesting in light of *Shauna: Every Man's Fantasy* as well.

Roberta Findlay often toyed with ironic juxtaposition, usually for comic effect; for example, the opening sequence of *Anyone But My Husband* (1975) features an extramarital sex scene playing against neglected housewife C. J. Laing in the kitchen, stuffing various shaft-like vegetables into the orifice of a chicken she is preparing for her unfaithful husband.[27] While ironic juxta-position between the spoken text and the visual text has a deliberately jarring quality, in *Shauna: Every Man's Fantasy* it feels even more disruptive, because it makes the audience complicit in something that transgresses moral bound-aries, in a way that is much more common in confrontational avant-garde and experimental film. "While the verbal narrative gives us these heartfelt clichés," writes scholar Thomas S. Johnson of *Shauna: Every Man's Fantasy*, "the visual text disturbs them."[28]

Juxtaposition is a key alienation device in many experimental theater and film theories, such as the Brechtian concept of *Verfremdungseffekt*, or the "estrangement effect," which seeks to shatter the empathetic bond that typical entertainment invites audiences to share with the characters of the drama.[29] It calls attention to its own artifice, creating a critical distance. As Johnson points out above, the incongruous relationship between the film's text and images in *Shauna: Every Man's Fantasy* has a similar effect, inviting active criticism rather than passive enjoyment. While Joyce James's direct address appeals to the emotions—particularly sadness and outrage—the onscreen imagery contrasts this text with orgasmic ecstasy. In the space between lies humor, which is perhaps what Roberta Findlay excels at most of all.

Each layer of the film dismantles the other layers; Joyce James's interrogation of moral responsibility dismantles the possibility of arousal, and the humor dismantles the possibility of earnestness. The intertextuality and its complicated construction dismantle what a porno film is and what it is supposed to do. "*Shauna* . . . uses biting visual irony to create a travesty of bourgeois sentimentality in its verbal text," writes Johnson, and this attack on bourgeois sensibilities aligns Findlay's work further with the traditions of the avant-garde.[30] Findlay disputes this notion. "I was just trying to put the thing together for expediency," she protests. "You're giving me a much higher motivation. I don't think I had any motivation at all."[31]

What resounds about the film is how unsafe it feels: you never know where it's going to go, and its content makes constant reference to real harm—a shotgun blast no less—to a physical body that is simultaneously presented for arousal. But it is not *Forced Entry* or *Wet Wilderness*, where what you see is what you get. It feels like an experimental prank, defiantly lacking in the compassion it urges viewers to consider.

Joan Hawkins writes of the performance or documentation of actual harm as a key element that aligns experimental art with documentary and pornography, referencing Yoko Ono's *Rape* (1969) and Mitchell Block's *No Lies* (1973) as examples of films that cross boundaries of privacy and compassion.[32] She talks about Ono's "Cut-Piece" in which the artist sits passively while the audience is invited to strip away at her clothing with a provided pair of scissors, which implicates them in real or potential violence.[33] Similarly, the documentary structure of *Shauna: Every Man's Fantasy* disrupts its potential to titillate and implicates the audience in Shauna's death. Since it was marketed as a regular pornographic film, there are certain expectations (to be entertained and/or aroused) that are—as Hawkins says of Ono's piece—"thwarted." In Ono and Lennon's *Rape*, a cameraman is hired to follow a random woman until she feels cornered. While the woman was later revealed not to be random—she was set up by her sister, whom she was visiting in London—the cameraman follows her right into her apartment, blocks her from accessing the phone, and, unable to speak English, she eventually collapses into a corner, terrified. Hawkins writes: "Ethical considerations become the structuring absence in a film that appears to purposely ignore and confuse categories such as observational and interactive, life and art, public and private."[34] When questioned about the film in a press conference, Ono told the reporters to "leave our morals alone." To

Ono, to Findlay, to many artists, there is compartmentalization, transgression, and re-compartmentalization.[35]

To aid in this compartmentalization, Findlay even throws in a therapy sequence. It is a method of critical distance she employs in other films such as *Altar of Lust* and *Anyone But My Husband*. Although common in sexploitation as a gateway for fantasy scenarios, in *Shauna* it performs double-duty, interrogating the industry's potential for trauma while delivering visually on that industry's obligation to the audience. Rachel Ashley plays a therapist specializing in sexual disorders who weighs in on the possible issues Shauna brought with her into the adult industry. She analyzes Shauna's blowjobs, concluding that Shauna "did not allow herself to release when she made love." She describes, and then illustrates, her recommended personal method of "mobilization therapy," a type of physical roleplay in which the therapist has sex with the patient to unlock the baggage causing their repression. This is similar to the function of therapy in *Altar of Lust*, but in the case of *Shauna*, Rachel Ashley's direct address to the camera is a claim of veracity that involves the audience in her findings.

Many writers who examine Roberta Findlay's work take on a similar role: that of therapist trying to unlock the secrets of this enigmatic character. The writing focuses on her contradictions as a woman while often dismissing the films themselves, which is a mistake; are there not things in those films that provide answers? While Findlay dismisses critical readings of her films, when I recite some of their synopses back to her she admits, "Oh gosh. They all sound terribly depressing. I guess I'm a depressive character. Well, that's me. I can't help it. You know, it's part of me, I guess, since I made the pictures."[36] *Shauna: Every Man's Fantasy* is aligned with Findlay's past work both in terms of its suicidal protagonist and its intertextual structure. If one can get past its ethical implications (as I did only on repeated viewings), it is ultimately an ambitious and fascinating film. Cirile, however, is not so sure. "I guess there's a way to make a documentary that has sex footage," she concedes. "I'm sure there is a way to do that. And some people would think it's not tasteful and others would think, well, that's artistic—but it's all in the intent. And that most certainly was not her intent."[37]

Intent has never been a subject about which Findlay minced any words. "I feel no moral responsibility at all to anybody ever," Findlay said in a press interview for her horror film, *The Oracle*, made the same year as *Shauna*. "I have a responsibility to make money and to keep making movies."[38] This refusal of accountability extends to any sympathy for the real Shauna Grant, a person she knew and worked with. While Shauna Grant evoked no particular ire from Findlay, the latter's distaste for women is something she has directly confirmed in multiple interviews, including my own. Such pronouncements are softened when speaking to female interviewers; for example, compare her slightly conciliatory tone in a 2017 interview with Alison Nastasi to a 2012 interview with *Third Eye Cinema*, in which she admitted that she finds pleasure in images of women being beaten, raped and otherwise degraded.[39] My own experience aligns with Cirile's in that Findlay was friendly and funny when I spoke to her. In fact, her frankness is hilarious, disarming and somewhat endearing. That Findlay is a feminist is without doubt given her pioneering role in cinema, and the centrality of women's health and pleasure in many of her films, but she is not like any feminist you ever met.

The thing is, Roberta Findlay may be a woman, but she is an exploitation director by trade and her decisions in *Shauna* are ultimately no more shocking than those of the Jewish David F. Friedman touring around carnivals with Holocaust footage. If your goals are to make as much money as possible with as little overhead as possible, then these are smart business ideas. And Findlay would not be the only one in the porn industry to be guided by such ideas in the wake of Shauna Grant's death.

EXQUISITE CORPSE: THE INDUSTRY RESPONDS

On May 6, 1984, the *Los Angeles Times* published a major article on Shauna's death, after which "a media battle began to define the public meaning and purpose of her life and death, and through that, the place of the industry in the cultural and economic life of Los Angeles and the country."[40]

Actor Jerry Butler, who had starred opposite Shauna in Roberta Findlay's *Glitter*, wrote an incendiary tell-all autobiography called *Raw Talent* in which he reflects back on Shauna Grant's death, and speaks out against Findlay's recycling of his scenes from *Glitter* for *Shauna: Every Man's Fantasy*. "I was very against doing the film; because I felt they were using a dead woman to make money, not to tell what a porno star's life is really like," he says. "I lost a lot of respect for Roberta when she did that *Shauna* film—especially because it had such a sick, sleazy feeling."[41]

One of the only academic works to exist on *Shauna: Every Man's Fantasy* is Thomas S. Johnson's impassioned essay "Feeding on Shauna Grant," about the industry's cannibalistic response to Shauna's death.[42] He likens Findlay's documentary to a display of necrophilia and cannibalism, noting that the porn media were quick to "fall onto Shauna's blood-spattered body and immerse themselves, and their viewers, in a self-consuming ritual feast over the freshly disinterred corpse."[43]

"Shauna was beautiful," says performer Kelly Nichols in Legs McNeil's *The Other Hollywood*, "and she made great print."[44] In the wake of her death and throughout the rest of the decade came a wave of retrospective articles, video compilations, and more. In the *Los Angeles Times* listing for Findlay's film when it opened in local Pussycat theaters, the blurb—it's clear the writer hadn't seen the film—noted that "her earlier films are playing on adult TV channels across the country. Tower Videos on Sunset Boulevard displays a special Shauna Grant collection."[45] As David Jennings points out in his book *Skinflicks*: "The 'previously unreleased stills' in *Gourmet*'s $40 magazine 'Inside Shauna Grant' featured harshly lit 'out-take' shots. *Cinema Blue* magazine put together a 'Shauna Grant Memorial' issue, digging up enough old photos of the late star to fill 16 pages."[46]

This *Cinema Blue* 'Shauna Grant Memorial Issue' of September 1984 has been digitized and made available in full on the *Rialto Report* website. In many ways it is a typical example of a porno mag from the era, if you ignore the oppressive cloud of suicide hanging over it. Several assertions are made in the editorial that the tribute is "very tastefully done," though as in Findlay's film, the eulogizing text is contrasted with hardcore imagery and bawdy wordplay.[47] Shauna even appears in a column entitled, "Yesterday's Porn Stars: Where Are They Now?"[48] "A tribute to the most beautiful woman ever to spread her thighs on film," the memorial article begins. "Yes, it's really true, Shauna Grant, the incredibly lovely, creamy-faced blonde with the prettiest pussy in the world, is dead."[49] The piece continues to articulate its appreciation of her in this way, while ironically pointing out that the "producers and distributors of X-rated material will continue to make dollar upon dollar on Shauna's perky tits, her lovely face, and that indescribably scrumptious ass."[50]

When I remind Cirile of her substantial role, not just in Findlay's film, but as the editor of the Shauna Grant issue of *Cinema Blue*, she explains she was still expected to operate within the limitations of an existing formula, especially if it was a high-profile issue like the Shauna tribute, and that being editor of the magazine didn't necessarily ensure *carte blanche* on the content:

> With all the magazines . . . you could pretty much write whatever you want, but every once in a while, someone would actually look. So, if they looked down at a page, there had better be a lot of keywords that are dirty, that they recognize. And every third page, you better have somebody giving a blow job. So, what I tried to do was create some kind of balance, and even to create a jarring lack of balance, where you get something on the left panel like . . . "The woman with the golden snatch has now been snatched from us!" And then, you know, a full page of her giving a blow job. And it's against the grain, but I think it's interesting intellectually to juxtapose things and to present things that are so obviously other.[51]

While Findlay historically used ironic juxtaposition, a mainstay of black humor, in her work, as we have seen, it seems that in this manner she and Cirile were aligned. Cirile, though, maintains her own use of it is much more conscious and calculated to achieve a certain effect. "I still think, although this could be really ass-backward thinking, that when you get someone's attention with sex, then there's any number of other things that you can also bring to their attention that might be—in your mind—good for them to know," she says. "Like you can get a point in, you can get in a quote from your favorite writer, little messages like, 'Can porn kill?', in a porn film!"[52]

It is the same question asked by the PBS *Frontline* documentary "Death of a Porn Queen" in 1987, produced by Colleen Applegate's regional station, WCCO-TV in Minneapolis. In fact, both films start so similarly that it immediately invites a challenge to the sincerity of the *Frontline* special. "This is the story of an ordinary young woman who wandered into a strange world . . . and died," says *Frontline* host Judy Woodruff, before passing the reins of this special report to what appears to be an all-male team. "In that one year Colleen performed in 30 X-rated movies," the reporter chides. "She had an abortion. She contracted herpes. She performed on camera with 37 men." The *Frontline* documentary may not juxtapose eulogizing with penetration shots, but it certainly doesn't tastefully hold back. Nevertheless, when it debuted in June 1987, the *LA Times* praised it for covering the story "simply, movingly and unsensationally"—even as they visit the evidence locker to show off the actual rifle that she used to kill herself and reenact how she did it.[53]

Director Bobby Hollander—who christened Colleen Applegate with the name we know her by—refers to Shauna as a "Jekyll and Hyde" type character, and the dualistic notion that Colleen Applegate and Shauna Grant are distinct and even conflicting personas, underscores the whole special. "These are like the belongings of two people," the reporter comments, looking through the things she left behind at a former apartment, "When did one person become the other?" The film gathers a different cast of characters than Findlay's film, among them Laurie Smith, makeup artist, onetime roommate and close friend of Shauna Grant, who dropped out of the industry after Shauna's death. Smith states that Shauna did not enjoy doing sex pictures—or having sex, period. "She hated it," Smith says, "She just lied there and let it happen." This corroborates what Jerry Butler says in his autobiography *Raw Talent*, describing Shauna as "a reluctant partner onscreen," and "a pillowy mannequin who looked prettier wearing clothes."[54] Butler also appears in the *Frontline* special, speaking somewhat venomously about the industry and its exploitation of this clearly reluctant young girl.

The 1988 made-for-TV biopic *Shattered Innocence*, in which participants are given fake names and some characters are condensed for expediency, seizes upon Shauna's financial problems and the pressures of externally fueled shame from parents, old high school friends, and anti-porn protesters as the source of her anguish. But here Shauna is presented as a bratty teen, who wants her own way and will lie to get it, thinking nothing of the consequences. If anything, it reinforces photographer Steve Hicks's assertion in the *Frontline* special that an eighteen-year-old is not emotionally equipped to handle major decisions, but does not invite sympathy for Shauna Grant as an individual.

Likewise, sympathy for Shauna Grant is not something that *Shauna: Every Man's Fantasy* genuinely attempts. A long-standing rumor holds that Roberta Findlay was ostracized from the industry after making the film. As Jill C. Nelson reports in her book *Golden Goddesses*,

> Some industry insiders believed Findlay's final adult submission, *Glitter* [sic], effectively ended her association with the pornographic movie business as the feature resulted in some disgruntled campers when it was perceived Findlay's intentions to make the Shauna Grant picture were less than compassionate.[55]

But while such reports have persisted, they do not hold up to scrutiny.

When the film was released in August 1985, every newspaper ad billed it as a regular porn film starring Shauna Grant rather than as a documentary, and its grim investigation not even hinted at. There aren't many reviews of *Shauna: Every Man's Fantasy* in adult publications that survive from the time, but Findlay doesn't recall any controversy surrounding the film; in fact, she remembers that the film performed as well as any of her other pictures despite its depressing subject matter.[56] Likewise, while Cindy Cirile was no longer editing *Cinema Blue* by the time the film was made, she recalls no such backlash against Findlay.[57] But perhaps such rumors can be dispelled most authoritatively by the fact that Findlay did not actually stop working in the adult market after *Shauna*; she went on to make several more adult films (more on these in the interview with Findlay that appears at the conclusion of this volume), while transitioning willingly to the horror market:

> I don't remember anybody saying that that's disgraceful or anything. We kept shooting dirty movies. The reason we stopped was that video just had started coming in. And our main source of income was, believe it or not, domestic theatrical, and all the theaters started changing over. They didn't need prints anymore. They just went to the video store and rented a cassette. And so, all that royalty, they didn't bother paying. And what were we going to do? Sue 300, 500 theaters or however many there were? No, no. That's why we stopped.[58]

Whatever *Shauna: Every Man's Fantasy* ended up contributing to Shauna Grant's legacy, Cirile laments that an opportunity was missed:

> The film [could have been] more high class, more empathetic, like the porn business embracing one of its own and seeking to truly know what

happened to her and grieving her. Because honestly that's what was going on . . . people were so upset because she really had something. I don't know, maybe it was a certain air of something, maybe an air of melancholy? Like she's kind of untouchable. For all the things that she did that were so "penetrating," she herself seemed like you couldn't really get near her. There was definitely a wall up. So, I think a lot of people felt that.

Actors Kelly Nichols and Tim Connelly were both on set for *Matinee Idol*, the Ron Sullivan/Henri Pachard film that Shauna was set to appear in at the time of her death, and they were with her best friend, makeup artist Laurie Smith, in the immediate aftermath of the event. "Any time a girl dies, it's like a little piece of us dies," said Nichols in Legs McNeil's *The Other Hollywood*. "It feels a little like, if we're not careful, that could be us." Connolly agreed: "Shauna's was the first death by suicide in the industry, and it really had an impact. I mean, it was like there was a huge cloud hanging in the air. Things got kind of weird."[59]

Grant's death was not actually the first suicide in the pornographic industry at large—Germany's Claudia Fielers and the UK's Mary Millington both predate Shauna in 1975 and 1979 respectively—but it was the first high-profile case stateside, and a sobering event that figures in the autobiographies of many adult film performers of the time, including those of Hyapatia Lee and Jerry Butler. "Shauna was the fragile kind of girl you expected suicide from, sooner or later," Jerry Butler wrote in *Raw Talent*. "She was a victim: of sex, of the industry, of herself." While he recalls her with a certain flippancy betraying the high moral ground he takes throughout the book, he does acknowledge that a year after her death he suddenly broke down crying in the street. "Maybe time and distance helped me see the pure sadness of it all," he writes, "whatever anybody in this business goes through, whether it be suicide, AIDS, or drugs, we ALL go through."[60]

Shauna Grant would never escape her own image, which was rendered immortal with her death. But just as that image was etched onto film and then projected for her audience, so too did that audience, and her colleagues in the industry, project things onto her. Thomas S. Johnson refers to Findlay's film as an example of social ritual, in which Shauna Grant is a scapegoat for the ills of the industry,

[who] takes on the guilt of the people, and is sacrificed so the people can cast away their sins and inhibitions, and make their atonement to themselves and their world . . . At the same time, the victim is digested in order that the people may take in and absorb an object of desire, the strength of which becomes a power in them. Finally the remains are eliminated, purging the social body of both its burdening evils and its excessive power, bringing the people back into a state of balance.[61]

The notion of Colleen Applegate/Shauna Grant as a destabilized body of fragments has dominated all discussions of her, and it parallels the hybrid structure of Findlay's film. This compartmentalization also extends to the corporeal in a literal sense: when she died, parts of her were donated; someone out there got Shauna Grant's eyes. I too had to compartmentalize to see *Shauna: Every Man's Fantasy* for what it is: a complicated artifact that reflects rather than reveals. The slivers of Shauna Grant that are refitted to various uses and contexts in the aftermath of her death never uncover any quantifiable whole through which we can claim to know her. Shauna Grant is the ghost of this film; she is the absent subject, a source of fascination, obsession, and ultimately speculation. No one can know what was going on in the mind of Shauna Grant that night in March of 1984. Least of all Roberta Findlay.

NOTES

1. John David Ebert, "On the Metaphysics of Being a Porn Star," *Cinema Discourse*, November 19, 2013, https://cinemadiscourse.com/on-the-metaphysics-of-being-a-porn-star/ (accessed May 26, 2022).
2. Roberta Findlay, personal interview, November 29, 2021.
3. Bravman had been a producer with Ed Adlum for softcore sexploitation films like *Blonde on a Bum Trip*, and was part of the circle that included Adlum and Mike and Roberta Findlay, who worked together on *Invasion of the Blood Farmers*, *Shriek of the Mutilated*, and so on.
4. Findlay, personal interview, November 29, 2021.
5. Cynthia Cirile, personal interview, November 3, 2021.
6. Cynthia Cirile, personal interview, November 3, 2021. Findlay conceded this was probably the origin of the film's core idea. Personal interview, November 29, 2021.
7. Alison Nastasi, "Flavorwire Interview: Exploitation and Adult Cinema Icon Roberta Findlay on Making 'Cheap' Movies, Getting Arrested with John Holmes, and Times Square's X-Rated Past," *Flavorwire*, December 30, 2017, https://www.flavorwire.com/609580/flavorwire-interview-exploitation-and-adult-cinema-icon-roberta-findlay-on-making-cheap-movies-getting-arrested-with-john-holmes-and-times-squares-x-rated-past (accessed May 26, 2022).
8. Cynthia Cirile, personal interview, November 3, 2021.
9. Cynthia Cirile, personal interview, November 3, 2021.
10. Cynthia Cirile, personal interview, November 3, 2021.
11. Cynthia Cirile, personal interview, November 3, 2021.
12. Susan Sontag, "The Aesthetics of Silence" (1967), rpt. in *Styles of Radical Will* (New York: Picador, 2002), 7.
13. "Roberta Findlay: A Respectable Woman," *Rialto Report* podcast interview, July 16, 2015, https://www.therialtoreport.com/2015/08/16/roberta-findlay/ (accessed July 28, 2021).
14. Roberta Findlay, personal interview, November 29, 2021.
15. Jill C. Nelson, *Golden Goddesses: 25 Legendary Women of Classic Erotic Cinema, 1968–1975* (Duncan, OK: BearManor Media, 2012), Kindle Version, Loc 2966.
16. Eric Schaefer, *Bold! Daring! Shocking! True!: A History of Exploitation Films, 1919–1959* (Durham, NC: Duke University Press, 1999), 71–2.
17. André Bazin, quoted in Laura Rascaroli, *How the Essay Film Thinks* (New York: Oxford University Press, 2017), 143.

18. Rascaroli, *How the Essay Film Thinks*, 145.

19. Findlay, personal interview, November 29, 2021.

20. Rascaroli, *How the Essay Film Thinks*, 146.

21. Lourdes Monterrubio Ibanez, "Women's Epistolary Cinema: Exploring Female Alterities: Epistolary Films and Epistolary Essay Films" *Feminist Media Studies* (2021): 1–20, cited at 1.

22. Rebecca Anne Sheehan, "Epistolary Forms and the Displaced Global Subject in recent films by James Benning and Jem Cohen," *Area Abierta* 19, no. 3 (2019): 363–81.

23. Schaefer, *Bold! Daring! Shocking! True!*, 61–2.

24. Findlay, personal interview, November 29, 2021.

25. Charles Ponce de Leon, *That's the Way It Is: A History of Television News in America* (Chicago: University of Chicago Press, 2015).

26. Martha Coolidge, comment on her Vimeo channel, 2014, https://vimeo.com/channels/835478/111304721 (accessed May 26, 2022).

27. Laing even breaks the fourth wall in this picture, demonstrating that Findlay was certainly aware of cinematic conventions and made use of them in her films.

28. Thomas S. Johnson, "Feeding on Shauna Grant: Ritual Cannibalism in Two Documentary Retrospectives" *Journal of Popular Culture* 36, no. 1 (2002): 25–43, cited at 32.

29. Bill Nichols, "Remaking History: Jay Leyda and the Compilation Film," *Film History* 26, no. 4 (2014): 146–56, https://doi.org/10.2979/filmhistory.26.4.146 (accessed May 26, 2022).

30. Johnson, "Feeding on Shauna Grant," 27.

31. Findlay, personal interview, November 29, 2021.

32. Joan Hawkins, *Cutting Edge: Art-Horror and the Horrific Avant-garde* (Minneapolis: University of Minnesota Press, 2000), 117.

33. Hawkins, *Cutting Edge*, 120.

34. Hawkins, *Cutting Edge*, 121.

35. Ono's screen work is directly tied to Findlay through the film eventually released as *Satan's Bed*—a picture starring a then-unknown Ono that was abandoned with a film processing company and sold off cheaply to someone who hired Mike Findlay to shoot some additional exploitation footage and turn it into something. Hawkins notes that this tendency—to salvage old films and repurpose them—gave their films "an oddly surreal, 'exquisite corpse' look and narrative structure that seems equally indebted to Bunuel and Godard and shares attributes with Paul Sharits's and Yoko Ono's Fluxfilms," *Cutting Edge*, 130.

36. Findlay, personal interview, November 29, 2021.

37. Cynthia Cirile, personal interview, November 3, 2021.

38. Candice Russell, "Director Making Gory Movies for Catharsis in hate-Filled Age" *Fort Lauderdale News*, April 13, 1986, 12G.

39. "Roberta Findlay!," *Third Eye Cinema*, June 17, 2012. https://thirdeyecinema.podbean.com/e/third–eye–cinema–61712–with–roberta–findlay/ (accessed May 26, 2022).; Jennifer Moorman, "Women on Top: The Work of Female Pornographers and (S)experimental Filmmakers," (Dissertation, UCLA, 2014), 155.

40. Johnson, "Feeding on Shauna Grant," 32.

31. Jerry Butler, *Raw Talent: The Adult Film Industry As Seen By Its Most Popular Male Star* (Amherst, NY: Prometheus, 1990), 258.

42. One must read the piece with a certain critical distance, as he makes excellent points yet they are buried in inflammatory language that sometimes undermines his otherwise valid observations.

43. Johnson, "Feeding on Shauna Grant," 27.

44. Legs McNeil, *The Other Hollywood: The Uncensored Oral History of the Porn Film Industry* (New York: Regan Books, 2004), 364.

45. John M. Wilson, "Images of Colleen," *Los Angeles Times*, November 3, 1985, 15.

46. David Jennings, *Skinflicks: The Inside Story of the X-Rated Video Industry* (Bloomington, IN: 1stBooks, 2000), 290.

47. Joyce James, "Shauna Entombed: The Legend Lives On," *Cinema Blue*, September 1984 (Shauna Grant Memorial Issue), 6, available at *Rialto Report* library, https://www.therialtoreport.com/2019/06/16/cinema-blue/ (accessed May 26, 2022).

48. Joan Jones, "Yesterday's Porn Stars: Where Are They Now?" *Cinema Blue*, September 1984, 17.

49. "Shauna: We Hardly Knew Ye," *Cinema Blue*, September 1984, 42.

50. "Shauna: We Hardly Knew Ye," *Cinema Blue*, September 1984, 42.

51. Cynthia Cirile, personal interview, November 3, 2021.

52. Cynthia Cirile, personal interview, November 3, 2021. In fact Cindy Cirile has a long career of employing ironic juxtaposition and hiding social or spiritual ideologies behind formulaic scenarios in her writing, her films like *Driller* and the novelization of *The Omega Code*, etc.

53. Howard Rosenberg, "'Death of Porn Queen: Stunning Storytelling," *Los Angeles Times*, June 9, 1987.

54. Butler, *Raw Talent*, 122.

55. Nelson, *Golden Goddesses*, Kindle Version, Loc 3030.

56. Findlay, personal interview, November 29, 2021.

57. Cynthia Cirile, personal interview, November 3, 2021.

58. Findlay, personal interview, November 29, 2021.

59. McNeil, *The Other Hollywood*, 364.

60. Butler, *Raw Talent*, 122.

61. Johnson, "Feeding on Shauna Grant," 30.

CHAPTER 7

Roberta Findlay's Bronx Tale: Notes on *Game of Survival*

Neil Jackson

"It seems like a moral tale to me!"

Roberta Findlay[1]

INTRODUCTION

Game of Survival (aka *Tenement* [1985])[2] stands as a curious test case in the broader sweep of Roberta Findlay's directorial career. As such, the ensuing chapter offers a critical account of its value and importance amid her latter oeuvre, reflecting upon the ways in which specific authorial quirks intersect with commercial and generic imperatives. This isn't necessarily to make a claim for a hitherto unrecognized specimen of exploitation art. On the contrary, it is clear to even the most forgiving spectator that the film is brazen and unapologetic in its salacious appeal, often running roughshod over any conscious (or unconscious) social critique otherwise embedded instinctively within the film. It manages to be both atypical and idiosyncratic, a "late period" work that is part-career anomaly and part-thematic throw-back, providing ample evidence of a filmmaker balancing the demands of the exploitation marketplace with an instinctual eye for the organization of the film's dramatic environment. Its assortment of exploitation cinema conventions serves the material in frequently startling ways, bestowing an alternative shape and form upon Findlay's previous portraits of the poverty, degradation, and disenfranchisement of New York's social outcasts. These were aspects that, perhaps unsurprisingly, went either unremarked or were simply swept aside in its limited and largely negative initial critical appraisal. Therefore, to properly consider its underlying cultural dynamics, it is important to measure them relative to an array of textual and extra-textual elements that reveal several layers of critical potential.

Set in the dilapidated South Bronx area of New York City on the cusp of Mayor Ed Koch's multi-billion-dollar program of urban regeneration in the 1980s, the film focuses upon the terminal conflict between a murderous street gang and a ragged community of tenement dwellers. The sustained and violent attack by the former upon the already fragile security and safety of the latter is centered upon the dominance, reclamation, and symbolic ownership of the building in which the action occurs.

Ashley West has suggested that Findlay's career can be broken down into distinct historical phases and categories:

> the 1960s black and white sexploitation films of her husband, Michael Findlay; the softcore films she made on her own for Allan Shackleton in the 1970s; the long sequence of hardcore films she made with famed New York music studio owner, Walter Sear; and the horror films she directed in the late 1980s.[3]

Conceived, designed, and promoted as an urban action-thriller, *Game of Survival* seems to be a significant authorial outlier amid West's overview, and if we are seeking to discern its place within an even vaguely definable auteur structure, it cannot be comfortably accommodated by his stated categories. Indeed, attempts to identify a structural relativity to the rest of Findlay's output would appear to be a quixotic task. Its chief characteristics are related as much to a melange of genre trends and patterns as they are to any vaguely discernible "personal" investment in the material, although that latter component should by no means be discounted altogether.

On the one hand the film sits conspicuously and uneasily between *The Oracle* (1985), *Blood Sisters* (1987), *Lurkers* (1987), and *Prime Evil* (1988), the horror titles that constitute a significant majority of Findlay's films at this stage of her career. These represented a not quite definitive break from her regular (and usually pseudonymous) assignments in hardcore pornography, where she had established apparent permanence since the mid-1970s.[4] On the other hand, it also marks a return to ideas familiar from prior phases of her work (which she didn't always necessarily direct), in which social privation is amplified by the emotional chaos, violence, and sexual depravity played out by the characters onscreen. While its veneer of social realism distinguishes it from the supernatural horror titles cited above, it is marked by a conceptual and narrative simplicity that develops in tension with its increasingly hyperbolic and confrontational displays of violent action. None of these latter films attained a "prestige" presence in the theatrical market, but they represent Findlay's closest ever brush with the mainstream. She signed the work with her own name, retained professional independence through Reeltime, the production and distribution entity she founded and co-ran with then established partner Walter Sear, and achieved wider exposure in both the domestic and global home video markets.[5]

THE EXPLOITATION GHETTO

The vagaries of exploitation production, promotion, and reception are fundamental to any understanding that we might develop regarding *Game of Survival*'s raw formal strategies and any (even if unintended) socio-cultural outreach it manages to achieve. These are often discussed as typical indicators of "bad" cinematic technique, a self-evident paucity of style and taste eroded further by the varied signifiers of moral derangement. Such aspects frequently mark the surface of *Game of Survival*, and the film compounds such effrontery by refusing elaborate exposition for its outré depictions of social dysfunction. It displays merely perfunctory justification for its graphically (but not always entirely convincingly) rendered presentation of drug addiction, animal slaughter, torture, beating, shooting, stabbing, impalement, throat cutting, slashing, scalding, castration, strangulation, electrocution, and rape. These are typical examples of content that has tended to offend liberal and conservative critical observers alike, lying at the center of affective strategies likely to incite anything from bemused shock through outright condemnation to the type of uncontained hilarity derived from the ironic counter-readings often favored by marginal cult audiences.

These commonly recognized (but methodically restrictive) traits of exploitation cinema have often proved anathema to critics seeking evidence of subtlety, textual unity, coherence, and complexity of expression. They are seen to infuse "low-level" product with an alternative system of articulation, but inevitably shunt it to the margins of acceptance or appreciation. Omayra Cruz has identified "very low budgets, tight production schedules, low paid inexperienced personnel, minimal production values and sensational selling campaigns"[6] as typical characteristics, while Linda Ruth Williams has noted the "sensational, shocking and taboo subjects (violence, perversion, drugs, cruelty, abnormality, sex and its perils)"[7] crucial to the commercial identity of films keen to attain some level of market distinction. *Game of Survival* certainly meets many of the criteria set out by Cruz and Williams (although Findlay was far from being "inexperienced" when she made the film), expanding to some degree upon exploitation tropes that extend as far back as the 1930s. Eric Schaefer has identified that period as the apotheosis of the "classical" exploitation film, during which filmmakers were complicit in "many of [society's] myths about the Other,"[8] a phenomenon defined frequently in terms of its exclusion, denial, and rejection of particular class, ethnic, or gender formations. Any nuanced representation of the "Other" was already acutely vulnerable to the representational demands of the Hollywood Production Code, and the classical exploitation film would merely sidestep or push beyond the code in ways which by no means had progressive or radical alternatives on its mind. All of this tended to display the "Other" primarily in terms of its perceived deviance, regardless of whatever form that happened to take.

Of course, levels of both screen permissiveness and social awareness had transformed radically between the classical exploitation era and the production of *Game of Survival*. The conditions it relentlessly describes have traditionally been the province of social realism, which has sought to form connections between broader socio-political and socio-economic patterns of impact and influence. However, its insistent emphasis upon lives ravaged or affected by poverty, drug abuse, alcoholism, prostitution, rape, sexual aberration, unplanned pregnancy, disability, generational conflict, and a simmering—almost unspoken—racial tension also seems like a compendium of "golden age" exploitation motifs. Here, they have been compacted into one dramatic setting, stripped of the hectoring, disingenuous moral lessons so crucial to the character of classical exploitation and filtered through five decades of tumultuous social and cinematic transformation. Moreover, its "othered" social demographic is isolated further through a confrontation that takes place beyond any form of institutional interest or intervention. Excepting their nominal presence at the beginning of the film, the police are an absent social force, any communication with them neutralized by the gang's cutting of the phone wires that represent the only immediate means of contact with the wider community.

The film never explicitly foregrounds and thematizes the "social problems" so fundamental to the moral fumbling of the classical exploitation film. Instead, they are organized and absorbed into a multi-stranded action narrative, all of which is contained within the physical site of the tenement building that houses the brittle communal bonds of its occupants. To appreciate its apparent indifference to sustained or systematic social commentary, one need only compare the politically charged vision of Spike Lee's *Do the Right Thing* (1989), a film released four years later that went some distance to speak both upfront and beyond its resolution of the multi-layered racial tensions underpinning its Brooklyn-based scenario. Essentially, *Game of Survival*'s entire *dramatis personae* embody the social "Other" in some shape or form, defining both its heroes and villains as outsiders and miscreants. From the basement to the top floor, each apartment space in the building becomes the site of social malady, with each occupant serving as a reminder of the South Bronx's population history. Furthermore, the very idea of a siege serves as a simple but expansive metaphor for the borough's image at the time it was produced, a series of heightened, exaggerated, but threadbare action sketches somehow linked inextricably to dire social reality. This invocation of the siege narrative is founded in historical confrontations that have since passed into myth (such as the 1836 Battle of the Alamo) and that found prior cinematic expression in anything from *Rio Bravo* (1959, dir. Howard Hawks) to *The Alamo* (1960, dir. John Wayne), *Night of the Living Dead* (1968, dir. George Romero), *Straw Dogs* (1971, dir. Sam Peckinpah), *Assault on Precinct 13* (1976, dir. John Carpenter) and *Siege* (1983, dir. Paul Donovan and Maura O'Connell). While the last title is a more immediate contemporary, the shadow of the others looms large, feeding directly into the design and purpose of Findlay's film. Through its self-contained interpretation of this time-worn scenario, the diverse constituents of an oppressed underclass are pitted somewhat paradoxically against each other, a self-defeating, nihilistic process couched in ironies from which the remaining combatants emerge as brutalized but empowered avengers in the final moments.

RESISTANT AUTEUR/RELUCTANT FEMINIST

Alexandra Heller-Nicholas has argued that, regardless of Findlay's three decades of activity as cinematographer, editor, writer, and director, her work offers significant problems for both auteurist and feminist reclamation. She suggests that it is "tempting as a site for retrospective canonization, but the reality of her practice makes such missions difficult to say the least,"[9] querying the assumption that women filmmakers should be obliged to make "progressive" feminist interventions ripe for the appropriation of a radical critical mindset. Any confluence of auteurist and feminist appreciation of Findlay's output would have to concern itself largely with the hardcore and softcore sex films that dominate her filmography. However, while her career developed in synchronicity with feminist film theory and its identification of the dominant male cinematic gaze,[10] Findlay became a model of the underground journeywoman, whose output demonstrated diversity and cack-handedness in equal measure. Put more uncharitably then, she might be described as a professional exploitation hack, moving from project to project while bearing an indifference to sociocultural responsibility, thus inviting a critical separation from those qualities of command, control, and formal rigor demanded for the "auteur" designation.

Out of this, one is tempted to pose the question: should women filmmakers be content just to be "hacks" too? Just as her incursions into pornographic cinema have inspired an oft ill-founded critical debate for feminist reclamation, then one could be forgiven for seeking out a similar "feminine" point of view in *Game of Survival* that might in some way inform its social perspective. Despite its range of female archetypes, it is far from being "female-centered," concentrating its attention instead upon the potentialities of the broader social collective. However, it also allows for the somewhat unorthodox presence of female cast members in the action set-pieces, an inclusive strategy that has the curious result of foregrounding the participation of both infant girls and pregnant or elderly women. Regardless of its narrative outcomes (and the gender makeup of those cast members left standing when the end credits begin to roll), it neither aspires to nor achieves the status of feminist statement, merely allowing for such readings according to whichever character progression one chooses to isolate. While there are thematic elements that have regularly exercised feminist thought (for example, sex work, pregnancy, motherhood and sexual violence), these are absorbed into the general flow of the action, serving more as convenient devices than points of sustained or reflective exploration.

Therefore, any attempt to reclaim Findlay for auteur-feminist discourse is bound to struggle in such a critical and theoretical quagmire. J. R. Taylor has commented that whether one's impulse is toward serious critical appreciation or mere nostalgic affection, the likelihood is that "Roberta Findlay thinks you're crazy."[11] Similarly, Anthony Timpone has argued:

> [we should not] look for any feminist or political statements in Roberta Findlay's horror flicks, unless stabbing a pregnant lady, or the disembowelment of college co-eds by abominable snowmen, or the epic battle between yuppies and the occult really hides some sort of message.[12]

Such comments are wholly indicative of the lowered expectations brought to bear upon any filmmaker working in the exploitation sector. They also demonstrate how readily critical judgment can be brought into line with a professed authorial indifference, a tacit acknowledgment that if the artist doesn't take the work seriously then there is no reason why the spectator or critic should either. While working in the outer reaches of popular culture may have been impedimentary enough, any significant outreach for Findlay's work has been affected further through her status as a female filmmaker working within a resolutely patriarchal infrastructure.

PLAYING THE CRITICAL GAME

The film's alternative title of *Tenement*, adopted for home video release in the United States, points at least ostensibly toward a rudimentary social conscience, prioritizing the building's symbolic importance amid its central narrative conceit. Prior to release however, it was promoted in the trade press as *Game of Survival*, suggesting a generic, action-oriented exercise wherein the "fight to the death" elements have been foregrounded to maximize any commercial potential. The thematic implications of both titles were incorporated succinctly into a trade advertisement in *Variety* on May 1, 1985 (see Figure 7.1). This proclaimed Findlay's authorial status, but misspelled "Laurel Films Inc." (presented on the

Figure 7.1 *Variety*, May 1, 1985.

advertisement as "Laural"), playing directly into the hands of any observer keen to decry some of the shoddier practices of exploitation hucksterism. The illustration neatly condenses the narrative core of the film, prioritizing a cross-section of assorted protagonists and antagonists in their battle to attain dominion of the building, and even pointing to the kind of high concept reductivism that was gathering pace in so many Hollywood films at the same time. The tagline ("The gang is out for blood. Fight back or be killed") merely underscores the motivational *raison d'être*. Emphasizing the race and gender mix among the film's cast, it privileges the figure of the reluctant black male hero as embodied by Sam (Joe Lynn), his defiant stance and posture astride the edge of the rooftop aligning him again not only with the protagonists of *Night of the Living Dead* and *Assault on Precinct 13*, but also in accordance with archetypes familiar from the marketing images of multiple blaxploitation films of the 1970s. In a curious inversion, it also manages to foreground other characters regularly dissociated from such modes of representation, including the infant, Charlie (Jorge Baqueiro), the elderly Jewish woman, Ruth (Mina Bern), the white female sex worker, Carol (Corrine Chateau), and the alcoholic superintendent, Rojas (Larry Lara). While this does not seem to be the consequence of any conscious marketing ploy to expand the promotional or representational parameters of the action film, such a spread of characters in the marketing material seemed to be reaching for a broader commercial appeal that the film itself could not possibly hope to achieve.

Even allowing for its limited theatrical release, reviewer response was unenthusiastic, exemplified by *Variety*'s notice following its Cannes market screening on May 15, 1985:

> [a] bloody, tacky affair without redeeming features . . . Roberta Findlay and her team have provided a ragged, silly pic with copious scenes of stabbing, hacking, shooting and mutilating, none very convincing thanks to poor acting and obvious make-up and effects. It gets to be so bad that even when a gun is fired it sounds more like a cap pistol than the real thing. All pervading sadism of the piece is complemented by the total lack of rudimentary filmmaking skills.[13]

Citing Findlay's direction explicitly (thus ascribing both responsibility and blame), the review condemns both the film's violence and its technical execution, couching its objections in terms of both moral and creative failure while simultaneously demanding that the film should somehow "redeem" itself. While curiously neglecting an extended rape sequence amid its litany of cinematic sins, incompetence is seen to impede ethical judgment. Such a confluence of shortcomings affects any impulse to ascribe discernible value, its abject failure presented not only as both technical and aesthetic, but also at the level of moral integrity. Barely concealed is a mockery of its budgetary impoverishment and, by implication, a more general dismissal of the exploitation sector.

Such condemnation might stand as a damning epitaph for Findlay's career in general. It implies that *Game of Survival* provides no evidence of development, improvement, or progress despite two decades of professional employment. Even Bill Landis, perhaps the most forgiving insider-observer of New York's local exploitation scene, could only describe the film in retrospect as "a cheap, boring exploitation mess."[14] That which the *Variety* reviewer found so objectionable was also clearly in line with MPAA sensibilities of the period. Just a week later, the ratings board bestowed an "X" rating upon the film,[15] a decision upheld in June despite an appeal lodged by Laurel Films. Across the Atlantic in the United Kingdom, the film was never a candidate for theatrical distribution, but its 1987 submission by Lazer Video to the British Board of Film Classification (BBFC) for a home video certificate was rejected outright. This meant an effective ban in that territory, instantly rendering it a desirable object on the burgeoning underground video trading circuit that had emerged in the wake of the 1984 Video Recordings Act. Institutional judgments such as these effectively condemned the film before it had even properly entered the popular consciousness. In tandem with critical opprobrium, this inevitably begat a disreputable cultural object.

However, the critical apparatus for dealing with such product have developed significantly since the 1980s, and retrospection has afforded a swell of contrary opinion. Reviewing its 2005 DVD release, both Shane m. Dallmann and Casey Scott offered responses informed by a more nuanced appreciation of the film's provenance and purpose. Dallman alludes more astutely to Findlay's reputation, stating "that such an extreme film was directed by a woman may have raised an eyebrow or two, but those people did not know with whom they were dealing."[16] Scott goes so far to describe it as Findlay's "masterpiece,"[17] and while this might seem an eccentric appraisal at face value, it seems less so if we allow for the degree to which the film meets its own requirements as exploitation product, a comprehensive fulfillment of modulated expectations in which films are expected to offend and outrage in ways that have nothing to do with the demands of middle-brow popular cultural tastemakers.

THE BRONX AS CINEMATIC SPACE

Both the harmonies and dangerous tensions so central to the Bronx's social formations fuel the internal dynamics of *Game of Survival*. Carolyn Mclaughlin comments that "the poorest half of New York's poorest borough is separated from Manhattan's wealthy upper east side by a few subway stops and yet these two areas couldn't be more different."[18] The public image of the South Bronx is founded in a complex local history far beyond *Game of Survival*'s restricted purview, but is fundamental to its generic strategies. As David Gomez points out, throughout the 1970s and early 1980s "an endless parade of presidential aspirants posed atop piles of rubble in nondescript lots, [and] the Bronx became synonymous with urban decay, poverty, crime and hopelessness . . . a punchline in the national consciousness."[19] Central to its identity has been the range of ethnic identities and communities, which fluctuated and transformed radically over the course of the twentieth century. Until the 1950s, the South Bronx had been home predominantly to white European immigrants, but the post-war shift of many manufacturing plants to other parts of the country meant that much of the population followed in their wake. The subsequent influx of Afro-Caribbean and Hispanic residents altered the prevailing mix sufficiently enough to drive out many other remaining white residents. Between 1970 and 1980, the total population of the South Bronx fell from approximately 769,000 to 454,000, an astounding 40 per cent reduction in its inhabitants.[20] Disrepair and dysfunction became emblematic of the South Bronx's overall image. Rampant drug abuse, criminal street gangs, and an increasingly fire- and rubble-scarred landscape became a dominant perception, a media-cultural shorthand that would resonate on both a national and global scale.

Inevitably, this had a significant impact upon a host of films emergent from the end of the 1970s intent upon utilizing its visual or thematic potential. Key in this regard were *The Wanderers* (1979, dir. Philip Kaufman), *The Warriors* (1979, dir. Walter Hill), *Fort Apache, the Bronx* (1980, dir. Daniel Petrie), and *Wolfen* (1981, dir. Michael Wadleigh). *The Wanderers* defines its 1963 Bronx milieu through the divisions and alliances between Italian-, African-, Chinese- and Irish-American gangs. *The Warriors* establishes the Bronx in its early scenes as a ground zero danger zone, with Van Cortlandt Park[21] serving as the gathering point for an ill-fated gang alliance aiming to control the entire city. Alternatively, *Fort Apache, The Bronx* privileges the perspective of Paul Newman's veteran Irish-American cop, his conscience pricked by the corruption of his white colleagues. However, the film's chief process of ethnic othering occurs through the figure of an African-American sex worker (Pam Grier) and Hispanic drug dealer (Miguel Pinero), key catalysts in the violence and chaos that the film depicts. *Wolfen* (1981) links the plight of the South Bronx to the wealthy corporate interests of Manhattan, relaying its critique partly through an expression of Native American spiritualism. This emphasizes how, despite their geographical proximity, the prominent beneficiaries of both the local and national economic infrastructure have insulated themselves from not only a despised array of immigrant groups but also an indigenous people for whom centuries of spiritual growth might easily unleash its own fearsome monsters in retaliation.

It would have been clear then to both domestic and international cinemagoers by the early 1980s that the South Bronx's problems might be negotiated through a range of generic motifs and structures, manifesting through anything from nostalgic reverie for the past to alternative spirituality or the modern tribal impulse of the street gang. This reached its *reductio in absurdum* in the Italian-produced *1990: The Bronx Warriors* (1982, dir. Enzo G. Castellari) and its sequel, *Escape from the Bronx* (1983, dir. Enzo G. Castellari). In these films, the borough became the landscape of a lawless future world, fusing its contemporaneous ruin with elements from action/science-fiction hybrids such as *Mad Max* (1979, dir. George Miller), *Mad Max 2* (1981, dir. George Miller), and *Escape From New York* (1981, dir. John Carpenter). Extracting its signifying weight from immediate social circumstances, these films transform the South Bronx into the realm of fantasy, bearing negligible allegorical value for Italian filmmakers less concerned with a community's collapse than they are with the opportunities its buildings afford as a ready-made dystopian backdrop. What these films also provided were other fantastical, hyper-exaggerated images of marauding gangs, their uniforms and accoutrements removed again from any reliably indexical relationship to social actuality, but synonymous with the iconography and criminal activity established in other contemporaneous films such as *Death Wish 2* (1982, dir. Michael Winner), *Class of 1984* (1982, dir. Mark Lester), *Exterminator 2* (1984, dir. Mark Buntzman), *Savage Streets* (1984, dir. Danny Steinmann) and *Death Wish 3* (1985, dir. Michael Winner).

BIOGRAPHY AND AUTHORSHIP

Game of Survival was clearly molded according to these cinematic trends. However, it is reasonable to argue that it offers more evidence regarding Findlay's personal investment than the horror films she directed in the 1980s. Noting to Ashley West her own Bronx nativity as the daughter of Hungarian Jewish refugees, she revealed that many members of her extended family did not escape the Holocaust.[22] Elsewhere, she has described the Bronx not as a borough but a "suburb" of New York, looking upon the original script by Joel Bender and Rick Marx as "a revisualization of where I grew up."[23] Allowing personal biography into critical discourse is rife with problems at the best of times, but this textual anchoring in lived experience and the utilization of authentic South Bronx locations lends a rudimentary level of "authenticity" to the film's frequently ludicrous scenario. Far from being a straight biographical account, it is a portrait of one corner of New York City as a dangerous yet cartoonish dystopia, a hyper-realistic portrait of street crime and violence run amuck. The very idea of a "revisualization" of experience lends another layer to the film's stark but seemingly empty-headed presentation of social breakdown. Furthermore, the slanted idea of the Bronx as suburbia strips that ideal of its own fragile connotations of economic stability, familial unity, and white middle-class conformism, a curious lens through which to observe the very different form of social entrapment the film depicts.

This sense of locality extended to Findlay's casting of local non-actors, including actual police officers in minor, non-speaking roles and the presence of actual gang member Manuel Cotto as the minor villain, Nines. Furthermore, the same disused South Bronx tenement building was utilized for both exterior and interior sequences, dressed accordingly to convey the lifestyles of each tenant and the sense of decay and abandonment gradually eating away at the stairs and corridors that separate them. Its function as an *ad hoc* soundstage demonstrates how the restrictions of independent exploitation filmmaking can be transformed into advantages, informing and intersecting with the elaborate *mise en scène* afforded those working in the higher echelons. This allowed for an effective microcosm of the area's contemporaneous state, conveying the dichotomy between the visible disrepair of the area and the diversity in lifestyle, hope and aspiration of the inhabitants obliged to live there.

WATCHING THE GAME

Excepting one sequence in which the gang is released from police custody before embarking upon their fateful journey back to the tenement, the film is confined exclusively to the immediate locale of the single building. This is founded as much in technical pragmatism as any expressive potential, but it enhances the idea of a social world that has been extracted from a broader socio-economic realm and immutably crushed into a single street corner. This is complemented by a visual style that, with isolated and notable exceptions, eschews any elaboration in its lighting and compositional choices, often utilizing a handheld camera to lend immediacy and spontaneity to the dramatic action. Thematic explorations are cursory at best, suppressed in favor of violent, melodramatic set-pieces key to the film's progression. This is starkly evident in its narrative structure, organized according to twenty intertitles (pointing again to the direct formal influence of *Assault on Precinct 13*). The first of these offers precise information regarding place and time ("The Bronx, August, 11:05am"), but for the most part they indicate either just the time or specific floor of the building in which the action takes place. This compresses almost seventeen hours of incident into a ninety-four-minute duration, imposing a temporal and spatial order that supports the film's exclusivity of location. The opening shots immediately establish an exterior geography that defines the social parameters, a montage comprising eleven images whose predominantly greyscale palette evoke an all-too-familiar urban decay. The garbage-strewn waste ground, discarded consumer objects, junked cars, stray dogs, burned out buildings, collapsed rubble, and twisted steel girders reinforce the sense of a community in terminal decline. While this topography is crucial to the film's allusive method, it can offer no progressive liberal-humanist solution for this state of affairs. Accordingly, panoramic vistas of the nearby Manhattan cityscape across the Harlem River are wholly absent from the film, retaining a sense of enclosure from any external economic or institutional force that might intervene in the tenant's plight. At the very least, and contrary to the withering putdowns of the *Variety* review cited earlier, it is clear from the outset that this is the work of a filmmaker who is wholly conversant with not just the expediency but also the potential of visual and narrative economy.

Although the film's score (composed by Walter Sear and William Fischer) is performed predominantly with a synthesizer (bearing distinct traces of a prog-rock influence), the opening montage is accompanied by a hip hop track, "Tenement" by Kool Krew, which is rhythmically upbeat and light in timbre, but lyrically reinforces the deprivation and neglect evident in the images ("a tenement is a place to live, some look so bad make you wanna shed tears"). This alludes directly to the Bronx's status as hip hop's historical seeding bed and its development as racially inflected, local musical reportage. However, the film never focuses primarily upon the social conditions of African-American youth so inextricable from the narrative of hip hop's cultural growth. Instead, it is the figures of Sam and the elderly black couple,

Mr. and Mrs. Wesley (Walter Bryant and Olivia Ward) that infuse the film respectively with a sense of reluctant communal involvement and a stoic but neighborly and liberal Christian tradition, an image of black America that is either middle-aged or elderly and responding in very different ways to the conditions people endure.

In this light, a breakdown of the expansive cast of characters, highlighting the groupings, sub-groupings and loosely defined racial, familial or marital identities is instructive:

The Tenants	The Gang
Sam Washington (Afro-Caribbean) *Widowed*	Chaco, the Leader (Hispanic)
	Hector (Hispanic)
Mr. and Mrs. Wesley (Afro-Caribbean)	Chula, the 'Moll' (Indeterminate)
Married	
Carol (WASP) and Poppo (Hispanic)	Nines (Hispanic)
Unmarried Couple	Sal (Italian)
	Monk (Indeterminate)
Anna, Anita, Charlie and Maria (Hispanic)	Rudy (Indeterminate)
Mother, daughter and grandchildren	
Leona and Jeanne (Afro-Caribbean)	
Mother and daughter	
Ruth (European Jewish)	
Mr. Rojas (Hispanic)	
Mr. Gonzales (Hispanic)	

The casting in an early role of the relatively well-known Paul Calderon (as Hector) encourages a sense of that character's ethnic foundations,[24] but the largely unknown cast means that no established screen personae are imposed upon any characterizations. Although positioned as foes, both groups are markedly multi-ethnic, but the film never systematically elaborates upon each character's deeper identity. Communal bonds among the tenants are tinged with petty resentments, with families, friendships and neighborly relations already breaking before the gang embarks upon its night of terror. This casual emphasis upon collective (dis)unity subsumes the racial theme, but it is clear that the melting pot is close to boiling over. Overt racism emerges through brief (but deliberate) details such as the casual racial epithet that Mr. Rojas hurls at Sam during a verbal quarrel. Alternatively, however, the image of the gang smashing a portrait of Martin Luther King in the apartment of Mr. and Mrs. Wesley alludes to a more expansive rejection of racial idealism. The film's broadness of racial characterization confounds any progressive impulse, while the construction of certain characters (for example, Mr. Rojas as a sweaty, over-weight and feckless alcoholic) conform to specific, insidious ethnic stereotypes. Nevertheless, these can be balanced and measured against the triumph of Sam, Anita (Gy Mirano), and Ruth by the film's conclusion, unlikely saviors whose unity develops through necessity, positing a future founded both in pragma-tism and a solidarity that crosses racial, generational, and gender divisions. Hints of their interior lives are provided through details such as the framed photographs of Sam's dead wife and a child, while his saxophone and pinned cuttings of playbills suggest a former career as a jazz musician. Alternatively, both contented adherence and frustrated resistance to Catholic dogma are conveyed by the crucifixes that adorn several apartments, spilling over in the inter-generational conflict between Anita and her mother, Anna (Martha De La Cruz), over the former's determination to be a single mother of multiple children (including the one she is currently carrying).

Traces of Findlay's own family past also inform this community dynamic. These are present most explicitly in the form of Ruth, elderly and adamant in her refusal to move from the building on the grounds that she has resided there for forty years. Her European accent[25] and the stated timescale of her residence, suggests that she is a Holocaust survivor herself, the adornment of her apartment with black and white photographs depicting her lost (extermi-nated?) relatives given extra resonance by the brief sequence in which she per-forms a lone prayer ritual amid these mementos (see Figure 7.2). The heedless criminality of the gang will soon trample literally over these objects, and Ruth's later defiant wielding of a baseball bat[26] against them plays on the surface like a casual deployment of the plucky pensioner archetype, a cheap visual joke designed to offset the violent action. While it would be an exaggeration to read Ruth as some form of authorial avatar, her final emergence as survivor adds curious weight to the film's title, alluding covertly to a much broader historical movement that it never explicitly delves into elsewhere.

The film's racial conundrum is brought into sharpest focus in a rape-murder sequence positioned as a pivotal shock moment, illustrating the extent to which it

Figure 7.2 Mina Bern as Ruth in *Game of Survival*.

is prepared to brandish its confrontational edge.[27] Established as the most dynamic and opinionated African-American presence, the victim, Leona (Rhetta Hughes), had previously enchanted her infant daughter, Jeanne (Chyann P. Robertson), with dreams of an escape to a Fifth Avenue apartment adorned with servants and consumer desirables. Jeanne's innocent riposte that she actually likes her home merely infuses pathos, a sense that the hollowness of the fantasy will in all likelihood pass through the generations. Moreover, Leona also admonishes Carol, the film's sole representative of young white femininity, of relinquishing her privileged position through resorting to sex work to support her partner, Poppo (Angel David), in his heroin addiction. That this assertive and charismatic presence (and outspoken critic of the "fallen" white woman) should be subjected to an assault by the gang comprising four minutes of screen time, placing explicit emphasis upon both her physical and psychological anguish, seems unavoidably like a silencing of a radical voice, a cynical extinguishment of the life she had imagined for both herself and her daughter. She is forcibly held, gagged, and spreadeagled by five men on her bed, her chest cut with a knife as a preliminary to her rape. The intercutting of bodily close-ups with the gurning, mocking faces of the attackers (underscored by taunts that "she likes it"), merely emphasize and accentuate the horror of the attack, offering no recourse to a perspective that might offer even a sense of objective distance from the events occurring onscreen. This is compounded not only by the cutaway that emphasizes that Jeanne is hearing the rape occur from her room, but also by the repeated punching of the victim after her brief resistance (she forces a pair of scissors into one attacker's eye) and the grotesque *coup de grâce* whereby a broom handle is violently inserted into Leona's anus. Leaving her bloodied and lifeless on the bed, she is reduced to a status equivalent to Mr. Gonzales (Alfonso Manosalvas)'s dog, ruthlessly slaughtered and mutilated elsewhere in the film. None of this is in the service of a sustained commentary on the socio-psychological or cultural foundations of sexual violence, or even a cursory observance of the historical inflections of the black female victim.

Somewhat alarmingly, Findlay has referred to the rape as a "comeuppance" for Leona's assertiveness,[28] its foregrounding as a set-piece bearing significant trace elements of the sexploitation roughies she had worked on in various capacities in the 1960s and 1970s. It stands also as a model example of what James Ferman, the former director of the BBFC, defined as "porno-rape,"[29] in which the victim is controlled, dominated, and even in some instances brought to submissive pleasure, the fragmented visual details of coercion, assault, and submission standing in for the close-ups of real (and consensual) penetrative sex so central to the visual affirmations of pleasure in hardcore pornography. Such a sequence (and Findlay's casual reading of it) certainly encourages a reluctance to even entertain the notion that her films might speak of anything but the lowest common denominator, significantly diminishing the potential for a sympathetic critical hearing. Furthermore, it partly defines her work as a betrayal of the apparent obligation to at least pay lip service to feminist critiques of the "male gaze."

Therefore, the film demonstrates contradictory impulses in both its gender and racial discourses, capitalizing upon an underlying sense of toxic antagonism while simultaneously emphasizing the necessity for integration and collectivism. While homicidal and often perverse in its actions, the gang itself is racially diverse, something that Findlay herself has described as being a somewhat fanciful dramatic conceit as far as the Bronx's real criminal problem was concerned.[30] Its uniform is not defined in terms of identificatory colors, adhering just as closely to an assortment of sartorial rock star clichés of the time, such as black leather, spandex, chains, studded wristbands, bandanas, and exposed chests and midriffs. Their initial internal bonds and loyalties also provide the film with an ironic expression of familial unity, albeit one cemented by a range of personal compulsions and addictions presided over by the vengeful, destructive path of its leader. Cutting straight from the first intertitle (over an establishing shot of the tenement) to an extreme close-up of a scavenging rat, the crude symbolism elaborates upon the realist emphasis of the title montage, immediately equating the basement-dwelling gang with the vermin that infest it. The basement also situates the gang literally at the very bottom of the tenement's totemic structure, their outward bravado and menace merely masking a social abjection manifest in anything from sexual violence to drug addiction. From its first appearance onscreen, the building itself stands as the obvious visual signifier of a phallic quest for power, however insignificant it might be outside the confines of the community itself.

The gang's gradual ascent of the tenement, murdering its inhabitants and desecrating their homes, seeks gradually to remove any vestige of a conventional domesticity, a process founded primarily in the drive to reclaim the building's symbolic authority after their ejection in the film's opening moments. This is a mission that has no function besides the claim to futile ownership, channeled and enabled primarily through Chaco (Enrique Sandino)'s sense of dominion over his underlings. It is his quest to reclaim the building as his own that drives the narrative, his apparent connection to a higher sense of purpose merely a delusion fueled by the various drugs in which he and the rest of the gang indulge. Consequently, he emerges as the film's most explicit embodiment of the ethnic other, particularly through his thick accent and faltering English, aurally exaggerated when Sandino (a native Colombian)'s naturally higher pitched voice was amended in the final sound mix.[31] His is a flamboyant but destructive masculinity, initially calm, authoritative, and detached from the rest of the gang (save for his intermittent, violence-fueled bouts of ritualized sexual activity with Chula [Karen Russell]), but he is gradually provoked into an increasingly hysterical response as the fulfillment of his ambition is frustrated. Through ritualized behavior and speech patterns (he frequently refers to himself in the third person) he is a genre surrogate for the Native American chief in the Western, embodying the threat to the film's sole vestige of civilization. In this sense, the film can transfer the root social causes of the tenement's plight onto his cartoon villainy, but all while developing him as the primary source of its chaotic formal energy.

From his vow of vengeance to his climactic hysteria in defeat, his presence dictates the film's most elaborate stylistic flourishes. For example, the reverse tracking shot of the gang leaving the police station positions him from a low angle while striding imperiously front and center frame, flanked by his associates as they torment an assortment of hapless citizens and assert their power amid their wider urban surroundings (see Figure 7.3). In addition, the low-angle 360-degree shot, isolating and framing him centrally against a clear blue sky as he delivers a short monologue ("My head is filled with blood! My dream is filled with blood!"), gives prominence to his oath to reclaim the building and destroy everyone and everything in it. In the climactic rooftop confrontation, the film resorts to a jarring pathetic fallacy, Chaco's internal anguish and impending defeat given a final expressive audio-visual grandeur through the lightning storm that has suddenly engulfed the neighborhood. Battered and burned from the sustained resistance to his homicidal quest, the sequence places him at the pinnacle of the very structure that has symbolized his phallic reclamation, but it sees him defeated by the pregnant Anita. This is in stark contrast to the realist aesthetics that have shaped the film up to that point, the *deus ex machina* of a lightning bolt striking the steel rod upon which he has been impaled suggesting that God Himself has put paid to the demi-god status he enjoyed within

Figure 7.3 Enrique Sandino as Chaco in *Game of Survival*.

the gang. Following his demise, the film's final stylistic gesture is a crane shot that pulls back to a high angle, revealing some of the remaining tenants spilling onto streets that bear absolutely no trace of the storm that was engulfing it only seconds before. Whether by editorial accident or design, the shot liberates the community from the subjectivity of Chaco's hysteria, restoring at least a semblance of harmony and balance to a now depleted community that has stood defiant in spite of its insurmountable differences.

CONCLUSION

If *Game of Survival* achieves anything beyond the mere affirmation of its detractors' barbs, it is to blithely expose—while indeed gleefully exploiting—the fragile social bonds that fuse its marginalized community together. This dual strategy suggests limited potential for unity amid social estrangement, evincing an oblique awareness of the tensions within a territory that has been neglected to the point of total relinquishment. Despite the film's formal and generic efficiency, even Roberta Findlay herself would no doubt dismiss demands that it should proffer even rudimentary levels of socio-political insight, contenting herself instead in the outlandish or even quasi-mythic possibilities afforded by the material. If social insight has been sacrificed to marketable sensation, the film's (and its director's) refusal of overt analysis might reasonably be seen to be part of the many problems besetting the Bronx at the time of its production, one more ugly, unheeding portrait of a borough in socio-economic freefall.

However, there *is* a conscience buried in its cynicism and opportunism, both its micro-tensions and its grand rivalries serving as dramatic foci for a community formed exclusively of social "Others" forced to negotiate the absence of any institutional authority that might even begin to take an interest in their plight. The film conflates and complicates the very idea of the "Other" while obfuscating the vast complex of (self)interests that have resulted in the desolation they endure. It is a film about defiant outsiders by a defiant outsider, a ghetto tale rife with confusion and contradiction and formed of conflicted obligations to the exploitation marketplace and the community it has deigned to put up on the screen. Despite itself, it demonstrates how a roundly despised popular cultural object can offer incidental insights and observations that color broader perceptions of social actuality. In that sense, and as Casey Scott suggested, it may well yet prove to be Findlay's masterpiece.

ACKNOWLEDGMENTS

Thanks to Johnny Walker for discussing several aspects of the film and Findlay's 1980s career with me.

NOTES

1. Quote from the *Game of Survival* DVD commentary (Shriek Show/Media Blasters), 2005.
2. *Tenement* was the title was utilized for the film's home video release in the United States (on the USA Home Video label), although trailers for this release actually present the title as *The Tenement*.
3. Ashley West and April Hall, "Roberta Findlay: A Respectable Woman—Podcast 53," August 16, 2015, *Rialto Report*, podcast, https://www.therialtoreport.com/2015/08/16/roberta-findlay/ (accessed July 28, 2021).
4. Findlay made one more hardcore film amid this late-stage career activity: *Shauna: Every Man's Fantasy* (1985) a pseudo-documentary account of the life, career and personality quirks of the recently deceased porn star, Shauna Grant. Its self-serving attempt to maintain a west coast, freewheeling pornotopian façade is about as far removed from the dystopia of *Game of Survival* as it is possible to imagine.
5. This late career surge came to a self-imposed (and terminal) halt after the failure to find a distributor for *Banned* (1989), a diversion into comedy that Findlay herself has written off as a mistake from the outset.
6. Omayra Cruz, "Tits, Ass and Swastikas: Three Steps Toward a Fatal Film Theory," *Necronomicon Book 2: The Journal of Horror and Erotic Cinema* (London, Creation), 89.
7. Linda Ruth Williams, "Exploitation Cinema," *The Cinema Book (Third Edition)* (London, BFI, 2007), 298.
8. Eric Schaefer, *Bold! Daring! Shocking! True! A History of Exploitation Films, 1919–1959* (Durham, NC and London, Duke University Press, 1999), 13.
9. Alexandra Heller-Nicholas, "What's Inside a Girl: Porn, Horror and the Films of Roberta Findlay," *Senses of Cinema*, Issue 80, September 2016, https://www.sensesofcinema.

com/2019/20-years-of-senses/whats-inside-a-girl-porn-horror-and-the-films-of-roberta-findlay-issue-80-september-2016/ (accessed July 10, 2021).

10. Key works in this period included Molly Haskell, *From Reverence to Rape* (New York, Holt, Rinehart and Winston, 1974); Laura Mulvey, "Visual Pleasure and Narrative Cinema"; *Screen* 16, no. 3 (Autumn 1975), 6–18; and E. Ann Kaplan, *Women and Film: Both Sides of the Camera* (London and New York, Routledge, 1983). Needless to say, Findlay did not figure in any of these pages.

11. J. R. Taylor, "The Curse of Her Filmography," *New York Press*, November 11, 2014, www.nypress.com/news/the-curse-of-her-filmography-LYNP1020050727307279985 (accessed July 10, 2021).

12. Anthony Timpone, "Queen of 42nd Street," *Fangoria* 52 (March 1986), 50.

13. Strat, "Game of Survival" review, *Variety*, May 22, 1985, 20. In her DVD commentary, unless she is staking her claim as the ultimate wry, ironic observer of her own work, Findlay misremembers this as "a pretty fair review . . . a good review!"

14. Bill Landis and Michelle Clifford, *Sleazoid Express* (New York, Fireside, 2002), 45.

15. Anon, "X rating for *Game of Survival*," *Screen International*, June 22, 1985, 8.

16. Shane M. Dallman "Tenement—Game of Survival" review, *Video Watchdog* 126 (July/September 2006), 12.

17. Casey Scott, "Tenement" review, *DVD Drive-In*, https://www.dvddrive-in.com/reviews/t-z/tenement85.htm (accessed August 3, 2021).

18. Carolyn McLaughlin, *South Bronx Battles: Stories of Resistance, Resilience and Renewal* (Oakland, University of California Press, 2019), 1.

19. David Gomez, "Foreword," in McLaughlin, *South Bronx Battles*, xi.

20. See McLaughlin, *South Bronx Battles*, 59.

21. The production did not use the actual Van Cortlandt Park, opting instead to use the presumably more practical (and possibly safer) site of Riverside Park in Manhattan.

22. Quoted on West and Hall's "Roberta Findlay: a Respectable Woman" podcast.

23. Quote from DVD audio commentary.

24. Calderon was born in Puerto Rico, of mixed-race descent. Just prior to *Game of Survival* he was visible as one of many Hispanic villains in the *Miami Vice* TV series, but has established himself in a long and successful career as a character player in both film and television, performing for renowned auteur filmmakers such as Spike Lee, Abel Ferrara, and Quentin Tarantino.

25. The actor, Mina Bern, was born in Poland in 1911, fleeing the country after the Nazi invasion.

26. This detail curiously prefigures Donny "the Bear Jew" Donowitz (Eli Roth) in *Inglourious Basterds* (2009), who wields the same weapon to mercilessly club Nazi foes to death.

27. In its duration and detail, the sequence is not uncommon in the exploitation realm, but it seems to be drawing significant stylistic sustenance from a similar attack portrayed in *Death Wish 2* (1982).

28. Quote from DVD commentary.

29. James Ferman, "James Ferman Talks to Himself," *Shock Xpress* 1 (London, Titan Books, 1991), 8.

30. As suggested in DVD commentary.

31. As revealed in DVD commentary.

CHAPTER 8

By the Numbers: Roberta Findlay, Home Video, and the Horror Genre

Johnny Walker

Roberta Findlay's association with horror cinema rarely extends beyond *Snuff* (1976, dir. Michael Findlay): the infamous Manson-inspired exploitation film which, in its promotional ballyhoo, falsely purported to depict the genuine murder of its lead actress. Protests that were sparked in New York City upon the film's theatrical release, followed by its banning as a "video nasty" in Britain in the early 1980s, has helped transform an otherwise run-of-the-mill exploitation film into an exemplar of boundary-pushing horror cinema.[1]

However, despite the film's infamy, foregrounding *Snuff* in academic and popular discourse has come at the expense of sidelining Findlay's directorial efforts in the horror genre: four films made between 1985 and 1989, *The Oracle* (1985), *Blood Sisters* (1987), *Lurkers* (1987) and *Prime Evil* (1988), which are yet to be the subject of meaningful analysis.[2]

Findlay's gender is grounds enough for a scholarly reappraisal of her horror output, given that, as Alison Peirse argues in the introduction to her pathbreaking collection, *Women Make Horror: Filmmaking, Feminism, Genre*, "there are [sic] a vast number of women filmmakers completely absent from our written horror histories and that by not including the outputs from 'half the human race,' our histories are faulty."[3] The present chapter is, in part, a contribution to Peirse's revisionist project, but this is not, I should make clear, its sole purpose. Nor is it my intention to champion Findlay's horror films as offering a "perspective" that challenges patriarchal hegemony, or to claim that they advocate for women or comment on "female experiences." There remains an assumption, which Peirse challenges, that, "a woman director . . . will make a woman-centred film" or that woman-directed horror films de facto lend themselves to "feminist" readings.[4] Frankly, it would be disingenuous to fold Findlay's horror films into this discourse.[5] While Findlay identifies as a woman and her horror films have female leads, she is not a feminist ("I don't think much of the movement in any aspect at all"),[6] has on numerous occasions expressed her dislike of working with women ("I don't like women . . . I just find them very annoying"),[7] claims to have never felt in any way subjugated on film sets because of her gender ("Never! Not once"),[8] has claimed that her films are not concerned with making any political statements whether about feminism or otherwise ("I don't know if a movie is one thing or not"),[9] and, as a cinematographer, insists she is referred to as a "camera-*man*" on set ("doesn't *cameraperson* sound ridiculous?").[10]

Alexandra Heller-Nicholas's argument that Findlay is best understood as an "anti-auteur" is a befitting label in this regard.[11] Unlike the intentions that her (male) horror contemporaries such as Wes Craven, David Cronenberg, and George A. Romero have purported, Findlay's chief aim when making horror movies or, indeed, films in any genre, was always to place economic viability ahead of artistic intent.[12] Critics were quick to recognize this too, dismissing her films as "horror by-the-numbers" for the "nondiscerning [sic] B-grade homevid market."[13] However, comments such as these, pejorative though they are, bring to light the economic context within which Findlay was operating, and the low-risk investment that low-budget horror features held for filmmakers at the beginnings of the video age. This chapter, rather than treating *The Oracle*, *Blood Sisters*, *Lurkers*, and *Prime Evil* as in some way innovative or as worthy of interest because they happen to be directed by a woman, shows instead how these films prove apposite case studies because of what they reveal about contemporaneous industrial practices. Analysis of the films in relation to contemporary trade publications and associated promotional materials enables a broader understanding of the economic context that birthed them and, by extension, leads to a fuller understanding of the industrial history of US horror cinema in the 1980s.

SEGUEING FROM PORN INTO HORROR

As various contributions to this collection attest, Findlay spent the majority of her moviemaking career lensing soft- and hardcore features for theatrical distribution, a number of which she directed (mostly under pseudonyms). By 1985, however, her focus changed. It is suggested that her move into horror filmmaking was in response to the backlash she was said to face following the release of *Shauna: Every Man's Fantasy* (1985), a sex film that capitalized on the suicide of pornographic actress Shauna Grant, which allegedly "made [Findlay] a pariah in the world of adult entertainment."[14] In actuality, however, Findlay's decision to switch from sex to horror was a move born of economic necessity.

It is now accepted that the advent of the videocassette and the rise of "cheap, shot-on-videotape [adult] programming," rapidly usurped shot-on-film pornography and became a key component in the demise of the adult movie theater.[15] However, while the popularity of theatrically distributed celluloid porn was in decline, the popularity of R-rated horror films among VCR owners was on the rise. In 1982, the film trade press reported that video dealers throughout the country were claiming that horror films were much of the time renting and selling "even more strongly than many major releases," and that they were doing so without much in the way of promotion from their distributors.[16] Reasons given to the genre's popularity at this time include the fact that many such films were not shown on television, and could only be seen in theaters "sporadically."[17] Video, thus, was often the only—or at least the easiest—means of accessing the films in question.

The boom in horror product—and in other video genres such as action—encouraged some working in adjacent areas of the film business to take stock of their position, including those whose bread and butter was adult filmmaking. It was generally agreed among those in the trade that, while pornography was rarely viewed as a reputable line of work or one for which it was assumed discernible skill was required, the results told a different story, as filmmakers were able to produce crowd-pleasing and profitable movies very quickly—in a matter of weeks or even days—and in the most frugal of contexts. Moreover, by the time Findlay switched her attention to horror, a number of her contemporaries were doing very well from the genre. Wes Craven, a fully fledged horror auteur by the 1980s, had worked on numerous hardcore features around the time he directed *The Last House on the Left* in 1972, a widely controversial, yet popular horror film that played all over the world.[18] The success of his subsequent horror films, including *The Hills Have Eyes* (1977) and especially *A Nightmare on Elm Street* (1984), showed that the transition from porn to horror was not only possible, but also potentially highly lucrative. Similarly, fellow New Yorker William Lustig cut his teeth directing two hardcore features, *Hot Honey* and *The Violation of Claudia* (both 1977), prior to shooting the horror film that made his name, *Maniac* (1980), and several higher-profile R-rated horror films he made in the years that followed.[19] As hardcore stalwart and director of the R-rated horror film, *Deranged* (1987), Chuck Vincent, explained to *Variety*, "Filming adult features has been a tremendous aid for me [and others] in terms of experience,"[20] affording him and his contemporaries the ability to master industry-standard equipment and materials, such as 35mm film, and providing others, including adult film producer and producer of the horror film *A Hazing Hell* (dir. Paul Ziller, released as *Pledge Night* in 1988), Joyce Snyder, with unmatched knowledge of distribution and foreign sales.[21] Findlay, with the assistance of her partner, the composer and studio engineer Walter E. Sear, and their new company Reeltime Distributing (est. 1979), was well positioned to enter commercial filmmaking of this nature, by self-financing and shooting on location (as was usually the case with her adult features), and then exploiting her networks within theatrical, cable, and video distribution.[22]

HORROR AND HOME VIDEO

Despite the best efforts of genre theorists to neatly define horror, it has forever been, as film historian Peter Hutchings has it, "particularly hostile to pin down."[23] Nowhere was this clearer than on the shelves of video stores in the 1980s, where independent and major distributors alike earned fortunes from horror films of varying types and ages. As video became the primary means of accessing screen entertainment throughout the 1980s, the theatrical runs of independent horror films grew shorter. Producers and distributors increasingly opted for "small releases" for their horror pictures, in select cities, before releasing the film to video. Much of the time, theatrical exhibition was bypassed altogether.

Releasing a film to theaters brought with it considerable cost in terms of, for example, advertising, print duplication and the transportation of film reels from location to location. Commonly, the negligible box office returns such films were met with rarely justified the required expenditure, beyond additional (albeit very limited) exposure. Things were different in the video store, where a film's longevity was extended simply by the fact it could remain on the shelf indefinitely.[24] This was especially true of horror films, which remained popular "year-round."[25] In this context, any one horror video could continue to lure in consumers long after the expenditure injected by its distributor into its initial marketing campaign.

This is the context that Findlay's first horror film, *The Oracle*, entered. Shot in mid-1985, it was released briefly into theaters in early 1986, and then onto video in 1987. The film—about a woman who accidentally summons demonic spirits using a Ouija board-style device—is somewhat of an outlier when considered alongside Findlay's subsequent horror movies. Whereas her successive films, discussed below, ape popular film cycles or major theatrical hits, *The Oracle* does not. Rather, it appears to have been made just as Findlay approached her sex films: based not, as she declared to a trade magazine in 1981, on any awareness of what was likely to sell in the fluctuating marketplace, but rather, as an experiment in trial and error.[26] What the film does share with other films of the period, however, is gore and special effects. Throughout the film, characters are killed by demons from the spirit world in a variety of grisly ways. One character, for example, fights off small, fanged creatures with a knife, in the process stabbing himself repeatedly in the forearm, chest and face. In a later scene, a woman attempts to shoot one of the demons but misses, the bullet puncturing a drum of toxic waste, its contents then spraying her and causing the flesh on her face to disintegrate. Such sequences—which, as per other contemporaneous horror films, revel in the "destruction of the Body"[27]—serve to align the film more squarely with horror *video* culture of the period where "gore" was viewed as a core rental-driver.[28]

As numerous scholars have noted, whereas theatrically released horror movies were routinely cut by the MPAA to secure an R rating (the stronger

"X" rating was less desirable, as many movie houses refused to screen such films due to the rating's associations with pornography), horror films were routinely released on to video "unrated," and any gore trimmed by the censor was reinstated by their distributors.[29] Examples include, for example, *Blood Feast* (1963, dir. Herschel Gordon Lewis), *The Driller Killer* (1979, dir. Abel Ferrara), *Drive-In Massacre* (1976, dir. Stu Segall), *The Texas Chain Saw Massacre* (1974, dir. Tobe Hooper), and *Snuff*, all of which were released onto video "uncut" and unrated in 1982. The rise in popularity of these so-called "splatter movies"—and the many films they inspired in the 1980s—was complemented, and indeed accelerated, by detailed coverage in the pages of the horror-themed magazine *Fangoria*, particularly in regards to the trade secrets behind their gruesome special effects.[30] And while, for some, the prevailing image of *Fangoria* was one of a publication whose articles simply amounted to "unpaid publicity" of "the 'hot' figures in the genre," in actuality much coverage was given to low-budget independent fare.[31] As I have argued elsewhere, "[b]y dedicating considerable space to the promotion of low-cost movies made by so-called mavericks," *Fangoria* and its ilk "fostered a culture whereby a film's cheapness was framed as admirable resourcefulness and that true talent could shine in spite of the most severe limitations."[32] *The Oracle*, as a cheaply made gory horror film of the home video era, swiftly became part of this discourse.

An article published in *Fangoria* in March 1986—doubling as a career overview of Findlay and a puff piece for *The Oracle*—is telling of the aforementioned context.[33] Expectedly, coverage is restricted to Findlay's horror output, which, given that *The Oracle* was her first horror feature as director, is sparse. However, in acknowledging her work as a "camerman [sic]" for two horror pictures, *Shriek of the Mutilated* (1974, dir. Michael Findlay) and *Snuff*, she is nevertheless presented as genre royalty—"The Queen of Splatter"[34]—with a career implicitly as worthy as those of other "ground-breaking goremeister[s]" that the magazine afforded retrospectives, such as the directors Herschel Gordon Lewis, Andy Milligan, and Ted V. Mikels, for whom home video made possible their (re)discovery.[35] As with Lewis et al., Findlay is framed as a maker of transgressive fringe-works. *Snuff*, the reader learns, "is one of the most controversial films of all time," while *Shriek of the Mutilated* is "a gore title that ranks right up there with *I Eat Your Skin* [1971, dir. Del Tenney] and *Twitch of the Death Nerve* [1971, dir. Mario Bava]": grisly exploitation films of the 1970s undoubtedly familiar to *Fangoria*'s readership.[36] *The Oracle*, as a result, is positioned by *Fangoria* as being worthy of its readership's attention on account of the fact it was made by a genre veteran.

Coverage granted to *The Oracle* itself extends to a brief overview of the plot and its production, but, as in countless other examples of *Fangoria*'s film reportage, it is the film's "Horror Effects" (HFX) that are presented as the chief area of intrigue (and, one can discern from the article, an anticipated driver in any sales or rentals from its forthcoming video release).[37] Indeed, of the four-page article, the two color pages are awash with images of the film's main HFX set-pieces: the face-melting (which takes up a half page), the fanged-critter attack, as well as images showing, respectively, a man's head being ripped from his shoulders, shards of glass protruding from a man's eye, and (admittedly, more anodyne) a floating skull. By foregrounding the HFX of *The Oracle*, and commending their effectiveness in spite of the film's frugal production context ("amazing . . . low budget oddities"), the article squarely aligns the film with the magazine's broader agenda to celebrate under-discussed figures and champion their resourcefulness.[38]

The Oracle was cultivated to help improve Reeltime's financial prospects, and it certainly achieved this. Unlike the film that Findlay made immediately afterwards, the action film *Tenement* (aka *Game of Survival*), which failed to turn a satisfactory profit, the domestic video rights for *The Oracle* were reportedly sold for ten times its budget to International Video Entertainment (IVE), a leading independent distributor with numerous subsidiaries that had recently welcomed investment from film producers Carolco, and for which its "USA Video" label—the label *The Oracle* would appear on—was generating lines in the trade press due to its success with independent horror films.[39] And, unlike the majority of Findlay's soft- and hardcore product, *The Oracle* was distributed on video all over the world, in markets where demand for horror remained high, such as the UK, Europe, and Japan.[40]

AFTER *THE ORACLE*

The success of *The Oracle* incentivized Findlay and Sear to continue in the horror genre. The horror films that followed—*Blood Sisters*, *Lurkers*, and *Prime Evil*—share some similarities with the former. Due to budgetary constraints, they were all shot in and around New York City, use recurring actors and production staff, were produced chiefly with the video market in mind, and therefore included varying levels of horror and HFX. However, Findlay's post-*Oracle* films are more resolutely commercial in that they appear, unlike *The Oracle*, to cull their basic plots and subject matter from higher-profile horror films.

Findlay's screenplay for *Blood Sisters*, for instance, sees a group of sorority sisters spend a night in a haunted former-brothel where they are tormented and murdered by the ghosts of sex workers, inviting comparisons from the trade press to the strong-performing slasher film of 1981, *Hell Night* (dir. Tom DeSimone), and modest exploitation film from the same year, *The Nesting* (1981, dir. Armand Weston); both of which were pushed hard on video by their distributors (and also involved hardcore filmmakers who turned to horror).[41] Similarly, *Lurkers*, in addition to borrowing liberally from Michael Winner's *The Sentinel* (1977),

Figure 8.1 Findlay's *Lurkers* (L) channels *A Nightmare on Elm Street* (R).

draws its most potent themes and imagery from one of the most lucrative horror franchises of the period, the *Nightmare on Elm Street* (1984–2010) series. The
film's basic premise, which sees a woman plagued by dreams of demonic figures
that turn out to be real, is culled directly from the *Elm Street* series, as are significant aspects of the film's iconography. Scenes featuring young girls playing
jump-rope and singing ominous rhymes, for example, echo similar sequences in
the *Elm Street* films, as does a scene in which the protagonist Cathy (Christine
Moore) has a nightmare about being murdered while asleep in the bathtub ("My
god, it was so real!" she later exclaims). Lastly, *Prime Evil*, a story about witchcraft
and satanism in New York, takes some of its themes and imagery from *Rosemary's
Baby* (1968, dir. Roman Polanski) and contemporaneous occult films, such as *The
Unholy* (1988, dir. Camilo Vila) and *Witchcraft* (1988, dir. Rob Spera), including
scenes of hooded figures performing ritual sacrifice.

The decision by Findlay and Sear to produce films that could be more easily
aligned with higher-profile horror releases harkened back to the commercial strategies of films she had previously worked on, including *Snuff*, which, despite its
legacy as a violent horror film, was at the time of its production made (under the
title *The Slaughter*) in response to the popularity of a cycle of similarly themed,
Manson-inspired "biker" movies.[42] Making overt references to horror films of
the day, or classics of the genre that continued to resonate with audiences, worked
on the assumption that a pre-established audience would be drawn to them. But
also, and most importantly from Findlay and Sear's perspective, was that such
allusions would hopefully register with the theatrical and video distributors that
they were trying to court, who would be able to anticipate their commercial performance based on their similarities to other films, should they acquire the rights.

The commercial orientation of Findlay's post-*Oracle* features was the result
of several strategic choices made by her and Sear to enhance their products' visibility in an ever-crowded marketplace. First, while Findlay, purportedly out of
necessity, wrote the screenplay for *Blood Sisters*, both *Lurkers* and *Prime Evil* were
scripts acquired from a little-known but nevertheless significant writing duo, Ed
Kelleher and Harriete Vidal.[43] While little is known about Vidal,[44] Kelleher—
unlike Findlay and the writer of *The Oracle*, R. Allen Leider, whose writing

credits comprised a series of sexploitation films—had greater knowledge of and investment in the horror genre.[45] While hardly a household name, Kelleher was a known quantity both to Findlay and horror enthusiasts, given he had written the screenplay for *Shriek of the Mutilated*, as well as *Invasion of the Blood Farmers* (1972, dir. Ed Adlum), another low-budget curio, the cult appeal of which led to the screenwriter being the subject of a two-page feature published in *Fangoria* in 1982.[46] Beyond this, Kelleher was also an accomplished industry commentator, having penned numerous pieces about current goings-on in horror cinema for the trade periodical *The Film Journal*, for which he was associate editor.[47] In partnership with Vidal, Kelleher was able to monitor and draw from industrial patterns and information that he was privy to on account of his position at the magazine.

COMPOSITE HORRORS

Findlay and Sear's strategy paid off. *Blood Sisters* was acquired for distribution by Sony, who released it direct to video in 1987. *Lurkers* and *Prime Evil* fared even better, with the former acquired for domestic theatrical distribution and international sales by the well-known producer and distributor of exploitation films, Crown International Pictures, which then financed and handled international rights for the latter.[48] They were also distributed, direct to video, overseas.

The intertextual nods to other horror films may have helped the films secure distribution, but the effectiveness of such allusions in the market proper hinged, of course, on *audiences* having seen them. The distributors, thus, had to convey a successful "narrative image" to capture the films' intended demographic(s). According to media theorist John Ellis, a narrative image is a "complex phenomenon that occurs in a number of media," and amounts to a "film's circulation outside its performance in cinemas."[49] The term refers, Ellis argues, to a range of paratextual factors, from poster images to taglines. Because distributors do not wish to give everything away about a film through its marketing, a film's narrative image is chiefly enigmatic, "[proposing] a certain area of investigation which the film will carry out." In another respect, for all its ambiguity, the narrative image will nevertheless seek to "locate . . . the film" for the prospective viewer via, for example, "[g]eneric indications" that "point to the similarity between the particular film being advertised and other films." The narrative image of a film, Ellis argues, "is the deciding factor in its commercial success."[50]

Creating an arresting narrative image was especially important in the crowded home video market. As Arny Schorr of the independent distributor Rhino Video explained to *Variety*: "when it comes to unknown [horror] titles, customers make most of their decisions by examining the packaging." Said packaging should, others working in the business concurred, be "bold" and

Figure 8.2   Video box art for *Blood Sisters*, *Lurkers*, and *Prime Evil*. Credit: VHS Collector (http://vhscollector.com, accessed May 26, 2022).

carry a "catchy" title.[51] Crucially, these factors did not apply solely to new movies. It was equally paramount for video stores to "stress older catalogue titles," too, as well as horror films in subgenres that were not as popular as others. "It makes it easier for people to find the kind of title they want," one storeowner argued to *Billboard*, "especially those people who might skip over the horror section entirely because they think that it's all 'slasher' movies."[52]

The promotional campaigns for the video releases of Findlay's post-*Oracle* horror films are indicative of the aforementioned strategy. Their distributors attempted to attract a comprehensive cross-section of the market by not discursively anchoring them solely to, say, one of the popular franchises of the period or one subgenre. Richard Nowell, writing in the context of the first US teen slasher cycle, argues that, as ticket sales dwindled for slasher product in the early 1980s, theatrical distributors of such fare looked to distance their other slasher films from the cycle proper, by, for example, having films' promotional posters carry ambiguous taglines and avoid the inclusion of the cycle's main iconography (e.g. teens under threat from a tool-wielding menace).[53] To this end, ostensible slasher films such as *Death Screams* (1982, dir. David Nelson) and *The Final Terror* (1983, dir. Andrew Davis) were distributed not as "slashers" but rather as "indeterminate horror films."[54] The situation that Findlay's films faced was slightly different. As in the context Nowell discusses, video distributors were keen not to limit their audience, but this, given the "year-round" popularity of horror video, was not due to such companies wishing to distance their product from one faltering subgenre (of which slashers, in the context of video, was not one such example; it just simply did not account for the popularity of the genre writ large). Distributors wanted to *maximize* appeal by spending as little money as possible, oftentimes through a small advertising campaign that might, in some cases, consist of the video box art alone. This was a situation made possible for horror titles by the genre's resilient commercial buoyancy, and the fact that video retailers would often go out of their way to direct their customers to the horror section by employing self-made gimmicks, or in some cases by having an entire room in their store dedicated to horror releases.[55] To this end, the advertising materials for Findlay's horror films appear—as in the case of many others on the market at that time—strategically conceived not as *indeterminate* horror films, but rather as *composite* horror films, comprised of numerous subgenres and iconography cultivated to appeal to as broad a church of horror movie viewers as possible.[56]

Consider first, *Blood Sisters*. On the box art of Sony's video release from 1987, the film's title, framed within a spatter of blood, anchors the film to the contemporary moment: specifically, a video-driven cycle of mid-to-late 1980s low-budget slasher films. While the popularity of theatrically released slasher films, as Nowell notes, was dwindling, it remained a go-to subgenre on video following the rental popularity of titles such as *Halloween* (1978, dir. John Carpenter) and *The Dorm that Dripped Blood* (1982, dir. Stephen Carpenter and Jeffrey Obrow), and the production of new films in a similar vein following the success of *Blood Cult* (1985, dir. Christopher Lewis), a microbudget slasher film and the first feature film made for the North American video market, which generated handsome profits for its makers in 1985.[57] *Blood Sisters*, originally shot under the working (and telling) title "Slash," is a prescient example of this strategy.[58] By virtue of its title alone, *Blood Sisters* was positioned by its distributors as the next in line of a series of slasher films hoping to replicate *Blood Cult*'s success, including *Blood Frenzy* (directed by yet another adult filmmaker/producer, Hal Freeman, 1987), *Blood Lake* (1987, dir. Tom Boggs) and *Blood Rage* (1987, dir. John Grissmer). In this way, as a title, "Blood Sisters" implies a degree of continuity with comparable works it was likely to share shelf space with, while its tagline, "Their Hazing Was a Night to Dismember," upholds the connection with slasher films, by invoking such films' associations with youth culture and bodily mutilation.[59] Beyond this, however, there are additional strategic nods to films from other subgenres of horror. The presence of a frightened, scantily clad woman, her hair fanning outwardly above her, appears to homage the theatrical poster and video sleeve used to promote *A Nightmare on Elm Street*, on which the female protagonist lies in bed, her hair dispersed across her pillow, while other elements, including the presence of a floating skull, a demonic, red-eyed rocking horse, and a gothic house emanating beams of light from its windows and front door infers similarity to other horror types, namely new haunted house narratives à la *Poltergeist* (1982, dir. Tobe Hooper) and its sequel *Poltergeist II* (1986, dir. Brian Gibson), as well as older films of a similar ilk that remained popular on video, such as *The Amityville Horror* (1979, dir. Stuart Rosenberg).

The artworks adorning the theatrical poster and video cover of *Lurkers* have subtle yet significant differences that serve to alter the films' narrative image from one to the other. Both feature the same photograph, a young girl looking outward, her shadow casting the impression of a large demon on the wall behind her. Yet, each carries a different tagline. On Crown's theatrical poster, for instance, the tagline suggests that the little girl may herself be the source of the horror in the film: "Cathy's not scared. She should be . . . She's one of THEM!" This works to align *Lurkers* with contemporary theatrical successes of the period such as *Damien: The Omen II* (1978, dir. Don Taylor and Mike Hodges) or *Children of the Corn* (1984, dir. Fritz Kiersch); both of which utilize the "monstrous child" trope in distinctive ways.[60] Media Home Entertainment's video artwork, however, foregrounds the film's focus on the nightmares that Cathy experiences as an adult, to which most of the narrative is dedicated—the tagline, reading "Cathy's childhood nightmares are back . . . and this time they're going to get her!"—and thus invites further comparisons with the *Nightmare on Elm Street* series, the latest installment of which, *3: Dream Warriors* (1987, dir. Chuck Russel), "set an all-time high pre-order record" for Media ahead of its release in August 1987 (300,000 units).[61] Moreover, the title "Lurkers" itself—changed by Crown from its shooting title, *Home Sweet Home*, ahead of its theatrical release—is ambiguous enough to resonate with films baring little to no similarity, such as Joe Dante's "mini monster" film *Gremlins* (1984) and the video hits it inspired such as *Ghoulies* (1985, dir. Luca Bercovici) and *Critters* (1986, dir. Stephen Herek)—which shipped hundreds of thousands of units on video, and from which *Lurkers* stood to gain being associated, if only on account of its duo-syllabic title.[62]

As in the case of *Lurkers*, the theatrical poster and the video box art used to promote *Prime Evil* are similar in some ways but different in others, their distinguishing factors evincing their respective exhibition contexts. The US one-sheet, for example, is somewhat of an outlier, insofar as it *does* anchor the film to a specific theatrical cycle, namely, a series of "occult"-themed "supernatural thrillers" that emerged in the latter half of the 1980s. By this point, film producers of the period were attempting to initiate new series, given the box office takings of the *Elm Street* series, of which the most recent, *4: The Dream Master* (1987, dir. Renny Harlin), was the highest grossing of the franchise.[63] The "supernatural thriller" was one such cycle to emerge from this context. The posters for such films routinely conflated satanism, sex, and death through their imagery and taglines, and share redolent compositions, where the films' threat often adorns the upper half of their posters, beneath which the victim/the film's protagonist is typically positioned. Thus, the theatrical poster for 1988's *The Unholy* depicts the head of a mysterious woman shrouded in darkness, her right eye projecting a beam of light, beneath which a priest is positioned, dwarfed by the size of his adversary. The tagline promises "seduction," "submission," and "murder." Comparably, the theatrical poster for *Prime Evil* depicts one of the film's hooded cult members holding a candle, the image of which expands across the poster's top half, above the illustration of a woman raising her hand to her face, her naked body concealed only by a small bed sheet. The tagline intimates themes akin to that suggested by *The Unholy*: "A terrifying force that cannot be resisted is here . . ." The posters denote a tendency in so-called "high concept" advertising, insofar as they reflect themes and design choices inviting viewers to "draw parallels" between different films.[64] The posters are, as Nowell argues of advertising materials used to promote teen comedy films made in the wake of the smash hit *Porky's* (1981, dir. Bob Clark), "made to type, whereby previous films' poster designs provide intertextual filters through which potential audiences are invited to make connections to earlier films and their associated genres."[65] The composition of *Prime Evil*'s poster and its resonances with *The Unholy* and others, thus, place the film within the parameters of a film cycle known to audiences, and attempts to speak to said audiences through the vernacular of known promotional strategies.

New World Video's cover for *Prime Evil*, as anticipated, is a composite design drawing from numerous horror sources. An illustration of the hooded, candle-holding figure is also present, albeit in this case in a photograph pierced by a bloodied knife, the edges of the photo curling as it is gradually engulfed in flames. The presence of a hooded figure in this instance, as in the case of the theatrical poster, locates the film in proximity to the films of the aforementioned occult cycle, which were, by this point, appearing on video, but also to earlier classics that inspired them, such as *Rosemary's Baby*, which was reissued by Paramount on video in 1988.[66] The presence of a blood-spattered knife, however, pulls the film in a different direction, namely toward latter-day slashers such as those aforementioned, while the collage of "occult" and "slasher" imagery evokes newer "supernatural slasher" films, such as the *Elm Street* sequels and *Friday the 13th* parts VII (1988, dir. John Carl Buechler) and VIII (1989, dir. Rob Hedden), all of which were backed by lavish promotional campaigns to ensure their visibility in rental outlets.[67] As in the case of *Lurkers*, any connection between *Prime Evil* and the major franchises of the period is tenuous. Nevertheless, by harnessing the iconography of numerous horror subgenres and films, the film's distributors hoped to attract dealers and ensure the film was placed in the eyeline of consumers who may not have heard of the film, but who were seeking entertainment akin to films of a higher profile.

Marketing Findlay's latter-day genre films in the foregoing ways speaks to the resilience of the genre beyond the movie theater in the mid-to-late 1980s. The strategies that Findlay's horror films evince continued for a short while into the following decade. However, as video dealers and renters cottoned on to the non-discerning attitudes of video companies and the poor product they continued to release, the returns on such material became much lower for their rightsholders. Reeltime's inability to secure distribution for its final film, the horror comedy *Banned* (1989), as discussed in Alexandra Heller-Nicholas's chapter here, is a case in point.[68] By the middle of the 1990s, producers of low-budget horror films akin to Findlay's output found it increasingly difficult to secure the type of distribution deal needed to ensure longevity in the business, given that the Blockbuster Video chain routinely refused to stock specific titles or entire catalogues distributed by companies known for violent horror movies.[69] Blockbuster's aversion to such material hampered whatever visibility remained for such product, its horror section given over to output from companies with the backing of major studios, such as Full Moon Entertainment, whose horror and sci-fi films were contrived to meet the demands of the family entertainment marketplace of which Blockbuster was the public face.[70] The bourgeoning video sales, or "sell-through," market ensured that Findlay's horror films remained available to consumers, but the opportunity for them to find new audiences, beyond niche horror fan communities, was over.

CONCLUSION

Since their initial release, Findlay's horror films have been reissued several times on video, DVD, and now on Blu-ray in boutique collectors' editions, where they are regarded as cult classics. The acquisition of these films by labels such as Shriek Show and Vinegar Syndrome, replete as they are with director interviews and/or commentaries, has enabled those with an interest in Findlay's work to get a sense of how she regards the films looking back. Perhaps unsurprisingly, she has little positive to say. "We just made a bunch of films, I did what I had to do," she has since explained to audience members at the Offscreen Film Festival in Brussels in 2019, in her signature flippant and self-deprecating style.[71]

Findlay's bewilderment at the cult status of her films engenders much amusement whenever she makes her views known. During an interview for Shriek Show's 2004 DVD release of *The Oracle*, for example, you can hear audible laughter from the interviewers when she dismisses the film, and horror films more generally, as ephemeral trash. But these comments, jovial though they may be, also serve as reminders of the reasons why she made the films in the first place, and why they should be of interest to film historians. As Heller-Nicholas has it, her films were never intended to "open hearts or minds," but rather "our wallets."[72] As far as the history of horror cinema goes, Findlay's genre films are symbolic of the industrial imperatives that underwrote much horror film production at the beginning of the video age. For every major release there was a swelling of commercial product of which Findlay's output was a part, which, while routinely framed as marginal to the industry proper, was, in fact, a bedrock for many individuals working in the film and video business. They were films made by *and for* "the numbers": a reliable income stream on which independent filmmakers and the first video stores could rely.

ACKNOWLEDGMENTS

Thanks, as ever, to Neil Jackson.

NOTES

1. On the film's legacy in popular culture, see Charles Bramesco, Scott Tobias, and David Fear, "Banned and Brutal: 14 Beyond-Controversial Horror Movies," *Rolling Stone*, October 28, 2016, https://www.rollingstone.com/movies/movie-news/banned-and-brutal-14-beyond-controversial-horror-movies-115696/ (accessed May 26, 2022). On the film's history see, for example, Eithne Johnson and Eric Schaefer, "Soft Core/Hard Gore: *Snuff* as a Crisis in Meaning," *Journal of Film and Video* 44, no. 2/3 (Summer-Fall, 1993): 40–59; Mikita Brottman, *Offensive Films* (Nashville: Vanderbilt University Press, 2005 [1997]), 79–97; Mark McKenna, "A Murder Mystery in Black and Blue: The Marketing, Distribution, and Cult Mythology of *Snuff* in the UK," in Neil Jackson, Shaun Kimber, Johnny Walker and Thomas Joseph Watson (eds), *Snuff: Real Death and Screen Media* (London: Bloomsbury, 2016), 121–38; and Adam Herron, "'A Contemptible Movie Now Showing in Times Square": Cultural Distinctions, Space and Taste in the Exhibition of *Snuff* at the National Theatre', *Horror Studies* 11, no. 2 (2020): 1–17.
2. See Giuseppe Previtali's contribution to the present volume for an alternative assessment of *Snuff*, where he argues that an overconcentration on the film in academic and popular discourse has meant that the original film to which the "snuff" coda was affixed, *The Slaughter* (Michael Findlay, 1971), has been overlooked.
3. Alison Peirse, "Women Make (Write, Produce, Direct, Shoot, Edit, and Analyze) Horror," *Women Make Horror: Filmmaking, Feminism, Genre* (New Brunswick, NJ: Rutgers University Press, 2020), 1–23. Quote at 10.
4. Peirse, "Women Make," 10.
5. See also Alexandra Heller-Nicholas, "Anti-auteur: The Films of Roberta Findlay," in Ernest Mathijs and Jamie Sexton (eds), *The Routledge Companion to Cult Cinema* (London: Routledge, 2020), 402–10.
6. Roberta Findlay quoted in Anthony Timpone, "Queen of 42nd Street," *Fangoria* 52 (March 1986): 50–3. Quote at 53.
7. Ashley West and April Hall, "Roberta Findlay: A Respectable Woman—Podcast 53," August 16, 2015, *Rialto Report*, podcast, https://www.therialtoreport.com/2015/08/16/roberta-findlay/ (accessed July 28, 2021).
8. West and Hall, "Roberta Findlay: A Respectable Woman."

9. Findlay quoted in Timpone, "Queen of 42nd Street," 50.
10. Findlay quoted in Timpone, "Queen of 42nd Street," 53.
11. Heller-Nicholas, "Anti-auteur," 402.
12. Heller-Nicholas, "Anti-auteur," 410.
13. Lor, "Blood Sisters," *Variety*, June 17, 1987, 21.
14. Heller-Nicholas, "Anti-auteur," 402.
15. Lawrence Cohn, "Pornmakers Surface in Mainstream," *Variety*, March 9, 1988, 3, 26. Quote at 3. For a nuanced account of the "effect" of video on the adult movie business see Peter Alilunas, *Smutty Little Movies: The Creation and Regulation of Adult Video* (Berkeley: University of California Press, 2017).
16. Laura Foti, "Cult and Horror Movie Titles Prove to be a Howling Success," *Billboard*, April 24, 1982, 55.
17. Foti, "Cult and Horror Movie Titles," 55.
18. Little is known about the late Craven's adult film career, although he has stated in interviews he worked on more than one. One such example is *The Fireworks Woman* (1975). See, for example, Craven's contributions to the documentary *Never Sleep Again: The Elm Street Legacy* (Daniel Farrands and Andrew Kasch, 2010). It is also worth mentioning that *Last House* was originally conceived as a hardcore film. On the history and legacy of the film see David A. Szulkin, *Wes Craven's Last House on the Left: The Making of a Cult Classic* (Godalming: FAB Press, 2000).
19. On the success of *Maniac* see, for example, Jim Robbins, "Lustig Sells Big Contracts at Cannes," *Boxoffice*, June 9, 1980, 5. Lustig went on to direct popular horror films such as those in the *Maniac Cop* (1988–93) franchise.
20. Vincent, quoted in Cohn, "Pornmakers Surface," 26.
21. Cohn, "Pornmakers Surface," 26.
22. Jeffrey Wells, "Sex in the Home (Where It Belongs)," *Film Journal*, June 28, 1982, 20, 22. Quote at 20.
23. Peter Hutchings, *The Horror Film* (Harlow: Pearson Longman, 2004), 33.
24. Daniel Herbert, *Videoland: Movie Culture at the American Video Store* (Berkeley: University of California Press, 2014), 58.
25. Jim McCullagh, "Horror Video," *Billboard*, September 17, 1988.
26. Dan Bottstein, "Roberta Findlay: Outspoken Lady of Porn," *Film Journal*, March 23, 1981, 22. There are similarities to be drawn between *The Oracle* and the later *Witchboard* (dir. Kevin S. Tenney, 1986), yet the latter did not materialise till December 1986, almost a full year after *The Oracle*'s theatrical release.
27. Philip Brophy, "Horrality— The Textuality of Contemporary Horror Films," *Screen* 27, no. 1 (January/February 1986): 2–13. Quote at 8.
28. David Everitt, "Splatter in the Living Room: The Booming Business of Video Violence," *Fangoria* 18 (1982): 24–7.
29. Mark Bernard, *Selling the Splat Pack: The DVD Revolution and the American Horror Film* (Edinburgh: Edinburgh University Press, 2014), 76–81.
30. Johnny Walker, "Blood Cults: Historicising the North American 'Shot on Video' Horror Movie," in Ernest Mathijs and Jamie Sexton (eds), *The Routledge Companion to Cult Cinema* (London: Routledge, 2020), 223–332. Citation at 224–5.
31. David Sanjek, "Fans' Notes: The Horror Film Fanzine," *Literature/Film Quarterly* 18, no. 3 (1990): 150–9. Quote at 152.
32. Walker, "Blood Cults," 224.
33. Timpone, "Queen of."
34. Timpone, "Queen of," 50.

35. Bill Landis, "Milligan!," *Fangoria* 20 (1982): 36–8. Quote at 36. See also, for example, Landis, "Herschell Gordon Lewis Today," *Fangoria* 17 (February 1982): 23–7; and Landis, "I, Corpse Grinder," *Fangoria* 26 (1982): 29–32, 63.

36. Timpone, "Queen of," 50.

37. "HFX" is an anagram coined by Ernest Mathijs to refer to the primacy of special effects in horror film culture of the 1970s and 1980s. See Mathijs, "They're Here! Special Effects in Horror Cinema of the 1970s and 1980s," in Ian Conrich (ed.), *Horror Zone: The Cultural Experience of Contemporary Horror Cinema* (London: I. B. Tauris, 2009), 153–71.

38. Timpone, "Queen of."

39. On the fate of *Tenement*—it was awarded an X rating by the MPAA and banned in several international territories—see Neil Jackson's chapter in the present collection. On Findlay selling her horror films to video distributors see *Rialto Report*. On International Video Entertainment, its video label, its horror success and Carolco's investment in the company, see Jim McCullaugh, "Carolco Invests in NCB," *Billboard*, June 28, 1986, 6, 73. For context relating to the Carolco/IVE arrangement, see Frederick Wasser, *Veni, Vidi, Video: The Hollywood Empire and the VCR* (Austin: University of Texas Press, 2001), 124–5.

40. For example, in the UK, *The Oracle* was released direct to video by Braveworld, a well-resourced independent distributor specializing in "B product," of which Findlay's horror film was typical.

41. Lor, "Blood Sisters." On the video releases of *Hell Night* and *The Nesting* respectively, see Anon., "Arcade Video to release MHE titles," *Screen International*, April 10, 1982, 15 and Anon., "Scary Plans from Warner," *Billboard*, August 31, 1985, 44.

42. Prior to securing an X rating by the MPAA, *The Slaughter* was lined up for distribution by Fanfare, a company with a series of biker films on its roster. Upon the film receiving the "X" rating, Fanfare dropped it. See Anon., "X Trips Solomon, Who Deplores 'Em," *Variety*, March 3, 1971, 20. It was subsequently acquired by distributor Allan Shackleton who shot the infamous coda, and released the film under the "Snuff" title in 1975. See, for example, Brottman, *Offensive Films.*

43. In numerous interviews Findlay speaks of having to write scripts because it was easier than scouting for them and cheaper than buying them. See, for example, Findlay's interview with William Hellfire at the Offscreen Film Festival in Brussels, 2019, https://www.youtube.com/watch?v=8LYMDHsCeGo&t=2840s (accessed 26 May 2022).

44. I have been able to unearth very little on Vidal who, from database searches, appears to have worked as a commentator/executive for the music business prior to her screenwriting credits.

45. Leider's credits included screenplays for such films as *Liquid A$$ets* (1982) and *Glitter* (1983), both of which were directed by Findlay.

46. Farnham Scott, "Blood Farming with Ed Kelleher," *Fangoria* 24 (1982): 43–6.

47. See, for example, Ed Kelleher, "*The Bride*," *Film Journal*, September 1, 1985, 38; Ed Kelleher, "*From Beyond*'s Helmer Gordon Calls For Ratings Revamping," *Film Journal*, October 1, 1986, 26, 101; Ed Kelleher, "Florida-based Romero Eyes 4 New Chillers," *Film Journal*, May 1, 1987, 12, 33; Ed Kelleher, "Horror Author Barker Makes Directing Bow With *Hellraiser*," *Film Journal*, October 1, 1987, 14, 83; and Ed Kelleher, "Hurd Readies Pair of Film 'Rollercoaster Rides'," *Film Journal*, April 1, 1988, 8, 52.

48. See Anon., "Crown acquires rights to *Lurkers*," *Screen International* 630 (December 12, 1987): 1; and Anon., "'Prime Evil' Atop Crown Intl. Heap," *Variety*, May 4, 1988, 219.

49. John Ellis, *Visible Fictions: Cinema, Television, Video* (New York: Routledge, 2001 [1982]), 31.

50. Ellis, *Visible Fictions*, 30.

51. Al Stewart, "Direct-to-video: The Saviour of Schlock," *Variety*, April 11, 1990, 39–40. Quote at 39.

52. Tom Daugherty quoted in David Wykoff, "'Horror Video' September is Horror Video Month," *Billboard*, September 2, 1989, 48.

53. Richard Nowell, "'Where Nothing Is Off Limits': Genre, Commercial Revitalization, and the Teen Slasher Film Posters of 1982–1984," *Post Script* 30, no. 2 (2011): 57.

54. Nowell, "Where Nothing," 56–8.

55. For example, *Variety* reports in September 1989 that, "Northside Video in St. Petersburg, Fla. turned a previously unused storage area into a horror room with a casket, skeleton, and creepy audio tapes. The room draws customers all year long . . ." Wykoff, "Horror Video," 48.

56. The notion of the "composite horror film" as a promotional tactic should be distinguished from the types of "hybrid" marketing that Nowell identifies across promotion of the first teen slasher films, the distributors of which oftentimes used iconography and subject matter from other non-horror "youth" films of the period in their marketing, "to boast significant audience appeal." See Nowell, "Where Nothing," 48. In the case of composite horror marketing discussed below, the aim of the distributor is not to disperse their wares across a variety of film genres, but to endeavor to remain within the parameters of horror (however defined), given that, whereas the theatrically distributed slasher films of which Nowell writes were competing in theatres with non-horror films, in video stores, genres were typically grouped together.

57. *Blood Cult*, for example, was shot on a budget of $125,000 and, after selling a remarkable 25,000 units, ended up grossing $800,000. See Walker, "Blood Cults," 226–8.

58. Lor, "Blood Sisters," 21.

59. Nowell, "Where Nothing," 48. See also Nowell, *Blood Money: A History of the First Teen Slasher Film Cycle* (London: Continuum, 2011).

60. Anon., "'Corn' Finds Green For Embassy Video as Summer Seller," *Variety*, June 27, 1984, 41–2.

61. Anon., "New Line Video Dream Comes True," *Screen International*, September 19, 1987, 8.

62. See, for example, Anon., "New Line Video Dream," 8.

63. Anon., "New Line's Street Cred," *Screen International*, October 22, 1988, 212.

64. Nowell, "Where Nothing," 48.

65. Nowell, "Where Nothing," 49.

66. McCullagh, "Horror Video," 48.

67. James Kendrik, "Slasher Films and Gore in the 1980s," in Harry Benshoff (ed.), *A Companion to the Horror Film* (Oxford: Wiley-Blackwell, 2014), 310–28. Quote at 318.

68. On *Banned* see Mike Watt, *Fervid Filmmaking: 66 Cult Pictures of Vision, Verve and No Self-Restraint* (Jefferson: McFarland, epub, 2013), 85–103.

69. For example, Lloyd Kaufman of Troma Entertainment, a producer and distributor of low-budget exploitation films in the 1980s, has said that Blockbuster refused to handle his product, despite it routinely achieving an R rating. See Kaufman and James Gunn, *All I Need to Know About Filmmaking I Learned from The Toxic Avenger: The Shocking True Story of Troma Studios* (New York: Berkeley Boulevard, 1998), 193–4.

70. Full Moon's videocassettes were distributed by Paramount. On Full Moon, see David Jay, *It Came From the Video Aisle!: Inside Charles Band's Full Moon Entertainment Studio* (Schiffer, 2017). On Blockbuster and its 'family' image, see Raiford Guins, *Edited Clean Version: Technology and the Culture of Control* (Minneapolis: Minnesota University Press, 2009), 98–104.

71. "Roberta Findlay Masterclass," Offscreen Film Festival 2019, https://www.youtube.com/watch?v=8LYMDHsCeGo&t=49s (accessed May 26, 2022).

72. Heller-Nicholas, "Anti-auteur," 410.

CHAPTER 9

The Beginning and the End: Transitioning Careers and Roberta Findlay's *Banned* (1989)

Alexandra Heller-Nicholas

Marking the end of a rollercoaster and frequently controversial career straddling exploitation cinema, hardcore pornography, and horror, Roberta Findlay's long-unreleased final film *Banned* (1989) has been the subject of dedicated fan speculation. After failing to gain distribution for the film, which was intended to profit from a trend for wild youth-oriented comedies on cable television, Findlay effectively quit filmmaking and returned professionally to the subject she studied at university—music—through her work at the legendary esteemed Sear Sound studio at 353 West 48th Street in New York's Hell's Kitchen (founded by and named after Findlay's long-term partner and collaborator, Walter Sear).

From this perspective, the little-seen *Banned* can be viewed as both the end of Findlay's film career, while simultaneously also flagging a transition to a second career, which at the time of writing she currently maintains. With much of *Banned* itself set in a recording studio, the film follows the antics of a milquetoast middle-class rock guitarist and vocalist who becomes possessed by the spirit of a dead killer punk rocker via a haunted toilet. With his middle-of-the-road jazz fusion group called Banned (whose name is a pun intended to play on its similarity to the word "band," and also connotations of the forbidden or censored), the largely insufferable Kent (Dan Erickson) is driven by almost naive ambitions of success. A last shot of hope comes in the shape of cheap recording time at a newly reopened music studio that was the site of a fatal massacre a decade earlier at the hands of punk rock singer Teddy Homicide (Neville Wells), lead singer of the band Rotting Filth, who drowned himself in the studio's bathroom straight after. Unfortunately for Kent, Teddy's spirit has lain dormant in the toilet, possessing the young man while he relieves himself and prompting his transition into an equally non-conforming punk rock antihero, escalating the band's fame but leaving a stream of violence and other broadly shabby behaviors in his wake.

While in its own way just as audacious as Findlay's more notorious works, *Banned* is not merely what is to date a sadly unseen finale to a complex and fascinating film career, but—more optimistically—it also bookends her career with a return to her first passion: music. However, in the case of Findlay, "passion" may not be exactly the right word to use here. As Jill C. Nelson wrote, "Roberta Findlay inferred her life has consisted of a series of random acts, and that she moved whichever way the wind happened to blow without a specific direction or objective in mind."[1] How much of this is retrospective self-mythologizing and how much is unambiguous fact is, in the case of as enigmatic a figure as Findlay, seemingly always up for grabs. But as Nelson wisely adds, regardless "it would be a challenge to attempt to contradict the dogged and refreshingly blunt Findlay."[2]

Raised in an almost completely Jewish community in the Bronx until she reached Junior High, Findlay was one of three children in a Hungarian immigrant family who grew up under intense family pressure to become a concert pianist. She began to play the instrument at the mere age of four and dedicated her life to it until she was sixteen, when she ran away from home to live with—and later marry—her boyfriend Michael Findlay, with whom she would make their notorious "roughies" in the 1960s (including *Her Flesh* trilogy from 1967–8 and *The Ultimate Degenerate* in 1969), branching out into horror in the early 1970s (*Slaughter* in 1971—which would famously have a notorious meta-coda added, to be released as *Snuff* in 1976—and *Shriek of the Mutilated* in 1974).[3] Growing up in a poor neighborhood, Findlay has described the area as a "slum,"[4] and much of the family's collective ambitions appeared to depend on the young Roberta's success as a concert pianist; thus, her running away to a very different life must have come as a shock. Findlay's mother was a bookkeeper and her father a dry cleaner, and they worked hard in "a hardscrabble life," but it was, Findlay has said, "a happy childhood."[5]

According to her version of events, Findlay excelled in school, skipping both the fourth and eighth grade, and was in "special classes."[6] Joking in her signature straight-faced, deadpan style, Findlay claims she "studied piano for 200 years,"[7] which led to her being accepted by the City College of New York to study music at the age of fifteen where she graduated at nineteen. But by her own account, she was there in accordance only with her parent's wishes:

> I studied music, which is a totally useless occupation and pastime. At the age of seventeen, I had no concept of what it is to live or what one does with one's life. My parents thought that I would be a great concert pianist. Unfortunately, I'm very dexterous and I can play very quickly, so they thought that's what I would be: a world-famous pianist that had come out of poverty or misery or whatever.[8]

She continued:

> It's not that I didn't like it, but it came to me when I was about nine or ten that I could never be a world-class pianist. It was silly—out of the question. My parents didn't know Liberace from Horowitz.[9]

For Findlay, however, classical music was her life. When pushed (and, at times, she has had to be pushed[10]), she has identified among her favorite composers as "the usual suspects . . . Beethoven, Mozart," as well as Bela Bartok and Robert Schumann ("I was a big Schumann expert," she said in 2019, but "no Bach, it's much too complicated").[11] Her focus on classical music necessarily entailed a rejection of what was then popular music, stating emphatically that "I assiduously avoided the noise of the Beatles and their ilk as I was growing up."[12]

Findlay was apparently, then, very much creatively contained within the terrain of the highbrow ambitions of her working-class parents; pop cultural forms and phenomena lay well beyond her zone of interest. Upon meeting Michael, however, everything changed. "My parents thought the world had ended—that marriage would end my career." But, she adds, "my career had ended long before that."[13] (To be more specific, Findlay has claimed she had "no sense of rhythm—zero."[14]) Nevertheless, it was through music that Findlay and Michael first crossed paths. Describing him as a "film nut"[15] and "an honest to god film freak,"[16] they met when she replied to an advertisement that he placed for a pianist to provide musical accompaniment to the silent films he would play at a film group he belonged to at City College.[17] While the Theodore Huff Film Society was, apparently, primarily dedicated to B-grade cinema of the 1930s and 1940s in particular,[18] from Findlay's recollections silent cinema was also a major component of their programming.

Her first performance was for a screening of a D. W. Griffith film,[19] and although completely unaware of film up until this point, she saw this very much as her awakening. An interview in the City College undergraduate newspaper *The Campus* from Wednesday December 6, 1961 provides fascinating insight into the pre-exploitation world of Roberta Hershkowitz and "Mike" Findlay, as they were referred to in the article. "Silent movies shows [*sic*] at the College used to be pretty quiet affairs before Roberta Hershkowitz decided to liven them up," it begins. "Roberta is a sophomore music-education major who thought that the films, presented on two days each week by the Board of managers, should have original musical accompaniment."[20] It continues, "She and the films series' [sic] director, Mike Findlay '64 had been a little perturbed by the audience's disrespect for the 1920 silent classics." Discussing her process in depth, the article describes Roberta's focus on the mood and tone of particular scenes ("'fear' and 'panic' are her favorites," we are told, a foreshadowing perhaps of her later work in the horror genre as a director).[21] Riffing on themes from Schumann and Rachmaninoff, Roberta composed her musical accompaniments a few days before the screening; Mike would record them on a tape recorder and play it back accompanying the live screening. As the article then notes, what was so impressive about Roberta's music was that she had in all cases never seen the film previously, so was improvising the score on first viewing—on top of that, she would write her compositions in one sitting, without taking a break. With particular relevance perhaps to the struggles she had with *Banned*—so much so that, as noted, it effectively ended her film career— even in these early days, Findlay struggled with comedy. But regardless, the interview highlights what drew her to the project; total creative autonomy. And yet again—once more providing a glimpse of the work of Roberta Findlay the filmmaker to come—in her list of complaints about scoring silent films, the final line of the article notes she lists as a primary problem the fact that "she doesn't get paid."[22]

Regardless, it was this period where, through Michael, she discovered a love of classical Hollywood cinema in particular, including movies such as *The Crowd* (1928, dir. King Vidor), *The Passion of Joan of Arc* (1928, Carl Theodor Dreyer), *The Thief of Bagdad* (1924, dir. Raoul Walsh), *I Married a Witch* (1942, dir. René Clair) and Orson Welles's *A Touch of Evil* (1958).[23] Threatened by the music department, who were horrified she was participating in something as lowbrow as a film group, Findlay persevered, and by her account provided musical accompaniment for twenty-five films alone in the first year, and she continued doing so when she and Michael left their studies and ran the program independently in a coffee house in the East Village.[24] Despite being one often (if not always) to downplay her accomplishments, this period stands out as a time where not just the discovery of cinema would leave a lasting impression on Findlay; she also speaks highly of the experience of providing these live soundtracks, describing it as "challenging and interesting."[25]

From here, it was with Michael that Findlay's career would take a dramatic turn away from the career path envisaged by her parents and her work in film began. It was through *Slaughter* and its transformation into *Snuff* that, after Findlay and Michael separated, her paths would cross with notorious distributor Allan Shackleton, whose claims to notoriety would of course be the brain trust behind the decision to add the controversial *Snuff* coda. But perhaps more importantly, it was through Shackleton that Findlay first met Walter Sear, the onetime professional tuba player who was famously a key adviser in the design of the iconic Moog synthesizer. Meeting in Shackleton's office when Findlay was still personally involved with the latter, Sear gave Findlay his business card, which Shackleton promptly ripped up, Jill C. Nelson speculating that he was "sensing an obvious connection between Findlay and Sear."[26] Findlay, however, memorized his contact details, and upon contacting him, their decades-long personal and professional relationship began in earnest (the latter culminating in the vast work they did together under the umbrella of Reeltime Distributing Corporation, in which they were partners),[27] making together what she counts as approximately thirty-five films across primarily hardcore pornography and horror movies.[28]

Banned would prove to be not just the final Roberta Findlay film, then, but the last film Sear and Findlay would work on together. The centrality of Walter to Findlay's post-Michael filmography and *Banned* in particular culminates nowhere more readily than in the fact that the film was largely shot in his legendary studio, Sear Sound in Hell's Kitchen.[29] He opened Sear Sound on West 46th Street in 1970 before moving to West 48th Street in the old Hit Factory studio in 1990, and it was during this period that his reputation as an outlier for refusing to let go of analogue technology grew within the music industry.[30] The lines between music and filmmaking span back far earlier than *Banned*, of course: regardless of which of these two addresses Sear Sound was located, it appears to have been a regular feature in numerous Findlay-directed Reeltime productions such as *The Playgirl* (1982), *Raw Footage* (1977), and the later horror film *Lurkers* (1988), for starters. But when it came to the studio itself, Walter emphatically refused to upgrade Sear Sound's analogue equipment to digital recording technology, leading to enormous industry respect. With Findlay as studio manager, Sear Sound drew a high caliber of diverse artists over the years, including Sonic Youth, Steely Dan, Lou Reed, Joanna Newsom, U2, and Björk. Sear died in 2010. The legacy of his film work with Findlay was, at least by April 2011, still apparent even just within the front door of Sear Sound, where large posters of her horror movies *Blood Sisters* (1987) and *Prime Evil* (1988) hung in pride of place in the visitor's lounge.[31]

FROM FILM TO SOUND: *BANNED* AND PROFESSIONAL TRANSITION

And then came *Banned*. As noted previously, Findlay has retrospectively cast her professional life almost as a series of unintentional wanderings that led her from job to job because opportunities came up and she simply had nothing else to do at the time: "I wasn't going to earn a living playing piano . . . [so] it seemed like making dirty films was a good idea."[32] Likewise, that she has ended up managing one of the most well-respected music studios in the world also seems like it happened more because she had nothing better to do than the result of a concrete decision ("What do I care about sound," "I have nothing else to do," "We ran the place, and that was it."[33]) *Banned* arrived after a series of what Findlay has called a "successful" run with horror movies,[34] but was made more out of desperation than inspiration. Of the film, she is hardly nostalgic; "the last one we made was a total disaster," she said in a 2019 interview.

"It's awful, it's unsellable . . . we lost too much." She continues, describing it as "a comedy—a sex comedy. It's stupid. Dumb."[35] According to Findlay, *Banned* was solely the result of a recommendation from Reeltime's accountant, who said it would be in their interest to "shoot something before the fiscal year ends."[36] Whether true or not (and there's no reason to believe it is not), this was not the first time Findlay had claimed such a motivation for making a film, saying that *Blood Sisters*, too, was made solely as an attempt to avoid issues with her tax (this, she says, was her specific "inspiration" for that film).[37]

Desperate to find something to shoot, Findlay recalls that "there was a kid working here [at Sear Sound] who said 'I have a script,' and I read the script and it was terrible. So we shot it."[38] That "kid" was Jim Cirile, who had worked as a producer's assistant on a number of Findlay's horror films (*Blood Sisters*, *Lurkers*, *Prime Evil*), and had worked at Reeltime. But in 1987, he also appeared in John Fasano's horror comedy *Rock 'n' Roll Nightmare*, written and starring cult icon Enclose "and onetime Mr. Canada" in parenthesis Jon Mikl Thor. A thoroughly over-the-top exercise in hair metal excesses and a puppet-centered demonic invasion, Cirile played the drummer of Triton, a band whose members cloister themselves in an isolated country house / recording studio to work on their new album. One by one, they find themselves and their girlfriends possessed by the demonic forces who have invaded the space, leading to the final confrontation between Thor's character, John Triton, and Beelzebub himself. While not identical to *Banned*, *Rock 'n' Roll Nightmare* does provide concrete evidence of where Cirile's inspiration to write a screenplay focused on a rock band where horror and comedy are the primary generic elements may have come from. Reflecting on the project, Cirile said:

> I was a fan of punk and had played in a couple of punk and metal bands. But I'm also a jazz fan, and a bit of a musical snob. So the idea of combining those two disparate influences into one character was a milquetoast jazz jackass and an ultraviolent, corrosives-snorting braindead Brit punk star. Teddy was obviously cribbed off Sid Vicious, but wackier. The subtext of it all was to skewer punk and jazz by pointing out the cliches of both.[39]

Cirile has, in the years since, spoken at length about his involvement with *Banned* and Sear in particular. As he tells it, he met Sear when he was looking for a job as an office boy, and he became involved with Reeltime just as the film component of the company was transitioning from porn to horror. "Company founder Walter Sear saw the writing on the wall—videotape was slowly killing off traditional theatrical porno film distribution," said Cirile. "He decided ultra-low-budget horror movies were the way to go."[40] After a few years of working on Reeltime productions, Cirile had climbed the internal company ladder, but with *Banned*, he confesses "I more or less sank the company." As he puts it:

Figure 9.1 Jim Cirile in *Rock 'n' Roll Nightmare* (John Fasano, 1987), a film whose shared rock horror comedy haunting-based premise surely influenced his screenplay for Roberta Findlay's final film, *Banned*.

I had been pushing Reeltime to expand from the shrinking low-budget horror market (foreign sales markets were drying up due to oversaturation of schlocky horror flicks.) My thinking was that Reeltime should rebrand itself as a quirky, cult-movie indie. In order to do that, we made BANNED, a screwball horror comedy (which I wrote), about a young, Milquetoast [sic] jazz guitarist who becomes possessed by the spirit of a dead, psychotic Brit punk rock star a la Sid Vicious. It was like ALL OF ME meets REPO MAN. To their credit, Roberta and Walter rolled the dice and made BANNED with their own money. Unfortunately, they couldn't give it away.[41]

He continues:

The problems were many. While the movie was pretty damn funny, it was also pretty damn crappy on a technical level. And I must take some of the blame, too, as the quirky script, while designed to be "bad-proof" due to its ruthless poking fun at itself, wasn't all it should have been. And so the cult classic we were all hoping for hit the American Film Market with a tremendous thud. BANNED was the first film Reeltime made that they were unable to find any significant distribution for, foreign or domestic. Reeltime took a pounding.[42]

Banned remains officially unreleased at the time of writing, though an official Media Blasters release is on the horizon.[43] Although rare, there are some reviews available suggesting that, despite the seemingly cursed nature of the film and its "undistributability" (for want of a better word), it does in fact have its charms. The 2010 book *Destroy All Movies!!!: The Complete Guide to Punk on Film*, for example, features a rare review of the film: "The great unreleased bonehead party comedy of all time," it declares with some degree of fanfare, making the important observation that "to my knowledge, this is the only film where punk behavior is created as a variation on demonic possession." But aside from this, the real virtue of the film is its glee; "from boners to banana peels, no joke is too low, but all are delivered with an eagerness that makes even the heaviest groaner forgivable."[44]

Because of this spirit alone, *Banned* can be considered a comfortable fit in Findlay's filmography. Because of this spirit alone, *Banned* can be considered a comfortable fit in Findlay's filmography, despite marking a shift away from sex films and horror movies towards comedy. She is a filmmaker who has in many ways so actively resisted the industrial and critical discourse upon which traditional auteur studies so heavily relies.[45] As I have written elsewhere:

> Roberta Findlay is an important cult film director because despite the fact that few would attempt to defend her work as necessarily "great," the aggressive, unrelenting tastelessness, rawness and general spirit of don't-give-a-fuckness that marks her films is for many of us unparalleled. These films are marked by a unique blend of sleazy honesty: they are what they are, and never seek to apologise for it. They may not be perfect or even very good, but the films of Roberta Findlay are all the things that cult film at its best should be: shocking, confrontational, and fundamentally wild. For all the pouty, sassy bad-girl posturing of 90s postfeminism, this is a woman who—if her work is anything to go by, at least—suggests they were made by someone genuinely untouched by conservative morality.[46]

I continue:

> No matter how hard we try to push her, Findlay resists orthodox auteurist frameworks, even those we tweak and modify for the often gonzo-ridden outlaw terrain of cult filmmaking. Her "filmography" (itself an unstable concept) and the drastically different production contexts in which she worked deny us any such critical comforts.[47]

From this perspective, then, *Banned* does what Teddy Homicide in his British vernacular would describe as "taking the piss" out of itself; as punk rock in spirit as Teddy himself, the film is both self-aware and self-effacing in a flagrant, chaotic manner that as a whole acts as an enormous "fuck you," not just to cinema in general, but to *itself* as well. As such, it is the perfect swan song to Findlay's directorial career, one that spanned arguably the most notorious film genres imaginable. While a notoriously ephemeral and unstable concept, punk has been critically framed as "a social practice, or sets of social practices" by a group of people

> [who] were sick and tired of the crap that mainstream culture was shoving down their throats, whether it was music, art, literature or fashion, and so they decide to make their own cultural products . . . it was a two-part process: a rejection of the status quote and an embrace of the do-it-yourself ethos."[48]

This is not to suggest that Findlay was punk per se—either literally or more metaphorically—but rather, that this parodic punk spirit of *Banned* is actively brought to life here. Findlay was an outsider and was perfectly happy being so. Attempts to shoehorn her into more orthodox notions were actively resisted by the reality of who she was and the work she made; attempts to champion her as a celebrated woman filmmaker in the traditional mold, for example, are continuously challenged by her explicit dislike of working with women[49] and her vocal disgust at attempts to frame her as a kind of feminist arthouse filmmaker.[50] Of her earlier films, Findlay again resists attempts to reduce her to a misunderstood artist, as she has spoken with open disdain at the fans of such work; as she has famously stated, "people who like those old movies seem to have deep psychological problems."[51]

As much as Findlay has perhaps quite rightly dismissed the film (it is hardly her magnum opus), it is less an earnest (non-parodic) spirit of punk that leaps out of *Banned*, but rather her love of classic cinema,[52] especially when manifested in some of the film's more charming visual gags—a repeated motif of Kent falling into potholes, for example, contains echoes of more classic screen comedy than the kind of rough-and-tumble schlock that much of the film's more then-contemporary elements might indicate (such as the focus on punk music, the attempt to mimic 1980s teen sex comedies, etc.). The film begins with a black screen with wild punk music playing over its opening credits. Beginning ten years before the bulk of the film's action, we see the original Teddy Homicide recording of the studio massacre from which the film's narrative largely stems. "I'm so fucking bored," screams Homicide with a seemingly deliberately over-the-top British accent, while his unimpressed producer complains about his lack of talent, and yet refers to him respectfully as "Mr. Homicide." A mysterious figure enters the building, and, despite a build-up of tension, is revealed to be the movie's first intentional gag—it is just a humble pizza delivery man. And yet, this is enough to provoke Teddy, who uses a machine gun to massacre everyone in the studio (including the pizza delivery man), and gives a signature punk rock two-fingers up before drowning himself by flushing his head in the toilet (to verify the film's dedication to visual comedy, he literally kicks a bucket as he flails, dying). Jumping forward to the film's then-present moment, Banned plays to unenthused passers-by in Times Square. Losing money and losing interest, Kent is the only band member with any seeming ambition for the group, with Serge (Fred Cabral), Chelsea (Brent Whitney), and Willie (Roger Coleman) all either disinterested, distracted, or increasingly fed up. While drinking margaritas to drown their sorrows, Willie notes to his bandmates that his brother recently purchased the old Impulse recording studio, which was bankrupted and forced to close after the Teddy Homicide massacre. Suggesting Banned could be just the test group the studio might need to make sure it was all running smoothly before reopening, they plan to record an album there at a discounted rate. Kit, seeing it as "the chance of a lifetime," is excited, and the group busily make plans to record. Early on in proceedings, however, the distorted voice of Teddy Homicide can be heard emitting from the toilet, claiming he is stuck "in the bleedin' bowl." While others hear strange noises, it is Kent who is finally possessed by Teddy, changing not just the energy of the band themselves, but his newfound punk rock attitude, and a burst in confidence and dramatically increased libido find his relationship with his girlfriend Rachel (Amy Brentano) under significant pressure.

Banned—again—may not be perfect, but it is at times funny in a consciously cheesy way that has a joy to its self-knowing status as a kind of corny, silly comedy. For example, when Serge is taken over by an increasingly hysterical televangelist persona, Wallie rescues him by pushing an electronic device on his chest, with Rachel providing the scene's much-anticipated and delightfully cringeworthy punchline: "it's good that you've got that surge suppressor." A running gag with Lebanese terrorists that has perhaps not aged as well as it could have finds Kent advising them on the best ways to advance the cause of their attacks, redirecting them from the cheaper café where he and Chelsea are eating lunch to the far more profitable Tavern on the Green in Central Park as a better place to rob if they wish to make money. Most charming, however, is the little-seen but important character of Percival the Priestly Plumber (Adam Fried), a camp ex-plumber priest wannabe who was rejected from the church and so founded his own religious-themed television talk show. Feeling like he could have come straight from a John Waters film, Percival has the dubious privilege of being the figure who performs Kent's exorcism, returning Teddy Homicide to the toilet from whence he came while shouting, toilet brush in hand "let's do religious things!"

Being a Findlay film, that there are numerous comedy sequences centered around sex—as softcore as they may be—is perhaps unsurprising. Serge's sex addiction and habit of throwing ignored alarm clocks at his bedroom wall as his bed is increasingly crammed full of a growing number of sexual partners is another running gag throughout the film, and a sex scene between Kent and Rachel early in his transformation that initially looks like it is nonconsensual rapidly devolves into a bouncy, silly comedy sex scene, complete with trampoline-assisted acrobatics and an exceedingly goofy soundtrack. One of the most memorable scenes in the film features Kent with two groupies, one played by cult horror figure Debbie Rochon (now a director in her own right who became a leading scream queen in the 1990s, especially due to her work with Troma and the like). Recalling a trash film reimagining of the group sex scene in Michelangelo Antonio's *Blow-up* (1966) with David Hemmings and Jane Birkin, this scene again strongly echoes Findlay's background working in sex films, and even from a contemporary perspective stands out as one of *Banned*'s most striking and memorable sequences.

As one of the only "big" names associated with the film today, despite Findlay's dislike of working with women behind the camera, Rochon still holds nothing but praise for Findlay and recalls the project positively:

> I thought it was clever. It's about the leader of a hip young jazz band that becomes possessed by Teddy Homicide a punk rocker who died in the same recording studio the jazz group rented for their first album. It was very funny and a real slice of the 80s.[53]

Rochon continues:

> Roberta is a really funny, unique person. One minute she's having a laugh and the next minute she's screaming at everyone calling them names. I have to give her a ton of credit. When we made *Banned* in 1989 she had been in the business for a couple of decades at that point and female directors were just not working in the capacity that she was. She is a true New York character! Eccentric and brash and to the point. It made me a little nervous at the time, but I look back now and love it! Makes me laugh—in a good way.[54]

While Rochon would, from this point, only continue to develop her career in the film industry, for Findlay *Banned* was the end of an era. But considering that she would from here transition more concretely to working solely at Sear Sound in the capacity of studio manager, the emphasis in *Banned* on the actual practical mechanics of day-to-day life in a music studio, while standing out somewhat clunkily in terms of the film's plot and dialogue, do give insight into how this aspect of how Sear and Findlay were evolving and merging to focus more singularly on the music recording side of their business. Take, for example, the detailed yet widely unnecessary discussion between Chelsea and Kent as they schedule their time in the recording studio, the emphasis on bands setting up their equipment, and the unabashedly extreme figure of music executive Sid

Figure 9.2 The low quality of the image reflects the fact that the film has yet to receive any kind of formal distribution, and low-resolution screen captures are currently all that is available at the time of publication.

Wesenthal, a small, older Jewish man who—after doing lines of his favorite drug of choice, beef adrenal tissue (!)—becomes a large Black man whose dramatic change in appearance seems to surprise no one.

After *Banned*, Findlay stopped making films and became more formally established in the Sear Sound recording studio side of the business (until then, she says, she just "hung around" the office).[55] While she still tends to downplay the significance of Sear Sound, her love, respect, and pride in Sear remain inescapable. And, even in *Banned*, despite the film's objective failure, Sear left his stamp there also, it being one of the many films Findlay directed that he provided the music for (of particular note here is an admirable punk cover of Wagner's "Ride of the Valkyries," which appears at choice moments in the film's final third act). Beyond their work at the studio—of which Findlay would continue without him after his death in 2010—Findlay and Sear continued to share in their love of music, frequently attending the opera together.[56] While Findlay is very much on the record for her disregard for *Banned*, it is somewhat ironic that its decades-long absence has rendered it a kind of cult film holy grail for a particular niche of trash film fans. But stepping away from the quality and history of the actual film itself, that Findlay's film work was by this point so literally and symbolically set at Sear Sound speaks not only of the endurance of their personal relationship as it developed and evolved over the many decades they spent together, it also marks Findlay's return—quite fittingly—back to where she started, long before she met Michael Findlay: music. As ambivalent about that journey as she may be, one cannot deny its satisfying symmetry. And with as self-depreciating and unrestrained an iconoclast as Roberta Findlay is, perhaps this symmetry is the tidiest way her wild, euphoric, sometimes cynical and often very challenging filmmaking career could wrap up.

ACKNOWLEDGMENTS

The author would like to thank William Wilson, Richard York, and Heather Buckley who facilitated access to the film. Special thanks to Debbie Rochon who appeared in the film and recalled her experiences of working with Findlay.

NOTES

1. Jill C. Nelson, *Golden Goddesses: 25 Legendary Women of Classic Erotic Cinema, 1968–1985* (Duncan, OK: BearManor Media, 2012), 168.
2. Nelson, *Golden Goddesses*, 168.
3. As I have discussed elsewhere, Findlay's precise involvement in her own filmography is hazy, see Alexandra Heller-Nicholas, "What's Inside a Girl?: Porn, Horror and the Films of Roberta Findlay," *Senses of Cinema*, September 2016, https://www.sensesofcinema.com/2016/american-extreme/porn-horror-roberta-findlay/ (accessed May 26, 2022).
4. Nelson, *Golden Goddesses*, 170.
5. Nelson, *Golden Goddesses*, 171.
6. Nelson, *Golden Goddesses*, 171.
7. "Gear Club Podcast: #71: Nimble . . . As It Were with Roberta Findlay," *Gear Club Podcast: The Art & Science of Music Recording*, 27 August 2019, https://www.gear-club.net/episodes/2020/roberta-findlay (accessed May 26, 2022).
8. Nelson, *Golden Goddesses*, 171.
9. Nelson, *Golden Goddesses*, 172.
10. In 2019, she calls a question about who her favorite composer is "silly," answering "how do you choose the best filmmaker, it's impossible!" See "Gear Club Podcast."
11. "Gear Club Podcast."
12. "Gear Club Podcast."
13. Nelson, *Golden Goddesses*, 172.
14. "Gear Club Podcast."
15. Nelson, *Golden Goddesses*, 172.
16. "Gear Club Podcast."
17. "Gear Club Podcast."
18. Gerald Peary, "Woman in Porn: How Young Roberta Findlay Finally Grew Up and Made Snuff," *Take One*, September 1978, 28.
19. Findlay has, at different points, named this film as Griffiths's *Intolerance* (1916) and *The Birth of a Nation* (1915), See Nelson, *Golden Goddesses*, 172; "Gear Club Podcast."
20. Martins (no Christian name provided), "Coed Records Mood Music for Silent Film Program," *The Campus* 5, December 6, 1961, http://digital-archives.ccny.cuny.edu/thecampus/1961/DECEMBER_109_18/00000149.PDF (accessed May 26, 2022).
21. Martins, "Coed Records Music for Silent Film Program," 5.
22. Martins, "Coed Records Music for Silent Film Program," 5.
23. Peary, "Woman in Porn," 29–30.

24. Nelson, *Golden Goddesses*, 172.
25. Nelson, *Golden Goddesses*, 172.
26. Nelson, *Golden Goddesses*, 179.
27. Nelson, *Golden Goddesses*, 179.
28. "Gear Club Podcast."
29. "Gear Club Podcast." Although the film is dated 1989 and the *New York Times* obituary for Sear dates the move to 48th Street in 1990, it appears that it is the latter where the film was shot. Like many things Findlay related, facts are often hazy and tricky to pin down. See Ben Sisario, "Walter Sear, an Audio Engineer with a Passion for Analog, Dies at 80," *New York Times*, May 6, 2010, https://www.nytimes.com/2010/05/07/arts/music/07sear.html (accessed May 26, 2022).
30. Sisario, "Walter Sear."
31. Nelson, *Golden Goddesses*, 196.
32. "Gear Club Podcast."
33. "Gear Club Podcast."
34. "Gear Club Podcast."
35. "Gear Club Podcast."
36. "Gear Club Podcast."
37. Fever Dreams Productions, "A Blood Sisters Reunion," *Blood Sisters* (Roberta Findlay, 1987) DVD extra. New York: Media Blasters, 2004.
38. "Gear Club Podcast."
39. Zack Carlson and Bryan Connolly (eds), *Destroy All Movies!!!: The Complete Guide to Punks on Film* (College Park: Fantagraphics Books, 2016), 30.
40. Jim Cirile, "I Wanna Be Seared," *Stormblog*, July 14, 2007, https://coverageink.blogspot.com/2007/07/i-wanna-be-seared_14.html (accessed May 26, 2022).
41. Cirile, "I Wanna Be Seared."
42. Cirile, "I Wanna Be Seared."
43. "Media Blasters: Roberta Findlay's Banned Prepped for Blu-ray," Blu-ray.com, August 11, 2020, https://www.blu-ray.com/news/?id=2725 (accessed May 26, 2022). Editors' note: John Sirabella of MediaBlasters confirmed to us that the film is scheduled for a 4K release.
44. Carlson and Connolly (eds), *Destroy All Movies!!!*, 30.
45. See my previous article and book chapter: Alexandra Heller-Nicholas, "Anti-auteur: The Films of Roberta Findlay," in Ernest Mathijs and Jamie Sexton (eds), *The Routledge Companion to Cult Cinema* (London: Routledge, 2020), 402–10; Heller-Nicholas, "What's Inside a Girl?"
46. Heller-Nicholas, "Anti-auteur," 402.
47. Heller-Nicholas, "Anti-auteur," 409.
48. Kevin Dunn, *Global Punk: Resistance and Rebellion in Everyday Life* (New York: Bloomsbury Academic, New York, 2016), 11.
49. Nelson, *Golden Goddesses*, 185.
50. J. R. Taylor, "The Curse of Her Filmography: Roberta Findlay's Grindhouse Legacy," *New York Press*, July 20, 2005, www.nypress.com/news/the-curse-of-her-filmography-LYNP102005072730727279985 (accessed July 10, 2021).
51. Taylor, "The Curse of Her Filmography."
52. Nelson, *Golden Goddesses*, 197.
53. Alexandra Heller-Nicholas, *1000 Women in Horror, 1895–2018* (Albany: BearManor Media, 2020), 396.
54. Heller-Nicholas, *1000 Women in Horror*, 417.
55. "Gear Club Podcast."
56. Nelson, *Golden Goddesses*, 197.

CHAPTER 10

Roberta Findlay vs. Porn Studies

Whitney Strub, Peter Alilunas, and Roberta Findlay

*T*his *interview, edited and condensed for clarity, took place on September 21, 2021 at the Sear Sound studio in New York City. Whitney Strub and Roberta Findlay were at the studio, and Peter Alilunas joined over Zoom.*

Whitney Strub What are your thoughts on having an academic collection of essays about your work?

Roberta Findlay I've had many interviews with various people. I've lost track of some of them, actually. I find it to be like psychotherapy. So, I do it because it's head spinning. As far as your publishing an academic tome about my films, I can't relate to that. I just can't see it . . . they have no merit. The only remote merit that might occur is for First Amendment [battles] . . . that we fought here and there, but not much of it. But that's about all I can think of. I don't find any academic merit in any of this stuff. Later, as I went on and on, I thought the photography got pretty good. I called it "painting with light."

Peter Alilunas What about all the people who had such a good time watching your films, do you think that there's any merit in the pleasures that people had watching?

RF People have pleasure in reading cartoons, too. There's all kinds of junk in the world that gives people pleasure. This is one of them.

WS If an academic book about your films is going to exist, what do you think should be in it? I know you don't think it should exist at all, but if it's going to exist, what would you include and what kind of angles, what kind of interpretations? What would you focus on?

RF That's a good question. I don't know that there's a running throughline through any of this stuff, but I guess inevitably, if a person makes it, creates something, it is consistent that person will have some of themselves in the creation. A lot of this stuff was written by me after the serious episodes with Michael [Findlay], when I was on my own . . . that's where you could see any through theme, possibly. I've been interviewed by other people before, who found me hating women in films, I didn't even know it was there. That's it. I thought I hid that [laughing]. OK. So what would an academic approach to this [be]? What's yours?

WS One throughline I see is family dysfunction. If you look at early stuff like *Altar of Lust* [1971] and *Rosebud* [1972] all the way through *Blood Sisters* [1987], which begins with the little boy being taunted by the girl because his mother is a prostitute.

RF That is familiar to me. The mother part no. My mother was like a gray creature, disappearing into the woodwork. She was a European Jewish wife who didn't participate in anything. My father was a mean, dysfunctional alcoholic hateful man, yeah, who I hated.

WS That does seem echoed in some of the films.

RF I didn't have any feeling one way or the other for my mother. I guess that's in the films.

PA There's also a theme offscreen too, which is just that you were working as a filmmaker. You put in a lot of work making movies.

RF Yes, that's true, that's true. I worked very hard. That's absolutely true at all aspects of film because I was the director, the cameraman, the editor. [But] I hated the sex scenes, I hated them. I found them not morally reprehensible, but disgusting. I don't want to look at naked bodies, so I was interested in all the other material, and I loved to shoot and I loved to edit. Editing was a great puzzle and fun for me. I lacked the connective tissue between the sex scenes to me. I know it's far-fetched, but the format to me was like an opera, and in an opera you have some action and action, and then the soprano has to come out and sing, and that's the aria, that's a sex scene. And then she goes back, and a little more action, and the tenor and baritone have been singing, and so forth. So to me it was an operatic format.

WS Are you familiar with any of the academic work on Porn Studies, like Linda Williams's book *Hard Core*?

RF Are you crazy?

WS She argues that the hardcore feature is like a musical, in a structural way.[1]

RF Musical, exactly. To me an opera, because I'm a snob.

PA When you speak so eloquently about the operatic format of the films, there's tons of merit to what you're talking about.

RF Walter [Sear] and I got really fancy and went off the deep end and starting doing stuff that wasn't good for sex pictures. We got carried away [on pictures like *Liquid Assets* (1982) and *Mystique* (1980)]. I don't know what I was thinking. That was incorrect for the market.

WS So there was an artistic ambition there, though.

RF Yes, I guess that's right. Generally influenced through the lens. I wanted to make beautiful frames.

WS Some of what you're saying makes me think of Sidney Lumet because he always talked about his approach to film. It was kind of a formal question. He would shoot a western because he wanted to see what it was like to shoot in the desert instead of the city. It sounds a little like your approach. Kind of a formalist approach. Not really caring about the film itself as narrative, but caring about the craftsmanship.

RF Oh yeah. While we were shooting I was obsessed with two things. Of course the photography and I loved lighting. And I was very careful about the gaffer that we got and I directed the gaffer. Generally, we'd get it down to below F2 with the lights, using barn doors and gaffer tape. There was practically no light left by the time we were through lighting the set. Second, no matter what the picture was, I was completely obsessed with editing so that all I cared about was not directing the actors, but will the shots go together? We didn't have enough film to do coverage. Master, close-up, close-up, whatever. Nothing was repeated. So I had to make sure that in my head all I'm doing is editing instead of paying attention to what's being shot. And everything always matched.

PA Thinking along these lines of making a puzzle out of the production, and editing in camera, was there any substantial difference to you when it came to genre, with something like *Liquid Assets*, which is really funny and has a comic timing, compared to something like *A Woman's Torment* [1977], which has these really intense sequences that are not funny. What was that puzzle like for you in terms of genre?

RF Walter Sear thought he was making social satire [with films like] *Fringe Benefits* [1974] and *Slip Up* [1975]. My stuff's not funny.

WS You've got some pretty grim, serious films, but you do have the comedies from the 70s. *'Sweet Punkin' I Love You* [1976] and *Dear Pam* [1976].

RF That's Walter's.

WS *Dear Pam*, really?

RF Yes, I was the cameraman. I shot that for him and that's his film.

WS It's hard for us to keep straight because of all the pseudonyms.

RF He'd never used his real name, but I started [using my real name] in the 1980s.

WS Well, something like *Anyone But My Husband* [1975].

RF Is that a comedy?

WS It's got comedic moments, right? The opening scene where she's [preparing] chicken intercut with a sex scene reads as a kind of a joke on the audience. Was that a deliberate middle finger to the raincoat crowd? it's sexy and then it's deeply unappetizing. And then you go back and forth between the two.

RF I know surely that I was never thinking about what the audience wanted to see.

WS What was the logic of that for you? Why intercut those two shots?

RF I don't remember why. I guess I thought it was amusing.

PA There's a few of those moments where you have some graphic match cuts that are darkly funny.

Figure 10.1 The opening of *Anyone But My Husband*.

RF Oh, I love match cuts. Nobody does that anymore. I learned all this stuff at Michael's knee. He was a true film aficionado.

WS Do you remember an article from 1976 called "*Angel on Fire*: Three Texts of Desire," by Dennis Giles in a journal called *Velvet Light Trap*? Is that something that crossed your desk at the time?[2]

RF Are you kidding? The only thing I ever read was *Cahiers du Cinema* and *Sight and Sound*. I stole the script from *Goodbye Charlie* [1964, dir. Vincente Minnelli]. I just made it up. Plagiarized.

PA We think this is the first piece of writing by an academic about hardcore film.

WS He concludes that "we have reached a tentative identification of the dominant fantasy of *Angel on Fire*, represented in distorted form as unconscious and conscious fantasies of the film. The dominant fantasy is the original trauma of birth, as expulsion from the mother. This is transformed into the unconscious fantasy of punishing the mother for this unwarranted assault upon her child. The last transformation is a guilty reversal of this unconscious desire. It is the conscious fantasy of being punished for the sadism of the subtext."[3] What are your thoughts on that?

RF Sounds like gibberish. Like he had a thesaurus. Polysyllabic words. I don't know what that means.

WS I think the chapters in our book are going to be a little more readable. In another passage, Giles doubts whether you existed because it was credited to Roberta Findlay, a woman, and he says "although this name is possibly a pseudonym, we are confronted with a feminine persona as a creator of a fantasy for a predominantly masculine audience, it presents a female filmmaker assuming the point of view of a male spectator who in turn identifies with a female protagonist."[4]

RF I was born Roberta Hershkowitz, so he's right there.

PA What's interesting about it is that the author can't imagine that a woman could make this film.

RF There's a couple of practical reasons at that time, I guess. Why would a woman want to do this kind of stuff, I mean. All through my career and forever and ever, it was supposedly demeaning to women to be in any of these films, and they're being abused and so forth. But I didn't have any problems with anybody that I can think of or remember as far as being a female.

WS Molly Haskell wrote a short little piece for the *Village Voice* about the same film. She had a slightly different gloss. Whereas Giles thought a woman couldn't have directed *Angel Number 9*, she thought it had to be a woman because of the issues around pregnancy. She says, "For those who are not blue movie aficionados, pregnancy is a no no in sexploitation movies, a definite downer to Don Juan fantasies of quickie no fault sex."[5]

RF I don't remember, is there a pregnancy in *Angel Number 9*? Oh, that's right. And then he's hit by a car. Yeah, and then we go to heaven, which was built three blocks from [Sear Sound].

WS Oh yeah, where?

RF 45th and 9th.

WS Some loft?

RF No, it was a small shooting stage. We often hired female art directors.

WS Ok, that challenges your narrative [of not hiring women] a little.

RF A few. Three or four.

WS How did that work?

RF Two of them were excellent. But I would not hire any women to work on a film crew, ever.

WS With an asterisk.

RF The equipment then was much too heavy. [On one of our films] a female gaffer came in to replace the gaffer for two days, I think it was because he had another job. I almost killed him. Walter's walking around, carrying 100 feet of feeder cable because she couldn't carry the goddamn stuff. Women cannot do the same job as men, physically. I'm not a feminist. I don't even know what that's supposed to mean. Generally, it means, I guess it's changed a bit, but that women used to play at it until they got into trouble and then they would go back to their husband and be taken care of.

WS Did you ever have any direct interaction with [any anti-porn activists] like Andrea Dworkin, Catharine MacKinnon, Robin Morgan?

RF I never had intercourse, you should pardon the expression, with them, with any women, actually.[6]

We turned to Karen Sperling's 1973 film, The Waiting Room. *As described in the Introduction to this collection, Sperling had previously directed* Make a Face *(1971), which played at various film festivals and had established Sperling as a rising filmmaking talent. Her follow-up,* The Waiting Room, *featured an all-woman crew, in order, as Sperling noted at the time, to provide opportunities for women technicians, who had experience and education but a lack of opportunities.[7] Findlay was the film's cinematographer.*

RF [Sperling's] idea was to hire an all-female crew. I said, Karen, what's the point? And finally, after a few days, I said OK, do you give up? And she did. And I got some guys in to carry the dolly. Put it up on a stage. Take it down and so on. The other women remained a waste of time. Idiotic.[8]

PA I had a conversation recently with Sperling, and she had very vivid and strong memories of you being [a very hard worker], which matches up with everything that Whit and I have read about you and in your interviews about how seriously you took your job.

RF It's true. Officious. It's a very, very Protestant work ethic, ironically.

PA How did you get the job as cinematographer?

RF That wasn't easy. I had to cull out of trailers and stuff a reel to show her. I took some trailers and I had to cut up footage that was innocent and that looked like not what it was, and so I managed to get, you know, about 15 minutes' worth of film that I thought looked good, was lit nicely. This is before the horror films. There's nothing to choose from. Just dirty pictures.

WS How do you feel about the irony of the fact that you were part of the first all-woman crew, even as you yourself are pretty vociferous against exactly that?

RF I never saw the finished print. It was a job. She paid me very well. I didn't care. It made no difference to me. I said, we can't go on like this, these bimbos can't carry this stuff around. Look at me. I could hold the camera but I couldn't do anything beyond that. And a gaffer, a grip is especially dealing with heavy gear. I don't know that it's ironic, but yeah, it was a job to me. I just never had any use for women. Weak.

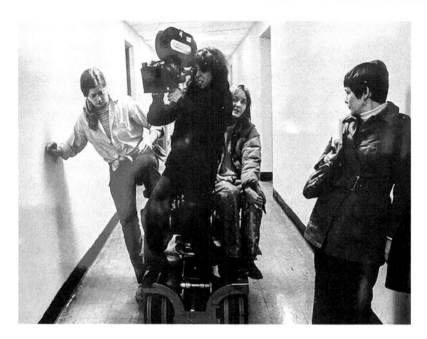

Figure 10.2   Roberta Findlay holding the camera on the set of *The Waiting Room*.
Photo courtesy of Karen Sperling.

Our conversation turns to pseudonyms, cameos, and lost films.

WS We wanted to ask you about authorship because you use your own name for *Altar of Lust* and then *Rosebud* and through *Angel Number 9*. And then you started using pseudonyms. So *Anyone But My Husband* was the year after *Angel Number 9* and you became Robert Norman and then you became all of these other names, so *Mystique* isn't under your name, *A Woman's Torment*, these were all different permutations of either Robert Norman or other pseudonyms. You use your real name for camera pretty regularly, but then the director credit would be these different pseudonyms.

RF I don't know why. There comes a point where it's just me, right? I directed *Underage* [1977]. [Walter] was too busy as production manager and soundman, which is a combination that you really can't deal with. So every once in a while, we would hire a sound man. No, he only directed *Sweet Freedom* [and] *Liquid Assets*. I didn't direct *Mascara*. It's Ron Sullivan [using the pseudonym Henri Pachard]. I said, Walter, we don't know how to direct sex pictures. We just don't do it right. We're no good at it. I'm ashamed and you don't know how to talk to girls. We'll hire the best in the business. So Ron comes in. He was a consummate asshole but he was very charming. Walter thought he was a jerk. But he was very enthusiastic in sex scenes. He got right in there with the players and so forth and urged them. However, he had no technical skill whatsoever. I said OK, Ron you're the director, what's the first camera position? The camera was parked in the corner to keep it out of the way, [and he said] that's perfect! That's the position. So from then on, I never asked him again, I just did it and let him enthusiastically direct the "amours." We never hired him again, but he was very funny. He said where's my bag of words? That was his script.

WS You did an interview in the *New York Press* in 2006, I don't know if you remember, called "The Curse of her Filmography."[9]

RF I never see any of this stuff after it's published.

WS [J. R. Taylor] asked you about a cameo as a cleaning lady at the end of *Raw Footage* [1977] and you denied . . .

RF Not *Raw Footage*.

WS That's what he called it. That's what I wondered because it was [originally titled] *Underage*, but they retitled it *Raw Footage* on VHS.

RF Oh, ok, no, it's not in *Underage* but I was a cleaning lady somewhere.

WS We both just rewatched it and you come in, Wade Nichols was in it.

RF Oh, really, ok.

WS I wasn't sure if when that interviewer asked you that if you were denying that you had been in it or if you just didn't recognize it by the title of *Raw Footage*.

RF I thought it was a different movie altogether, but ok, you're probably right. I just remember being a cleaning lady. If it's *Underage* and the [Muzio] Clementi piece that [Marlene Willoughby] plays [on a piano earlier in the movie], that was me.

WS Was it your actual hands on screen?

RF No. Recorded by me.

PA You're very funny in that moment.

RF I vaguely remember doing that. Walter probably dressed me for that.

WS Was it you who retitled it *Raw Footage*?

RF No, I don't know who retitled that, probably a video company.

Figure 10.3 Roberta Findlay as the custodian alongside Wade Nichols in *Raw Footage*.

WS What about Wade Nichols? He's an interesting guy. How did you feel about him? He was doing disco music, he was doing gay and straight stuff. Later he wound up on soap operas, very attractive. He recorded as Dennis Parker, he did "Like an Eagle," a disco hit in the late 1970s.

RF I don't know any of that. We used him a few times, I guess. I don't remember him. The few that I do, oh, Ron, of course.

WS Ron Jeremy?

RF Yeah, Ron Jeremy, because of the objection from everyone except Walter, who thought he was funny. The girls used to say, this is a long time ago, no animals, no blacks, and no Ron Jeremy.

WS The ugly side of Ron Jeremy is on trial right now. Have you been following this? He's in jail, he's facing some really serious sexual assault charges now.[10]

RF Are you kidding?

WS No, years of allegations from teenagers and adult women. So you weren't aware of any of that kind of behavior at the time?

RF No, no, I didn't know what it was they objected to, we didn't know. We thought maybe [his penis] was too big. I have no idea. But the girls loved John Holmes.

We made three or four films together at the very beginning. *Love in Strange Places* [1976], *Sweet Sweet Freedom* [1976]. We shot scenes for each together. We never had a problem with Uncle John except for once when Walter handed him the script for *Love in Strange Places*, which I wrote, and John said, what is this? It was like 100 pages. And he said, what are you, a dialogue freak? And he threw the script away and he was very funny, on his own, ad libbing. He wouldn't read anything.

WS In *New York City Woman* [1977] when he's recording his memories, is that him ad libbing?

RF Yes it is, but we gave him an outline because that's one of our, what we call free pictures. It costs nothing. We shot for half a day or whatever on Walter's terrace on 85th and West End. His wife was delighted. I pieced outtakes from all the films that he was in and put it all together. Cost nothing. Just his memoirs.

WS *Mnasidika* [1969] is a strange and unique and striking film.

RF I don't remember much of it. What I remember is it's a series of tableaux. Is that correct?

WS Basically, yeah.

RF I don't know what Michael was thinking. Oh, I know another thing, but never mind.

WS That sounds tantalizing.

RF *Mnasidika*, I guess I did shoot. It was shot in 16 [millimeter], the only one ever, because I was in no condition to shoot with a heavier camera. So there.

WS You don't want to elaborate.

RF No. Talk about bad form or bad behavior or what's the word, "immoral," "immorality." No, I didn't think so. I had a kid. We gave her away.

WS Ok, and that was during *Mnasidika*.

RF I also had poison ivy. At the same time. It was shot on 16 because I couldn't hold a 35 [millimeter] camera. I don't know why he thought that a bunch of tableaux would make a film. I don't think there's a story to the thing, is there?

WS No, not really. It's pretty surreal.

RF It was shot in Gloucester [Massachusetts]. In the forest. John [Amero] showed us places.

WS How did you feel about the film? It's just so weird. It's kind of got an art house vibe.

RF That was for Stan Borden, who, once again, didn't question Michael, but he should have. Stan said [imitating Borden] what is this? What is this? Massapequa?

WS Did that one make money?

RF I don't think so. How could it? I don't think so. That may have been the end of their relationship. No, it couldn't have been because Stanley paid for the 3D. I mean, he was the benefactor. His estate owns the patent.[11]

WS I want to ask you about a few films that disappeared. Do you remember *Erotikon?* You made it in Belgium [in 1967] and then customs confiscated it.[12]

RF Yes, I took the negative.

WS And then it never gets distributed.

RF That was made by, theoretically, by Michael, theoretically, for Stanley Borden. He financed *Erotikon*. I was still in school, so I guess that's when I quit school. I went back though afterwards and I guess I was seventeen. We went to Antwerp first, and picked up a production manager and then we went to Brussels and lo and behold, the cast only spoke French. Wow, what a surprise [sarcastically]. So I directed it in French. As well as I could. But Michael shot it in black and white. It was about a book that's called *The Erotikon* [Augustin Cabanes, 1966]. And he was copying a French director. You know, *Breathless* [1960].

WS Jean-Luc Godard.

RF So he's copying Godard.[13] There's scenes in a field with a tea service and two guys. There was a print, Michael cut it. Actually, a famous actor was in it. I want to say Maurice Ronet, is that possible? Anyway, there was a well-known actor in it. As far as the sex scenes go, I don't even remember that there were any.

WS This takes me a little out of order, but *Take My Head* [1970].

[Hands her a printed copy of the film's poster.]

RF I don't know that. That's not me.

WS The Internet Movie Database credits you and Michael with it from 1970.[14]

RF Not me.

WS Lawrence Cohn, who wrote for *Variety* and covered a lot of this stuff at the time, writes about it on IMDB [using his well-known alias lor_] and says that Michael's unmistakable voice narrates it.[15]

RF I don't know if I was still with him, but I had nothing to do with that. After I left, he was making gay films with John [Amero].

WS In a 1978 interview with Gerald Perry you mentioned another film after *Altar of Lust* [1971]. You say, "I wrote another script, produced and directed it and cut it. It wasn't much, it was just a stupid series of loops, later retitled *The Doctor Knows Best*." I've also never seen that mentioned anywhere.[16]

RF That's a lie. *The Altar of Lust* is *Doctor Knows Best*. It's the same picture.

WS So you just recycled it.

RF No, I didn't do anything. I gave it to [Allan] Shackleton and he called it *The Doctor Knows Best*.

WS One more film to ask you about: *Teenage Milkmaid* [1973].

RF That's Shackleton. That's *The Clamdigger's Daughter* [1974]. After *Angel Number 9*, he said, what are you doing, this is hardcore. And then he sold it to Joe Steinman [Essex Video], because he was afraid to go to jail, like me. The only hardcore film I made for Shackleton was *Angel Number 9*.

WS OK, so *Teenage Milkmaid* is straight up retitling, it's not recut or anything.

RF No. He couldn't release a picture called *The Clamdigger's Daughter*. Which was shot at Gloucester. I don't know why I went there. I have no idea. But Michael and I used to go up there to visit the Amero family. They came from Gloucester. And we were very familiar. We both grew very familiar with the town. So let's shoot up there. I'm shocked that he paid for such an expense, but he did.

WS You know, I like *The Clamdigger's Daughter* a lot. It's a moody, melancholy film. It really has this beachside kind of vibe. I feel like that's another through-line in your work. With *Mystique* and *A Woman's Torment*, you're good at capturing this kind of melancholy offseason beach feeling.

RF Yeah, I liked *Mystique*. Sex theaters didn't get the drift. Walter said yeah, that's really sexy, a woman dying of cancer [sarcastically]. By the end [of *Clamdigger's Daughter*], after it was finished, Shackleton owed me twelve grand and instead of paying me, he punched me in the eye. We had a fight and he beat me up. I had already met Walter. Walter got me a lawyer, and he called Shackleton and said she's gonna go to the police and will sue. Give her the money. And he did. That was the end of that. I never saw him again.

WS You narrate it very casually, but was that traumatic?

RF Yeah, it was. He'd already done it before. He already beat me up once when we first met, he came to my apartment, hit me, beat me. I tried to fight back the last time when he punched me in the eye, I threatened to break his glasses. He said, if you break my glasses I'll kill you. So I didn't break them, I thought that was wise.

WS I'm glad you fought back, but I'm sorry you went through that.

RF Michael tried to strangle me once. I'm not the most pleasant companion in the world.

We turned to Shauna: Every Man's Fantasy, *made in 1985, shortly after actress Colleen Applegate died by suicide in 1984. Applegate had performed as Shauna Grant in more than thirty adult films, including* Glitter *and* Private Schoolgirls *for Findlay in 1983. Ostensibly a "tribute" to Applegate,* Shauna: Every Man's Fantasy *is actually a deeply exploitative attempt to profit from the widespread publicity accompanying Applegate's death. The film intercuts hardcore outtakes from Findlay's productions with an "investigation" by a journalist played by Joyce James, then the editor of* Cinema Blue *magazine, in which she interviews adult film performers about Grant, with frequent voice-over narration on the topic playing over hardcore footage.*

PA I think one of the one of the sort of enduring mythologies about your career that gets circulated around is that you stopped making hardcore films after *Shauna: Every Man's Fantasy* [because] maybe people didn't want to work with you again. Is there truth to that?

RF That's not true. Why would we stop after that? *Shauna* is once again a free film. It's outtakes from the other pictures that she was in for us. I lied to [Joyce James] pretty good. I said this is a tribute to Shauna Grant. That wasn't Shauna Grant's narration [in the film]. She was too stupid to do that. Actually, I don't know if she was too stupid. She was completely, totally, all the time stoned. Most of the California cast were always stoned. The New York cast was not. I could care less. I have no heart in these things and it was just outtakes and a cheap film. But Reeltime made pictures after that. We made *Climax* [1985] and *Wet Dreams* [1985]. And *Can't Get Enough* [1985], which we bought. We didn't stop making hardcore films. It had nothing to do with people wouldn't work with us anymore. The market failed. What happened was we were selling to small video distributors in Europe, mostly in Europe. They all started disappearing and were bought up and our market dried up. Also, we made a lot of money theatrically in theaters across the country, and they switched to video. They didn't have to rent our films. They rent the video and you're going to sue thousands of theaters? So the business changed, that's why we stopped. That was the only reason.

WS Peter, do you know *Climax*? I don't, I don't remember ever hearing this?

PA No, I feel like this is a significant addition to the mythology about your career, that there were three more films after [*Shauna*]. *Wet Dreams* is credited online as being directed by Ron Sullivan, as Henri Pachard.[17]

RF He was there, I remember this. He was an actor. He wanted to be in [*Climax*] and he plays the character Sparrow [Arnold Stang] from *The Man with the Golden Arm* [1955, dir. Otto Preminger]. This jerky moron guy with a baseball cap that hangs onto Frankie Machine [Frank Sinatra] and won't let him go and tries to endear himself to him and that's the character Ron took in *Climax* and he did it all by himself. I thought what the hell? He was hysterically funny. I know nobody understood what he was doing except me.

WS What was *Can't Get Enough*? That's just a film you picked up?

RF I shot that—we shot together with Joe Sarno. [Walter and I] were crew and we bought the picture from Distribpix. I don't remember how we split it up or if Joe cut our picture. I think he cut it and we just bought it. It's terrible, it's just one sex scene after another, that's all it is.

PA I want to ask you for some of your recollections about *Tenement* [aka *Game of Survival*, 1985]. It was filmed in neighborhoods you were familiar with, and it does stand out a little bit in your filmography because it's not the sex pictures and it's not the horror pictures, it's this sort of other thing. I'm wondering what you might think about it now.

RF We bought the script, I didn't write that job. Joel Bender wrote the script and was supposed to direct, but Walter said he doesn't know what he's doing, so we got rid of him. But we thought it was an interesting script and it reminded me of where I grew up, although, frankly, the building wasn't quite as bad as the tenement [in the film]. But we did shoot in a neighborhood that I knew in the Bronx, just the exteriors, which was nearby to the Southeast Bronx where I grew up. The rest of the stuff was shot very cleverly on 125th Street in what's called an *In Rem* building that the city was going to rehabilitate, and so it was free. I know Walter found it, but it was a free set when we were there for a month. I liked the script very much. It seemed real to me, although the racial makeup of the gang is fake. I mean, it's not, it's not correct. When I was a kid, there were Puerto Rican gangs and there were Italian gangs. There were no Black gangs. I was in a Black neighborhood. The gangs were absolutely, completely 100% ethnic, whatever ethnicity that they were in. It was a very dangerous neighborhood. We lived in what I call the *shtetl*, which is a village in Poland, and that's where we lived in this Jewish enclave. In this little tiny piece of the Bronx near the Bronx Zoo. The people in the gang reminded me of gang members I used to see. I went to school with them or they'd show up every once in a while in school.

PA Did you ever think about making other pictures that were more like *Tenement*, action, thriller-type pictures?

RF No, I thought the horror films were much safer. [*Tenement*] was screened in California, by the MPAA, and they gave it an X rating. We appealed it, they came to New York, had a screening, and Richard Heffner, [host of] *The Open Mind* on PBS, very, very what you call the New York intelligentsia, led a committee for the appeal and they walked out after the first reel and that was the end of that. And their opinion was that it was disgusting. Believe it or not, we have R ratings on the [horror] pictures from the MPAA.[18] Oh, and one other thing. Another Walter brilliant stroke. The woman—there's a black couple, a middle-aged woman and man in *Tenement*—a woman, some pretty bad actress. Her name was Olivia Wade. What's the significance of that? Her husband was Benjamin Wade, the Police Commissioner of New York at that time. He realized that, I don't know how, and hired her instantly and we had police with us. Forever and ever and ever. They also reprimanded us for putting her in dangerous positions.

PA Do you ever miss making pictures?

RF Certainly shooting and editing, yeah. That was more fun than the *New York Times* crossword puzzle, which is what I'm relegated to now. My life has collapsed [laughing].

WS It seems like there would be interest in a return to filmmaking. Why not go for it, you've got fans.

RF Walter said after *Banned* [1989] we should make another film. All the pictures, everything that we ever made was with our own money. We'd just reinvest. I said, not a chance. I ain't puttin' no more money into these pictures. We never were able to raise one penny. We were terrible at it.

WS These days there's crowdfunding, GoFundMe, things like that.

RF I don't know how to do that. You do it, you do it and I'll shoot.

WS We'll produce your comeback, I'm in.

RF I've never even held a digital camera. Some films are still being shot on film. I would shoot on film and the equipment would be free because I still have all the cameras and a friend of mine has the lenses, but I'd take them back. We had a lot of lenses, yeah, lots of Cooke's, some very good lenses. 16 Distagon, that was my favorite lens. I have no lighting gear. We sold all that off to camera service when we moved in [to the current Sear Sound studio]. There's no place to put it.

WS If I recall, I think maybe this was your *Rialto Report* interview, you said your dream project was an adaptation of [Herman Melville's 1852 novel] *Pierre; or, the Ambiguities*.[19]

RF Either that or some more obscure [Anthony] Trollope. Not the Pallisers [a series revolving around a wealthy family], but something. I've read everything he's written.

WS Your tastes run pretty classical. In cinema, you're always invoking John Ford and classic Hollywood.

RF Oh yes. Billy Wilder, William Wyler.

WS Did you watch the films by your exploitation peers at the time? I mean, like Gerard Damiano, Anthony Spinelli's films? Or did you not even watch other hardcore movies in the 1970s? Did you watch other B horror movies in the 1980s when you were making that genre, like John Carpenter, Wes Craven or even lower budget?

RF I must have gone to a screening or two. Walter would only go if they were catered. I don't like horror films. I hate cheap crummy films. Although, I am sick of watching TCM, the same movie over and over. I'm not skilled enough to stream, I can't. I don't know how.

WS What about contemporary cinema? Do you watch things like, I don't know, *Moonlight* [2016, dir. Barry Jenkins]?

RF No, I saw *Green Book* [2018, dir. Peter Farrelly] and that was terrible. Like a sledgehammer. I do admire Roman Polanski. I think he's very good. A marvelous editor.

WS Politics. When we were on the phone, I don't remember how it came up, but it became clear that you certainly did not like Donald Trump and you were a big Hillary Clinton booster.

RF I was, yeah. Not anymore. She's not doing anything much. She could be doing more, maybe not. She's so unpopular. I don't know why. She was dismissed and abhorred. In New York!

WS Where do you see yourself politically? How do you identify? How do you vote or what words do you use to describe yourself?

RF I'm very moderate. I would say I wanted [Ohio Senator] Sherrod Brown to run for president. The Bernie Sanders/AOC wing, they're dreaming. They're not helpful. It can't work like that. How this fever gets broken, I don't know. John Kerry, I thought, was a good candidate. He's a smart man.

WS I see on your wall there are pictures of Barack Obama. Does that mean anything?

RF Of course, I adored [Obama] even though he could be doing more and he's not. We recorded some stuff here for free for him for social media. That had never happened in the history of Sear Sound. And I worked on his phone bank during the second campaign. They assigned me southwest Pennsylvania.

PA Can you reflect a little bit on the time you spent running Reeltime as a distribution company? What was that like? Do you have good memories of that?

RF It was exciting. I loved it. I had a big print book [for] moving prints around. Of course we were in Hollywood. We had, I think, like fifteen prints, maybe twenty for each title and I had to shift them from exchange to exchange because we couldn't make 100 prints or anything. [Cecil] Howard showed me how to run an operator print book and gave me the names of all of these area sub-distributors in every part of the country except the South—they don't want dirty films in their backyard. So there were [sub-distributors] in each territory. The Western exchange, California, Colorado, Washington state, and the Chicago exchange, which was the mob. And New York, which was the lowest paying, one of the lowest paying exchanges in the country. New York City? Can you believe that?

WS Why?

RF Because they could. So I would move the prints around and the trailers. I would ship all the trailers out. And then we had our foreign clients. Eventually we moved over to an agent who sold [foreign] for us. It was better and they could contact more people. Certain countries, of course wouldn't show hard-core films, like the UK. Germany was a big sale. Japan was a very, very big sale.

PA Sounds like maybe that was another kind of puzzle that you enjoyed.

RF I love distribution. I love paperwork. Keeping track of a million pieces of stuff. I like to do that. We were doing quite well until we weren't [laughing]. Our main source was theatrical, and that was over in the 1980s, I guess. I'd say 1983 or 1984. The theaters would just go to a video rental store. They wouldn't even buy the cassette, they'd rent it. We couldn't collect on that. It all ended with *Banned*. And we bought that script from [Jim Cirile] who was working for Reeltime. It's the accountant's fault. The year was ending for Reeltime, and he said you've made too much money this year. You have to shoot a film before the year ends. The only thing we could find was this guy's script. I said, Walter, this script is terrible. He said, how bad can it be? I said, it makes no sense. It was a sexy kind of rock-and-roll comedy. Comedy? For me? He said, it's got rock-and-roll and sex, how bad [can it be]. As I was editing, I said, boy is this terrible. And it is.

WS Did the bands that recorded here know about your work as a filmmaker? Is that something that would come up with Wilco or Sonic Youth or Paul Simon or whoever?

RF It depends. They all seemed to know before they got here. A couple of them, not the more famous ones.

WS It kind of blows my mind thinking about the intersection of some things that I really love. I mean the intersection of *A Woman's Torment* and Sonic Youth— did [guitarist and singer] Thurston Moore show up and know your films?

RF Walter and Sonic Youth went back years and years. He recorded their first album at the old studio, which is the Paramount Hotel, and he was very friendly with Lee [Ranaldo, guitarist] and Thurston somewhat. Thurston is nuts. He's the craziest one in the group.

WS We're both historians, and so we're both kind of obsessed with these questions of archives and paper trails and business records and memoranda. Can you say a word about what you preserved? What kind of archives do you have?

RF I don't have any archives. Those file cabinets [points] . . . that's it.

WS What about personal material? Did you keep a diary throughout your life, or letters that you would send?

RF No, nothing.

WS Is that deliberate, you just didn't keep things?

RF I didn't think of it.

WS Would you want an archive to have this stuff, like the New York Public Library? Is this something you'd be interested in? I think historians would kill for this, frankly.

RF Yeah, why not. I'm not selfish.

Figure 10.4 Roberta Findlay at Sear Sound in New York, September 21, 2021. Photo by Whitney Strub.

NOTES

1. Linda Williams, *Hard Core: Power, Pleasure, and the "Frenzy of the Visible"* (Berkeley: University of California Press, 1989): 130–4.

2. *Angel on Fire* (1974) was also titled *Angel Number 9* and is referred to by both titles throughout this interview.

3. Dennis Giles, "*Angel on Fire*: Three Texts of Desire," *Velvet Light Trap*, Fall 1976, 45.

4. Giles, *Angel on Fire*, 42.

5. Molly Haskell, "Are Women Directors Different?" *Village Voice*, February 3, 1975, 73.

6. Findlay here deliberately invokes Andrea Dworkin's blistering polemic, *Intercourse* (New York: Free Press, 1987).

7. Molly Haskell, "Moviemaking Without Men," *Village Voice*, May 10, 1973, 83.

8. Sperling disagrees with Findlay's claim, saying that she never hired men for the crew of *The Waiting Room*, and that a woman who worked as a dolly grip on the film was trained by a teamster member prior to shooting (email with Alilunas, October 4, 2021). During production, Sperling told Molly Haskell that "a professional cinematographer came out to help ours learn the trade. He was delighted when he saw how well we were getting along" (Haskell, "Moviemaking Without Men," 83).

9. J. R. Taylor, "The Curse of Her Filmography," *NY Post*, November 8–14, 2006, https://web.archive.org/web/20061108201842/www.newyorkpress.com/18/29/film/JRTaylor.cfm (accessed July 20, 2021).

10. Jeremy was indicted in Los Angeles, California on August 25, 2021 on a total of thirty sexual assault counts involving twenty-one women going back more than twenty years, and investigations are ongoing, https://da.lacounty.gov/media/news/adult-film-star-indicted-rape-other-sexual-assault-counts (accessed May 26, 2022).

11. Borden, in addition to financing and releasing some of the Findlay's films (including the original Flesh Trilogy in 1967), financed the development of Michael's 3D camera technology, called SuperDepth. Michael was killed on May 16, 1977 along with five other people in a tragic helicopter accident atop the Pan Am building in New York, while en route to the Cannes Film Festival to seek investors in the 3D camera venture. For more, see "Michael Findlay's Last Year—3-D, Funk, and the Tragedy on the PanAm Building: An Oral History," *Rialto Report*, July 21, 2019, https://www.therialtoreport.com/2019/07/21/michael-findlay/ (accessed May 26, 2022).

12. See the Introduction in this collection for more on the seizure of *Erotikon*.

13. In a curious return of this borrowing that appears to have gone wholly unnoticed until now, Godard made use of Findlay's work in the obscure, essayistic *Les enfants jouent à la Russie* (1993), a satirical lamentation on the state of post-cold-war Europe with a collage-like use of assembled film footage. As the narrator rues the fate of "the woman in the stairs of Odessa," who wound up "in a porno film on one of the twenty television stations controlled by the mafia," onscreen appears the image of C. J. Laing masturbating with a bottle from *Anyone But My Husband*, thereby cementing the link between Godard and Findlay for future film historians.

14. See https://www.imdb.com/title/tt0238651/ (accessed May 26, 2022).

15. See https://www.imdb.com/title/tt0238651/reviews?ref_=tt_urv (accessed May 26, 2022).

16. Gerald Peary, "Woman in Porn," *Take One*, September 1978, 31.

17. See https://www.imdb.com/title/tt0312016/ (accessed May 26, 2022).

18. For more on the MPAA rating and *Game of Survival*, see Neil Jackson's chapter in this collection.
19. Ashley West and April Hall, "Roberta Findlay: A Respectable Woman—Podcast 53," August 16, 2015, in *Rialto Report*, podcast, 1:14:05, https://www.therialtoreport.com/2015/08/16/roberta-findlay/ (accessed July 28, 2021).

Index